"*Development in Mission* is a timely, necessary book that examines what has often been problematic about mission work and advocates listening to, learning from, and partnering with people in vulnerable communities. By offering practical ideas, clear methodologies, compassionate approaches, and new theological insights, it feels both simple and groundbreaking. This book should be required reading for every Christian who places loving people in vulnerable situations at the center of their faith—which should be every Christian."

—**Jessica Goudeau,** author of *After the Last Border,* winner of the
J. Anthony Lukas Book Prize

"Churches have so internalized the message that helping can 'hurt' that they have become paralyzed and passive in the face of global poverty. In *Development in Mission*, Lynn, Gailey, and Reese share a prophetic call to action. Transformational development provides the church with a compassionate, redemptive, and effective way to join God's mission in partnering with vulnerable communities. This is a wise, timely, necessary, and profoundly important book."

—**Richard Beck,** Professor of Psychology at Abilene Christian University,
author of *Unclean* and *Stranger God*

"Jesus said that those who loved him would love and serve people experiencing hunger, poverty, sickness, and oppression. This book is for people ready to lead their communities into doing so. It covers the why, what, and how of global development work thoroughly and thoughtfully from a posture of humility. It engages the evidence we have and the mysteries that remain. I warn you only that it leaves no excuse for inaction."

—**Paul Niehaus,** cofounder of GiveDirectly, Segovia, and Taptap Send,
Associate Professor of Economics at the University of California, San Diego

"Inspirational, substantive, and comprehensive, *Development in Mission* shows how the way of Jesus is interwoven into current practices of holistic ministry and church engagement. This book comes at a time when Christians need to remember the creative possibilities of the gospel breaking in through history and hold fast to that hope. Herein, individuals and congregations will find a useful guide to transformational development for living into that hope both locally and throughout the globe."

—**Nell M. Becker Sweeden,** Director of Nazarene Compassionate Ministries

"A solid biblical, theological, historical, missiological, and development foundation enriched by strong research, *Development in Mission* is an invitation to churches and individuals to join with the Global South and jointly be transformed. Have a highlighter nearby because there is so much you will want to reference! A critical book needed for these days and the future."

—**Jo Anne Lyon,** founder of World Hope International, General Superintendent
Emerita of The Wesleyan Church

"*Development in Mission* is a tour de force into the complexity of poverty that confronts some two billion people in the world today. Lynn, Gailey, and Reese present an unvarnished look at the causes and implications of one of the world's greatest challenges, while guiding us toward proven solutions with a humility we must chase after in order to achieve results. This is more than a book; it's an invitation to participate in one of the greatest movements in history: ending poverty for millions in our lifetime."
—**Belinda Bauman,** founder of One Million Thumbprints, author of *Brave Souls*; and **Stephan Bauman,** former President and CEO of World Relief, author of *Seeking Refuge*

"You know you're reading a transformational book when its very title links global poverty with the need for us to be transformed ourselves. This is vital if we are to play the role God wants us to play alongside our sisters and brothers around the world. This is also an accessible book brought to life with stories that may well resonate in your hearts for many years. It addresses real, practical issues by drawing on the wisdom of Scripture and insights from our sisters and brothers in the Majority World and those who have humbly sought to serve alongside them."
—**Richard Lister,** Church and Community Transformation Specialist at Tearfund

"The authors provide a holistic perspective on transformational development. An insightful read offering tools and principles that strengthen the community development acumen of Christians. This book is a timely reminder that Christian development efforts need to be multifaceted and imbued with humility as they seek to draw all people into a deeper relationship with God."
—**JoAnn Flett,** Managing Director of PW Entrepreneurs, L3C Partners Worldwide

"Lynn, Gailey, and Reese thoughtfully combine mission with development to culminate in the redemptive process of transformation. To achieve that, they present a solid theological foundation for holistic mission and an extensive survey of transformational development sectors. This is a timely book that calls the church to humility, to listening, and to reimagining global mission, and provides congregations with practical tools for doing that. I find that this book provides a thoughtful, friendly, appropriate, timely, and practical corrective to global mission."
—**Elie Haddad,** President of Arab Baptist Theological Seminary

"Holistic mission meets transformational development in this well-conceived, well-organized work. This would be an ideal textbook for courses in faith and development, theology of mission, and other courses seeking to equip the church to be the agent of change that it is called to be among the world's most vulnerable."
—**Al Tizon,** Executive Minister of Serve Globally, Affiliate Associate Professor of North Park Theological Seminary, author of *Whole and Reconciled*

DEVELOPMENT
IN MISSION

DEVELOPMENT IN MISSION

A Guide for Transforming
Global Poverty and
Ourselves

MONTY LYNN
ROB GAILEY
DERRAN REESE

With a foreword by Brian Fikkert and
an afterword by Ruth Padilla DeBorst

DEVELOPMENT IN MISSION
A Guide for Transforming Global Poverty and Ourselves

Copyright © 2021 by Monty Lynn, Rob Gailey, and Derran Reese

ISBN 978-1-68426-4-216
LCCN 2021011068

Printed in the United States of America

ALL RIGHTS RESERVED
No part of this publication may be reproduced, stored in a retrieval system, or transmitted in any form by any means—electronic, mechanical, photocopying, recording, or otherwise—without prior written consent.

All Scripture quotations, unless otherwise indicated, are taken from the New Revised Standard Version Bible, copyright © 1989, the Division of Christian Education of the National Council of the Churches of Christ in the United States of America. All rights reserved.

Scripture quotations marked NIV are taken from The Holy Bible, New International Version®, NIV® Copyright © 1973, 1978, 1984, 2011 by Biblica, Inc.® Used by permission. All rights reserved worldwide.

LIBRARY OF CONGRESS CATALOGING-IN-PUBLICATION DATA
Names: Lynn, Monty L., 1959- author. | Gailey, Rob, 1970- author. | Reese, Derran, 1978- author.
Title: Development in mission : a guide for transforming global poverty and ourselves / Monty Lynn, Rob Gailey, and Derran Reese.
Description: Abilene, Texas : Abilene Christian University Press, 2021. | Includes bibliographical references.
Identifiers: LCCN 2021011068 (print) | LCCN 2021011069 (ebook) | ISBN 9781684264216 (trade paperback) | ISBN 9781684269297 (ebook)
Subjects: LCSH: Church work with the poor. | Missions. | Poverty—Religious aspects—Christianity.
Classification: LCC BV639.P6 L96 2021 (print) | LCC BV639.P6 (ebook) | DDC 261.8—dcundefined
LC record available at https://lccn.loc.gov/2021011068
LC ebook record available at https://lccn.loc.gov/2021011069

Cover design by Bruce Gore | Gore Studio Inc.
Interior text design by Sandy Armstrong | Strong Design

For information contact:
Abilene Christian University Press
ACU Box 29138
Abilene, Texas 79699

1-877-816-4455
www.acupressbooks.com

21 22 23 24 25 26 / 7 6 5 4 3 2 1

We dedicate this book to the hundreds of millions of people experiencing poverty and vulnerability around the world who reveal the very person and presence of Jesus Christ.

CONTENTS

PREFACE.. 11
FOREWORD   To the Church in the Global North, by Brian Fikkert 15

PART ONE
DEEPENING UNDERSTANDING

1 Blessed to Give and Receive 23
2 For God So Loves the Whole World 41
3 Effective Christian Poverty Alleviation 63

PART TWO
ENHANCING ENGAGEMENT

4 Transformational Development Sectors 95
    Children, Youths, and Older Persons 98
    Creation Care 102
    Education 106
    Food 112
    Freedom and Liberation 119
    Health 127
    Income Generation 139
    Migration and Refuge 146
    Peacemaking and Peacebuilding 150
    Relief 155
    Scripture Translation 164
    Shelter 168
    Sport 172
    Technology 173
    Water, Sanitation, and Hygiene 175

PART THREE
MOVING FORWARD

5 What Churches Can Do 181
6 Looking Ahead 211

AFTERWORD **From the Church in the Global South, by Ruth Padilla DeBorst** 223
APPENDIX A **Further Reading** 227
APPENDIX B **Development Organizations** 229
BIBLIOGRAPHY 243

PREFACE

Christian congregations and individuals often struggle to minister effectively in global, holistic mission. Many of us feel called to address poverty, oppression, and injustice; yet, for some, every step feels precarious, as if we were walking across a rickety bridge draped over a precipice. Might we harm those we aim to assist? Can we trust our partners? Will we be effective? Others of us advance in confidence, assuming that we are welcome pioneers in lands where few have trod. With a commission from God and a newly minted passport, we launch out on our own to change the world.

In actuality, both groups are missing the same critical resource: a humble pursuit of insights from vulnerable communities around the world and wisdom from servants who have gone before. Listening and learning from these voices can empower those held back by fear and uncertainty. Likewise, "world changers" can reimagine themselves as friends and co-laborers with God's faithful around the world.

This book is an attempt to help both groups—in fact, to help all of us—courageously and wisely engage in compassionate service to vulnerable populations by demonstrating how listening and learning from one another blesses everyone involved. As Jesus says, we offer *and* receive refreshing water from one another (Matt. 10:42; Mark 9:41). This ancient path of loving and transforming service reflects the nature of God and the way of Christ, and through it we participate in God's liberation, justice, and *shalom*.

Our goal is to welcome a variety of voices into the holistic mission and transformational development conversation. In particular, we believe that theology, missiology, global development, and local voices have valuable insights to offer to congregational and individual mission efforts. From this chorus, we attempt to offer a theological foundation for holistic mission, and we suggest principles that can guide poverty alleviation. We collect wisdom and best practices from a panorama of sectors such as water, sanitation, and hygiene; health care; disaster relief; peacemaking and peacebuilding; and education. And we provide practical suggestions for churches and disciples of Christ to advance and improve their partnerships with others. As we learn from others, we try to wash the residue of colonialism from our language and thinking (albeit imperfectly), believing that mission is best when everyone has agency and all are open to transformation.

The perspectives we propose grow out of our experiences in missions and global development in Africa, Asia, Europe, and North America. Rob has lived and worked in Eswatini, Malawi, and South Africa; Derran in Thailand; and Monty in Slovenia. Monty and Rob have worked with various faith-based agencies in global development, and Derran has served with the International Rescue Committee. Each of us has engaged in church leadership, and all three of us teach university-level courses in missions or global development.

Along the way, many individuals and communities have relayed insights to us, insights we are combining and sharing. It is appropriate at the outset that we extend our appreciation for a few of these transforming influences. Particularly formative for Monty have been Mac and Marty Lynn, who through lives of consistent service and ministry have shared all they are and have with many, most recently with the students of Nations University; and Vernon and Alice Boyd, who have helped many cross borders to love one another. Monty also thanks Dan Norell of World Vision and EconDev International for opening doors for him and for thousands of farmers. Larry and Hollye Conway and Keith and Grace Gafner opened their homes in Kenya, and Chris and Carolyn Chetsanga and Washington and Alice Mhlanga extended warm fellowship in Zimbabwe. The Oxford Centre for Mission Studies and Abilene Christian University offered much appreciated space and support for writing.

Rob wishes to thank his family, especially his parents, who first taught and modeled for him the importance of servant-led intercultural ministry and church engagement; cultural mentors and cherished friends in Eswatini, Malawi, South Africa, and the other locales where he has been blessed to engage in ministry and economic development; staff and friends at World Relief, Nazarene Compassionate Ministries, and the Microcredit Summit Campaign; administrators, staff, and faculty colleagues of Point Loma Nazarene University (PLNU), for their encouragement, support, and sabbatical funding; and PLNU students who supported and engaged with him inside and outside the classroom as he worked through many of the ideas and practices that informed this book. A special thanks goes to those who have been like iron sharpening iron (some directly, as dear friends, and some indirectly, as authors, and a few as both!), including Wanda, Jamie, Larry, Nell, Tim, Ron, Stephan, Park, Peter, Brian, Susan, Dean, Jesse, Wes, Paul, Bruce, Belinda, Josh, and Teresa, and authors Bryant Myers, Bryan Stevenson, Tony Campolo, Esther Duflo, Steve Garber, Henri Nouwen, William T. Cavanaugh, and Jeff Van Duzer.

Derran wishes to thank, first and foremost, his mission team in Thailand: Ryan and Ning Binkley, Haley Edmiston, Chris and Tonya Fikes, and his wife, Ann. They have shown him what loving your neighbor looks like in the flesh. He is also grateful to the Chiang Mai team for modeling what it looks like to participate in the mission of God and to the Thai brothers and sisters who are examples of faithfully following the way of Jesus. He especially wants to thank Thim, Na, and Auto, whose faith is a constant source of hope. Derran is also indebted to those who have taught him much about how to love and serve wisely and compassionately: Jackie Beth, Mark and Ali, Jessica, and friends at International Rescue Committee in Abilene, Texas. Derran also thanks the Railsback family for the space and Susan Lewis for the time so he could write. Finally, he is deeply grateful to his family for putting up with long hours of writing and, most importantly, for their allegiance to Christ.

Together, we appreciate insights shared by those who read portions of the manuscript: Brian Fikkert, Roland Hoksbergen, Paul Niehaus, Jesse Casler, and Nell Becker Sweeden and her staff. We are grateful for those who wrote letters to the church in the United States for this project, editorial assistance from Jason Fikes and Kaitlin Barr Nadal, Lydia Buchanan's assistance with images, a generous grant for editorial support from the Point Loma Nazarene University Office of Alumni Relations, and friends who encouraged us on this journey.

Our hope is that each of these gifts of compassionate insight and skill bears fruit in faithful and effective global, holistic mission.

FOREWORD

TO THE CHURCH IN THE GLOBAL NORTH

Brian Fikkert

The United States of America is not doing very well ...

The political process is in shambles, racial tensions are on the rise, families are fraying at the seams, and communities are losing all sense of, well, community. Unfortunately, the church is not faring much better: worldly methods and goals, widespread politicization, leadership scandals, and theological drift have only added credence to citizens' growing distrust of institutions, of authority, and even of truth itself.

Not surprisingly, all of this is taking its toll, as evidenced by the decline of numerous indicators of personal well-being. For example, life expectancy in the United States dropped in 2015, as death rates increased for nine of the top ten leading causes of death. Moreover, from the late 1930s to the present—a period of unprecedented economic growth and prosperity—depression, anxiety, and other mental health issues among college-age Americans have been steadily increasing, resulting in dramatic increases in the suicide rate.[1]

---

[1] Fikkert and Kapic, *Becoming Whole*, 30–31.

Jean Twenge, a leading social psychologist, summarizes the situation as follows:

> I think the research tells us that modern life is not good for mental health . . . Obviously, there's a lot of good things about societal and technological progress, and in a lot of ways our lives are much easier than, say, our grandparents' or great-grandparents' lives. But there's a paradox here that we seem to have so much ease and relative economic prosperity compared to previous centuries, yet there's this dissatisfaction, there's this unhappiness, there are these mental health issues in terms of depression and anxiety.[2]

Against this backdrop, there is a tragic irony at the core of many of our poverty-alleviation efforts: We are not doing well, and we are increasingly unhappy; yet we implicitly assume that the goal of our ministries should be to help poor people become just like us. Having been immersed in the story of the "American Dream" for so long, we assume that the goal is to increase poor people's freedom to pursue ever-increasing levels of personal peace and material prosperity. And we assume that the way to achieve this goal is the way we have always done it: "Pull yourself up by your own bootstraps, get an education, work hard, look out for number one, and one day, you too will have power and wealth." Yes, and one day, you too will be a hyper-individualistic, self-serving, materialistic creature who is increasingly miserable.

We need a better story, both for people who are materially poor and for ourselves. In *Development in Mission*, Monty Lynn, Rob Gailey, and Derran Reese call us to embrace the only story that is actually true—the story of the kingdom of God—a story that burst forth from a tomb roughly two thousand years ago and that promises healing for every square inch of the cosmos, both now and not yet.

As the authors point out, the kingdom of God is unlike the kingdoms of this world, which have different goals and methods. Indeed, as we read

---

[2]Twenge as quoted in Singal, "For 80 Years."

about God's kingdom in the pages of Scripture, there are times when it feels like we are reading science fiction—like we are being introduced to an alternative universe in which the "laws of nature" are all different from those in our universe: down is up, weakness is powerful, and death is life. But it is not an alternative universe—it is the way things work in *our* universe—because Jesus reigns over it, and he sets the rules. Unfortunately, we keep trying to go against the grain of Jesus's universe; we keep trying to live according to "laws of nature" that are not operative in his kingdom. And this is the reason the United States is not doing well. The way we are living simply does not work.

You see, in the kingdom of God, the goal is not to be a hyper-individualistic, self-centered, consuming machine; instead, the goal is to be transformed into the image of Jesus, who showed that to be human—to truly flourish—is to live in deep communion with God, self, others, and creation. And the way to achieve this goal—the way to become like the king of this strange kingdom—is by following his methods:

> In your relationships with one another, have the same mindset
> as Christ Jesus:
>   Who, being in very nature God,
>   did not consider equality with God something to be
>   used to his own advantage;
>   rather, he made himself nothing
>   by taking the very nature of a servant,
>   being made in human likeness.
> And being found in appearance as a man,
>   he humbled himself
>   by becoming obedient to death—
>   even death on a cross!
> Therefore God exalted him to the highest place
>   and gave him the name that is above every name,
> that at the name of Jesus every knee should bow,
>   in heaven and on earth and under the earth,
> and every tongue acknowledge that Jesus Christ is Lord,
>   to the glory of God the Father. (Phil. 2:5–11 NIV)

Ironically, as *Development in Mission* explains so well, we become like Jesus not by grasping for power and wealth, but by pursuing kenosis—spirit-empowered, sacrificial service in which we empty ourselves on behalf of those who are blind, lame, cast out, and in poverty. Indeed, it is only through such humble service that we join Jesus in his mission, pursuing his goals according to his methods.

Building upon this rich theological foundation, the authors move into practice, outlining wise principles and solid steps to assist churches and individuals to humbly participate in Christ's reconciling of all things. In addition, the book includes a comprehensive survey of the various sectors, organizations, and educational resources in the space of poverty alleviation, providing helpful guidance to what can be a bewildering array of options. The resources listed in the appendices and bibliography alone are easily worth more than the price of the book.

Lynn, Gailey, and Reese provide more than enough information to enable any church or individual to develop excellent strategies and plans for moving forward in effective poverty alleviation. But consistent with living into the story of the kingdom of God, the authors also provide this profoundly important caution:

> Unquestionably, churches and Christian organizations should seek out the best practices in the larger development landscape, but they must then filter these practices through a gospel lens. Regarding mission in general, Wrogemann provides a word of caution for US churches: "The pragmatic-activist trait characterizing much of US-American thought completely eclipses the motif of self-emptying, i.e., of kenotic mission. Christian mission is seen as action, planning, and strategy—not as suffering, waiting, or clinging in faith to a reality that is yet to be revealed."[3] For development work specifically, this means that individuals, churches, and organizations should pursue ways to empty themselves and give up power for the sake of those who are vulnerable.[4]

---

[3] Wrogemann, *Theologies of Mission*, 223–24.
[4] See Chapter Three of this book, page 75.

To the Church in the Global North

This is the way of Jesus; this is the only way that truly works in his kingdom, both for poor people . . . and for ourselves.

—Brian Fikkert
    Founder and President of The Chalmers Center at Covenant College
    Coauthor of *When Helping Hurts: How to Alleviate Poverty without Hurting the Poor . . . and Yourself*

PART ONE

DEEPENING UNDERSTANDING

1

BLESSED TO
GIVE AND RECEIVE

Doris, the oldest daughter of a successful business owner and recipient of a college education in Boston, Massachusetts, had always been deeply committed to her Christian faith. After marrying, Doris and her husband were called by God and commissioned by their church to serve as educators in Siteki, Swaziland (now Eswatini).

During her first term as a missionary, Doris was blessed to forge a friendship with Patricia, a wise and humble Swazi woman who lived nearby (see Figure 1.1). Patricia and her husband were well-respected church leaders, adept at bridging cultural divides. The Swazi couple served as cultural tutors to new and veteran missionaries alike.

One October morning, Doris looked out her window as Patricia walked past. Doris was surprised and excited to see Patricia carrying a beautiful round, orange pumpkin. These kinds of pumpkins, while common in the United States during the fall season, were not sold in the local market. In fact, it was the first such pumpkin Doris had seen in the country—and she was thrilled! Immediately, Doris realized the golden

Figure 1.1. Patricia and Doris, 1969

DEVELOPMENT IN MISSION

opportunity available: she could provide her two young US-born children a taste of the Halloween holiday that would soon be celebrated "back home." Doris stepped outside to greet her friend, all the while eyeing the treasure Patricia held in her arms.

"Patricia, where did you find that beautiful orange pumpkin?"

"It was a gift I received from a dear friend."

"That is so nice! Back home our friends are about to celebrate a holiday called Halloween. The holiday is a bit hard to explain, but orange pumpkins, like the one you are holding, feature prominently in the celebration."

"Wow, how interesting."

Doris, with an air of excitement, beseeched, "And, friend, I have a deal for you! I want to buy this prized possession from you right now. I will pay you cash and give you top price for it! My family would love having this pumpkin in our house so that we can celebrate this festive holiday with a tangible reminder of home."

Patricia placed the large gourd in her friend's arms, smiled, and happily declared, "Take it as a gift from my family to yours to enjoy!"

Doris was aghast at the quick turn of events and quickly calculated the economic loss this represented for her friend. Not wanting to cheat or harm her much poorer neighbor, Doris resisted: "Oh, don't be ridiculous! I am willing to pay handsomely for this special treat. You know, my father is a successful businessman in Boston. Early on in life, he taught me that when something is rare and precious and in high demand, it can command a higher price than it would under normal circumstances. Not only must I pay you a fair price for this rare item, you should be demanding a premium since I approached you." Doris was pleased with her clear logic and quick retort. She could not believe she found a Halloween goodie and, at the same time, could help her friend with some extra cash and an economics lesson.

Yet, for reasons Doris could not then understand, Patricia kindly replied, "Friend, I refuse to take your money. I want this to be a gift from my family to yours."

With pumpkin in hand, realizing her friend would not willingly accept payment for it, Doris threw enough money at Patricia's feet to pay a generous price for the pumpkin and quickly went inside with her precious acquisition, immediately feeling a sense of relief and justice.

Her self-congratulation, however, did not last long.

The next day, Patricia came knocking on Doris's door and asked to speak with her missionary friend about the previous day's events. Following a few words of introduction, Patricia looked at her friend with kind but serious eyes and said, "You missionaries preach and teach us that the Bible says it is more blessed to give than to receive. Why is it then that you try to keep all of the blessings for yourselves?"

The lesson hit hard, and Doris quickly accepted back the money she had thrown at her friend's feet. Doris kept the pumpkin as a special gift from her Swazi friend. With insight worthy of Solomon, Patricia had imparted wisdom that forever shaped her missionary friend.

Our Aim

The story of Patricia and Doris serves as a threshold for considering holistic mission and, more specifically, efforts to love, serve, and care for people in poverty. Scripture is replete with stories, exhortations, and laments about the plight of those experiencing need, oppression, and vulnerability. Yet, in seeming tension with the numerous calls to help others, Jesus declares that, in the upside-down kingdom of God, "Blessed are you who are poor" (Luke 6:20). This short phrase is indicative of the radical transformation of expectations and norms inaugurated in the reign of Jesus Christ. In a world in which the rich and powerful seem to have all the answers, Jesus lets us in on a little secret about the true nature of humanity: it is through those who are perceived as weak and vulnerable that the power and strength of Christ are made manifest. The presence of Jesus is found in and among those who are hungry, thirsty, strangers, naked, sick, or imprisoned (Matt. 25: 31–46).

Those of us who seek to extend aid to others must reassess our posture in light of Jesus's reshaping of humanity. If those in poverty are the ones who are blessed, then we might have just as much, if not more, to receive as we do to give. (Our guess is that Doris would give a hearty "Amen!") Yet God still calls us to give, and give we must. And while it certainly includes our finances, the call is to give of our very selves—our time, comfort, talents, status, prayers—for the sake of loving our neighbors.

The entire canon of Scripture witnesses to God's heart for the vulnerable and God's desire for us to love and care for others. This is evident throughout the Hebrew Bible in exhortations to care for and seek justice on behalf of vulnerable and oppressed populations (Deut. 24:17–22; Jer. 22:3), as well as warnings against causing harm to those in need (Deut. 27:19; Isa. 10:1–4; Amos 2:6–7). When the brokenness of the world is acute and overwhelming, God's faithful cry out, "Rise up, O Lord: O God, lift up your hand; do not forget the oppressed.... O Lord, you will hear the desire of the meek; you will strengthen their heart, you will incline your ear to do justice for the orphan and the oppressed, so that those from earth may strike terror no more" (Ps. 10:12, 17–18).

Though we could point to countless passages expressing God's call to love vulnerable communities, few capture it as clearly as Isaiah 58:6–7:

> Is not this the fast that I choose:
>> to loose the bonds of injustice,
>> to undo the thongs of the yoke,
> to let the oppressed go free,
>> and to break every yoke?
> Is it not to share your bread with the hungry,
>> and bring the homeless poor into your house;
> when you see the naked, to cover them,
>> and not to hide yourself from your own kin?

True fasting, a giving of ourselves, should be oriented toward care and concern for those who are hungry, without shelter, naked, enslaved, isolated, and victims of injustice.

This ethic found throughout the Hebrew Bible finds its fulfillment in the person of Jesus Christ. Jesus begins his ministry by underscoring the centrality of compassion and justice highlighted in Isaiah 61.

> "The Spirit of the Lord is upon me,
>> because he has anointed me
>>> to bring good news to the poor.
> He has sent me to proclaim release to the captives
>> and recovery of sight to the blind,
>>> to let the oppressed go free,

to proclaim the year of the Lord's favor."
And he rolled up the scroll, gave it back to the attendant, and sat down. The eyes of all in the synagogue were fixed on him. Then he began to say to them, "Today this scripture has been fulfilled in your hearing." (Luke 4:18–21)

Those words do not merely echo through the synagogue but become embodied in the life and ministry of Jesus. While Jesus walked the earth, he lavishly loved others and consistently called for his disciples to do the same. By his words and example, Jesus taught his followers to welcome children (Luke 9:48), to dine with those whom society marginalizes (Mark 2:15–17; Luke 14:15–24), and to touch and heal those suffering from diseases and medical ailments (Luke 5:12–15; Mark 2:1–12). Jesus broke down cultural barriers (Luke 10:25–37) and cared for those caught in sin (John 8:1–11). He called those who have extra to share with those who are without (Matt. 19:16–24; Luke 16:19–31).

The earliest Christians continued this radical way of love and service (Acts 2:44–45, 4:32–37; 2 Cor. 8:1–7). They aided others knowing that, in God's timing, their service would make a difference within themselves and for each person with whom they shared food, hospitality, and shelter. They saw Jesus in others and wanted to be formed in his likeness. And they called others, including us, toward embodied compassion and generosity (2 Cor. 9:6–15). As John writes: "How does God's love abide in anyone who has the world's goods and sees a brother or sister in need and yet refuses help? Little children, let us love, not in word or speech, but in truth and action" (1 John 3:17–18).

Our desire is to affirm this call for disciples and churches to love "in truth and action." As willing recipients of the blessings offered by vulnerable populations and joyous givers for the sake of others, God's people are called to participate boldly, courageously, and wisely in God's mission throughout the world. Joining God in this mission—a mission that can transform global poverty—means embracing and advocating for the transformation of all.

We make this appeal while quiet yet profound shifts in global mission are occurring. Many churches in the Global North are redirecting their attention and resources away from global missions and toward needs closer to home. Voices in the public space call for citizens to place their nation and its people's interests above all others. Yet these are not the example of the earliest Christians who served at personal risk, aiding one another across borders (Rom. 15:25–27). The followers of Christ assisted strangers, orphans, widows, enemies, persecutors, and the dying, both near and far. They aided one another and were transformed in the process.[1]

Many today also are retreating from global mission and poverty alleviation because of fear and uncertainty about their ability to make a positive impact. Steve Corbett, Brian Fikkert, and their colleagues at The Chalmers Center have sensitized many to the fact that well-intentioned efforts to help can sometimes make matters worse. We suspect, however, that some readers stopped short of the real meaning of *When Helping Hurts: How to Alleviate Poverty without Hurting the Poor . . . and Yourself.* Instead of being encouraged and empowered to more effectively engage global poverty, some walked away with a mindset that "intercultural and international poverty alleviation is risky, so don't try it!" That was not at all the authors' message, as the contents and subtitle of the book attest.[2] Rather, their message was that how we view others, ourselves, poverty, and God's love dramatically shapes our priorities and relationships with others. Too often, the "sending" church in missions has been blinded to its own ethnocentrism, missing the opportunity to see the gospel fully expressed and embodied in those living elsewhere. Christians in the Global North sometimes fail to see how their actions and behaviors can directly affect the lives of their Global South friends.

Meanwhile, Christian disciples in the Global South are growing in numbers and vibrancy, articulating and demonstrating how the Christian faith is lived out in different cultural contexts. We believe these converging circumstances create an optimal time to reimagine the roles of congregations and individuals in global mission.

In the following pages, our aim is to provide congregations, missionaries, relief and development workers, and individual Christians with fresh perspectives on holistic mission and transformational development. We pray

---

[1] For a history, see Lynn, *Christian Compassion.*
[2] Corbett and Fikkert, *When Helping Hurts.*

that timeless biblical teaching—such as what Patricia taught Doris—will expose new opportunities for learning and following. Additionally, we offer lessons learned from holistic mission experiences, global development research, and brothers and sisters from around the world. To distill insights, we have had to quiet our own thoughts and listen to church and mission leaders, development researchers, theologians, and missiologists from various contexts. We hope this synthesis of voices will propel disciples of Christ toward embracing and promoting the dignity and mutuality of all persons across cultures, geographic space, and economic disparity.

Terminology

As we begin, let's pause to define a few terms. We employ the term *holistic mission* to refer to Christian efforts that address the whole person and all creation with God's love. Holistic mission includes disciple making and church planting, as well as poverty alleviation, creation care, peacemaking, and justice.[3] Relatedly, we employ the terms *global development* or *poverty alleviation* to refer to faith-based or secular efforts that engage vulnerable, and particularly economically vulnerable, populations to help alleviate or eliminate poverty.[4] These two domains—holistic mission and global development—overlap, yet they often differ on fundamentals such as the nature and role of humanity, divinity, and the church.

When elements of holistic mission and global development are combined, we arrive at our primary focus, which is *transformational development*. Vinay Samuel describes Christian mission as "individuals coming to Christ, challenging corrupt and sinful systems, structures and cultures and enabling individuals and communities to experience God's transforming power."[5] Similarly, transformational development is the intersection of God's mission to renew all things and our efforts to compassionately engage

---

[3] We explore holistic mission in more detail in Chapter Two. See Padilla, "Holistic Mission," for an overview of the development of holistic mission in missiology.

[4] For development terms, see Horner, "Towards a New Paradigm." Similar whole-world nomenclature is being used in other sectors. "Global health," for example, emphasizes the linkages among all countries in health and disease. See Hotez, *Blue Marble Health*.

[5] Samuel, "Mission as Transformation," 244.

suffering in the world (see Figure 1.2).[6] Transformation happens because of Christ, and it occurs in all who remain open to it.

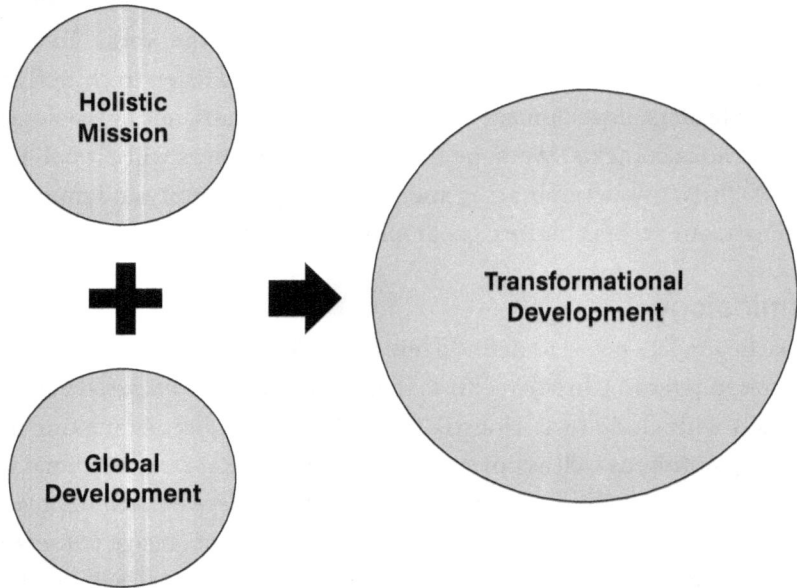

Figure 1.2. Transformational Development

Transformational development is a redemptive process focused on persons, communities, societies, and the connections among them. Instead of something done *to* someone else, transformational development is done *with* others. It invites participants who cross borders—cultural, social, economic, and geographic—to advocate for just laws and policies, utilize resources toward well-being for vulnerable communities, and live in ways that reflect an awareness of God's love and God's purposes for all creation. The intended effect is for all to participate in God's compassion and justice, which moves the world toward flourishing, or *shalom*. Just as seen with Doris and Patricia, it results in the transformation of all in the process (Rom. 12:2).

---

[6] Our definition is influenced by the thoughts of Bryant Meyer, who writes that we set "aside that which is not for life in us and in our community, while actively seeking and supporting all that is for life." See Myers, *Walking with the Poor*, 3. We also are influenced by views on a "preferential option for the poor," which "commit oneself to resisting the injustice, oppression, exploitation, and marginalization of people that permeate almost every aspect of public life." See Dwyer, "Preferential Option for the Poor," 755.

As a final note on terms, we acknowledge that geographical references often are inadequate to describe global complexities. Binary divisions between the third and first world, the developing and developed world, the minority and majority world, or the Global South and Global North have become increasingly blurred. Although imperfect, we employ the last of these pairs. We use *Global South* to refer to middle- and low-income countries primarily located in Latin America, Asia, Africa, the Caribbean, and Oceania. *Global North* refers to high-income countries, regardless of their location around the world.[7] By using these terms in the context of transformational development, we hope we will resist the historical elevation of high-income, Western nations and cultures and signal new ways of anticipating the blessing of learning and partnering around the globe. We invite all to imagine the world in new ways, as a south-up map suggests.

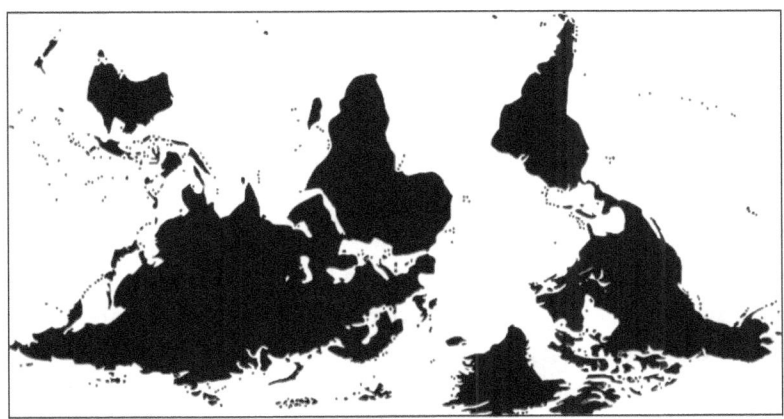

Figure 1.3. South-Up Map

Making Peace with Complexity

Anyone who has engaged in small- or large-scale holistic mission efforts knows how challenging poverty can be to understand or address. So, at the outset, we want to acknowledge that transformational development is complex. Famine, violence, and trafficking, combined with government policies, global trade, and aid architecture, create a cauldron of complexity. Water supplies require more than well drilling, livelihoods require more

---

[7] For a listing, see World Bank, "World Bank Country and Lending Groups."

than a loan, and food security requires more than a sack of grain. Often, institutions and contexts magnify the complexity, and any effort is made more intricate when pursued across cultures.

How Christians have thought about poverty in churches adds yet another layer of complexity. Many of us have witnessed debates over humanitarianism versus evangelism in domestic and international missions. We (and many others) believe that this is a false dichotomy and the vestige of mistaken theology. God's mission envelops all aspects of creation stewardship and human well-being and salvation, and Scripture repeatedly directs us to respond with courage and hope to the brokenness we find in the world, as we will discuss in Chapter Two.

The gospel of Jesus Christ is good news for the whole world. Mission involves our entire lives, as individuals and communities, witnessing to the gospel that, through the life, death, and resurrection of Jesus, God reigns.[8] Empowered by the Holy Spirit, we desire to follow the way of Christ and be transformed more fully into his likeness. Our love and care for the vulnerable throughout the world flow from Jesus's prayer: "Your kingdom come. Your will be done, on earth as it is in heaven" (Matt. 6:10).

Listening

One way to begin adjusting to global and local complexities is to listen to others. Although we can gather a variety of tools and experiences to equip us for different situations, we are almost always guaranteed to be misled if we don't begin in humility, listening to others.

A story that illustrates this point is recorded in the book *Nurturing the Prophetic Imagination*. A group of college students from Point Loma Nazarene University (PLNU) in San Diego, California, traveled to visit ministers and church leaders at a Nazarene seminary campus in Tecate, Mexico, just south of the US–Mexico border. The group was co-led by Spanish language professor Cynthia Ovando-Knudson and cultural anthropology professor Jamie Gates, along with Josh Sweeden, a student leader.

As part of the service weekend in Mexico, Josh asked pastors in Mexico to describe what it was like to receive assistance from churches in the

---

[8] See Stone, *Evangelism after Christendom*, for an incisive explanation of the holistic nature of evangelism as a practice of the church.

United States, or *El Otro Lado* ("the Other Side"). Listen in and see if you can detect the flaw that mirrors Doris's lesson about the pumpkin.

> Josh made arrangements for the group to meet some of the pastors with whom he had developed deep friendships. Everyone the group met with was asked a question that was difficult to answer and difficult to be received. The pastors were requested to be open and straightforward about the difficult aspects of receiving so many "*gringo*" mission(s) teams from "*El Otro Lado*."
>
> One of the pastors smiled when the term *gringo* was used. He recognized that the group was being confessional. He said that not all of the teams that come from *El Otro Lado* were in fact *gringo*, only the ones who wouldn't listen.
>
> Using the name *gringos* was a confession by the group of their complicity in the gross disparities created by the border between the U.S. and Mexico. *El Otro Lado* is more than just a phrase meaning "the other side" in Spanish. Living in San Diego, Jamie's Spanish-speaking brothers and sisters often use this phrase in reference to the United States. Rarely is *Estados Unidos* used; *El Otro Lado* has become a standard reference for the side of the border from which the group had come. It couldn't have been a better lesson for that weekend—the group was from "the other side." And members thought they had just arrived on the other side. They were the "other."
>
> It was as if the group's confession gave each person they met permission to speak about difficult relations and dynamics. Perhaps the most truthful and prophetic comments came from the caretaker of the campgrounds where the group slept. In telling about leaky pipes and cracked walls, about the old bunk beds still with the PLNU stamp on them and the newer buildings that mission(s) teams had built over the years, the caretaker reminded the group not just of the materiality of their faith and their fellowship, but of their participation in a church that is also a global economic body.

DEVELOPMENT IN **MISSION**

In his conversation about his difficulty in getting parts from *El Otro Lado* for the new showers in the old cinderblock dormitories, the caretaker made the uneven reality of the border come alive. Parts and people flow south across the border almost at will. Yet, crossing the border north for even the most mundane of needs is a monumental task. The social/economic/political/psychological/theological fence between north and south determines fellowship far too significantly. Those from *El Otro Lado* could zip down for a weekend leadership training retreat by flashing a driver's license to the border patrol; the caretaker and the pastors in Mexico had to apply three months in advance just for the chance to get a temporary permit to buy supplies or visit the PLNU campus just 20 minutes north of the border.

Cynthia asked the caretaker to reflect a bit more critically on the mission(s) teams that came down so often from *El Otro Lado*, particularly the difficult ones. The caretaker showed her a slab of concrete with a half-crumbled wall in the middle of a courtyard. He explained that there are a lot of very talented people with a lot of construction experience and expensive tools that come to help out. But the same dynamics that make it difficult for him to get supplies to fix the showerheads also make him cautious to use the latest and greatest technologies in his construction projects. He often chooses to use a simpler technique and technology because it is something he can fix once all the talent and tools leave.

When the caretaker has one of those teams that just won't listen or do things the way they need to be done in Tecate, he has them build a wall or two on that slab of concrete. When it's time for the team to go back to *El Otro Lado*, the team celebrates the work they've done together, prays, and parts in peace. The caretaker then tears down the wall and gets it ready for the next group that has too much to give and not enough time or patience to listen and learn. The group later dubbed this the "gringo wall" as they realized how profound a sign this wall was in representing their inability to listen to one another, to be reconciled to one another, to be agents of reconciliation as the Body of Christ in the world, to be witnesses to the reconciliation that God has already made possible in Christ.[9]

Though all of the well-intentioned work groups coming from the United States wanted to help the students and staff at the seminary in Mexico, the inability of some to listen and learn in humility made their efforts impotent.

Similarly troubling are the stories following disasters, of churches and businesses donating high-heeled shoes and fur coats to places where such donations are either not appropriate or not helpful in the context and climate of the receiving population. Sometimes, the donations are of such poor quality that they are useless: clothes that are ragged, electronics that cannot be repaired, dolls with eyes poked out or scribbled on, even used tea bags. In these cases, the recipient churches and nonprofits have to immediately discard the items, even though the donors spent considerable money shipping the unusable and impractical goods to the country. Donors may have given with the best of intentions, but they benefited more than did the receivers. These givers are the ones who are impoverished when contemplating their lack of listening, learning, and humility.

Churches and mission groups *can* yield long-term benefits in intercultural settings when they humbly seek out input from others, specifically through partnerships of trust and mutual understanding. Indeed, the world yearns for Christians in the Global North to assume earnest, faithful postures of listening and learning from others as together they engage in transformational development.

Global Poverty: What Is True?

To conclude this chapter, we want to begin *hearing* realities today that may invert our thinking about global poverty. Let's do this by way of a simple game.

In small group settings, people often play an icebreaker game in which an individual relays three personal statements about himself or herself that others likely do not know. Two statements are true, and a third is false. After the individual provides the three statements, the rest of the group

---

[9]Gates, Bollinger, and Gailey, "Nurturing a Prophetic Imagination," 236–37.

tries to guess which one is false. The conversations that follow each person's revelation of the true and false statements often provide memorable and informative conversations within the group.

We thought it worthwhile to begin our examination of global poverty in a similar fashion. Two of the following statements are true. Which one is contested?

1. During the past thirty years, global poverty has decreased at an unprecedented rate in world history.
2. Among countries of the world, the United States is the most generous governmental funder of international aid.
3. Since the turn of the twentieth century, the church has grown fastest in areas where economic poverty is relatively high, and thus more Christians now live in the Global South than in the Global North.

The following analysis of trends in global poverty will reveal which of these statements are true.

Declining Poverty

Global poverty has significantly declined over the past three decades on nearly every metric. Although poverty indicators ticked up during the global coronavirus pandemic, both the percentage and the number of people living in abject poverty have steeply declined since 1990. For example, the number of children each day who die from mostly preventable causes has dropped by more than half, from an average of 35,000 per day in 1990 to fewer than 17,260 per day in 2018. Maternal mortality (the number of women who die in childbirth, often due to poverty) has declined by 44 percent from 1990 to 2017.[10]

With fewer children dying, the average life span globally has increased. Literacy rates, particularly among women, are increasing. The improved chances a child will live past the age of five, along with increased access to health care and education, have resulted in a number of countries' birthrates declining sharply. Economic growth in several countries has resulted

---

[10] "Goal Area 1: Every Child Survives and Thrives," 1.

in families shifting from having many children—often as a hedge against high infant mortality rates and to ensure someone will care for parents in old age—to having fewer children and providing a better quality of life for them. This is evident in the growth rate of the world's population now being half of what it was in the 1960s.

In 2015, many countries in the Global South met or surpassed the Millennium Development Goals agreed to in 2000. These goals targeted grand outcomes, including eradicating extreme poverty and hunger, achieving universal primary education, and improving maternal health.[11] Many countries made laudable progress, and new Sustainable Development Goals were set to carry each country through to 2030.[12] Equally surprising to some is the realization that aid can be effective. Many global and missions commentators have raised concerns about aid and dependency, and these views need to be heard (see Chapter Three). But evidence also suggests that when given effectively, aid can materially and sustainably reduce poverty and disease.[13]

Despite these reductions in global poverty, many people in the Global North retain an image of dire poverty across the Global South. A recent Barna Group report indicated that while almost a quarter (24 percent) of Christians in the United States have volunteered to address global poverty, many declared they would do more if they thought their efforts made a difference.[14] The good news is that they can and they do! Many working in poverty alleviation around the world have renewed optimism that additional progress is possible.

Despite the progress, however, millions remain in poverty without clean water, without jobs, and without peace. As expressed throughout Scripture, God calls us to do what we can to offer compassion, extend justice, and participate in transformation. While we ultimately place our trust in God, we desire to be what economist Bruce Wydick terms "shrewd Samaritans." This does not mean that we elevate efficiency or effectiveness

---

[11] UN, "Millennium Development Goals Report 2015."
[12] China's economic growth has been massive in recent decades. Increasing average incomes within the country graduated more than 500 million people out of extreme poverty. Yet, China was not alone in experiencing reductions in economic poverty.
[13] Bill and Melinda Gates Foundation, "2014 Gates Annual Letter."
[14] "Good News about Global Poverty."

above other values, but that we love others enough to engage in actions that make a difference—actions that "loose the bonds of injustice" and "let the oppressed go free" (Isa. 58:6).[15]

Surprising Aid

Given these gains, one might imagine that the United States vigorously funds poverty-alleviation efforts. Indeed, it regularly leads the world in total monetary aid.[16] But considering why and how funds are given, and the percentage of national income this aid represents, puts these sizable sums into perspective.

Governments allocate most nonemergency aid strategically—that is, they offer aid to help their allies and further their own national interests and priorities. Some aid comes with strings attached that require the receiving nation to bend to the donor, or it is given in a way that benefits the giver. Even in the case of providing relief for natural calamities or prevalent diseases, some needs receive more attention, while others are ignored completely.[17] Despite the fact that, in recent years, the United States has provided the most official development assistance (ODA) among all countries (around 30 billion dollars), annual US government aid represents between 0.21 percent and 0.16 percent of gross national income. In other words, the United States gives about one-fifth or one-sixth of 1 percent of its economic income as aid to other nations.[18]

Private funding, such as from the Bill and Melinda Gates Foundation or from individuals contributing to humanitarian aid organizations, provides an amount roughly equivalent to US government aid. Eclipsing the size of both private and government aid flows, however, are remittances—the money that family members who are working outside their home country transfer to their families in low-income countries. So, the most

---

[15] Wydick, *Shrewd Samaritan*.
[16] OECD, *Development Co-operation Profiles*.
[17] See Epstein, "Crisis Mentality"; Eikenberry, "The Hidden Costs of Cause Marketing."
[18] OECD, *Development Co-operation Profiles*. In 1970, many Global North countries—including the United States—committed to give 0.7 percent of their national income in international aid. Some European countries have reached or exceeded the target; but not the United States.

generous funders are not governments, foundations, or individual donors but those who are working away from home—many of whom are in poverty themselves—to support their families back in their home countries. In sum, it is true that wealthy countries provide billions of dollars worth of aid, but these funds are often channeled to further self-interest and are only a tiny percentage of the overall economy.

The Growing Christian South

Amid these trends related to global poverty, the world is witnessing a dramatic increase in the number of Christians throughout the Global South. The statistical center of gravity in global Christianity slid from Europe to Africa after 1970 (which is discussed further in Chapter Six).[19] Though it should not be surprising if we look at the biblical witness and the early church, the fastest growth is in areas where economic poverty is relatively high.[20] The generosity and interdependence of communities of faith throughout the Global South is a catalyst for many coming to faith and extending mutual care.

With the church growing fastest in the Global South, and with capacity increasing among our brothers and sisters there, there is an increase in both need and ability. We believe the church everywhere has an enduring role to play in God's desire for wholeness and *shalom* throughout the Global South, as well as the Global North. Scripture and God's love compel us to bolster rather than relax our commitment, which can be supported by global metrics.

Returning to our game, the correct answer should now be evident. Global poverty has decreased globally, and the church is growing the most where significant material poverty remains. The United States is a significant donor, but its gifts are often conditional or strategic and they pale compared with the percentage of aid given by several other nations and shared by people in relative poverty themselves. With these perspectives in mind, we move forward in transformational development with cruciform hope.

---

[19] Johnson and Chung, "Tracking Global Christianity's Statistical Centre."
[20] Johnson and Zurlo, *World Christian Database*.

What Lies Ahead

In the chapters that follow, we will highlight perspectives and tools that we believe will strengthen Christians engaging in transformational development. We begin by laying out a theological foundation for how holistic mission and poverty alleviation fit within God's mission. We argue that *missio Dei* entails a renewing of all creation and that our love and care for vulnerable populations is grounded in Jesus being Lord. In Chapter Three, we attempt to detail what is unique about *Christian* poverty alleviation—that is, what is transformational development. We argue that the ultimate aim of transformational development is to participate in the life and mission of God, and we contend that we do this by following the way of Jesus. We suggest how kenosis can be embodied in transformational development, and we provide principles for faithful and effective engagement.

The longest chapter in the book, Chapter Four, surveys prominent sectors in transformational development and provides detailed information on how churches can engage in each sector more effectively. This chapter can be read in its entirety, or it can be read selectively according to sectors of interest. Chapter Five offers practical steps for congregational engagement and fostering healthy partnerships. In the concluding chapter, we explore four large waves of change already lapping up on our shores, and we make suggestions for the way forward. In the appendices, we offer additional resources (books and organizations) for further investigation and learning.

Along the journey of these pages, we will provide insights from others—community members, researchers, practitioners, missionaries, and others—and we will attempt to listen to the wisdom of all, seeing the world that receives "good news of great joy for all the people" (Luke 2:10) and imagining what it looks like when people are transformed and experience God's *shalom*.

2

FOR GOD SO LOVES
THE WHOLE WORLD

I (Derran) am certain he saw the shock in my eyes. It happened during the two years my wife and I spent as missionary apprentices in Chiang Mai, Thailand. Fresh out of college and newly married, we wanted to learn and experience mission work under the tutelage of a seasoned church-planting team before we launched our own long-term ministry in Thailand. Our primary focus, other than trying to master the Thai language, was discipling college students who were relatively new to the Christian faith.

On one of the many balmy Friday nights in that beautiful city, the small group of college students we had grown to love decided they wanted to go sing praise songs at the famous night bazaar market. Despite my reluctance, I soon found myself standing on a street corner overrun with local sellers and bargain-hunting tourists. My friends began singing newly learned songs as I watched from a few feet away. (I did not join in because, as my family will attest, no one wants to hear my pitchy crooning.)

As I softly hummed along, observing the excited faces of my friends and those who stopped for a quick listen, an older man—his clothes and accent revealing he was from the United States—approached me. He introduced himself, asked for my name, and then inquired who we were and why these Thai young people were singing. I explained that I was a missionary apprentice who was serving a Thai church there in Chiang Mai and that the chorus of voices belonged to friends of mine in the campus ministry of that church.

"So, what else do you and your church do other than sing at night markets?" he asked. His tone and demeanor were noticeably more irritated than a few moments before.

"Well, we meet for worship, and we have small gatherings each week during which we pray, read Scripture, and share our joys and struggles," I said. "We also look for opportunities to serve those around us, especially those who are facing difficult times because of poverty, health concerns, or other challenging circumstances. And sometimes we sing for tourists on the side of the road." I gave him a wink to lighten the mood of this now-awkward conversation.

"I don't know why you are wasting your time singing or doing those other things to help people," he said. "What you need to be doing is walking up and down this street telling these people that they are going to hell with their religion. That's what a missionary is supposed to be doing."

And with that admonition, the man walked off to a nearby booth to buy a wooden elephant. I could not help but notice that he did not tell the seller anything about the dangers of hell.

I am fairly certain that my mouth was agape. I know that I did not reply; I was too stunned. I was taken aback by his direct and confrontational behavior, in complete contrast to the typical demeanor of my Thai friends. But, more than that, I was shocked that he could boil mission work down to helping people avoid hell. At that time in my development, I could not have clearly articulated why that was such a flawed and reductionistic view of the gospel. But I knew it was.

Encountering the Gospel on the Streets of Brazil

Many years later, after completing seminary and serving as a missionary in a small town in northern Thailand, I was working as the director of global ministries for a church in Texas. The leaders sent me to visit a sister church in Itu, Brazil, to explore how we could expand our partnership with them and with Crescimento Limpo (CL), a nonprofit organization that had grown out of the life and ministry of the Brazilian congregation.

CL works to bring restoration to neighbors in Itu who are suffering from addiction and are living on the streets. This ministry grew out of the hospitality of two of the ministers of the church I was sent to visit, a married couple (a woman from Brazil and a man from the United States) who had begun inviting their neighbors on the streets to dinner in their home. As they listened to their new friends' stories around their table and even offered their extra bed at times, the complexity of issues that led to addiction and homelessness became more apparent. One of the biggest challenges facing these neighbors was that, even if they were able to get into rehab, there was no support system waiting to propel them toward whole and flourishing lives. Resolutely and compassionately, this couple established a halfway home for their neighbors, and they called it Crescimento Limpo ("Clean Growth").

I still remember walking into that halfway home for the first time. Some of the residents were busy preparing a meal for that evening, while others were cleaning the common room. One staff member was providing counsel to another resident in a private room. There was a lot of laughter in that place, and everyone greeted me with warmth and hospitality. Some of us walked down a few blocks to the community garden that CL had created. A couple of residents were tending the raised-bed garden. The couple showed me where they were developing an aquaponics system so the garden could be more efficient. The goal, which was already partially realized, was to sell their produce to nearby markets, thus making the garden financially sustainable. We then walked over to a corner of the property where they hoped to one day open a café where residents and community members could share a cup of coffee or snack together. (They have since realized that dream.)

This community garden provided an avenue for the CL residents to gain experience working and reconstitute their dignity as contributors to society. The CL staff worked alongside them, providing emotional and spiritual support, while also helping them find full-time employment. As we left the garden that day, one of the residents, who was covered in dirt from hours of tending the garden, told me he would look for me at the Bible study that night at the church. While, by that time, I had served as a missionary for years and earned a Master of Divinity degree, in that moment, overwhelmed by the presence of the living God in that space, I could not have clearly articulated why this was a full and embodied expression of the gospel. But I knew it was.

What Is (Holistic) Mission?

For those not immersed in missiological literature, discussions about theology and best practices related to holistic mission can quickly become confusing because of a single letter in the alphabet. While *mission* and *missions* are intricately related, it is important to clearly distinguish the meaning and significance of each term.[1] *Missions* most commonly refers to particular activities of a church, typically related to intercultural and international ministries. There is variation among churches and traditions about what exactly should be included within "missions" (e.g., church planting, service, short-term trips), but the distinguishing factor is that missions is a human endeavor in response to God's call for the church. Furthermore, the term denotes a subset of activities—one among many ministries (e.g., education, benevolence, worship)—initiated and carried out by a church or parachurch organization.

Mission has a much deeper and broader meaning. It is to this meaning and its theological significance that we now turn. The purpose of this chapter is to provide a theology of (holistic) mission. This theological account will reveal how missions and other ministries of the church, with special attention given to poverty alleviation and transformational development, flow from the mission of God and the church's participation in that mission. Our aim is to give God's people a robust foundation for engagement in poverty alleviation and transformational development. It can also serve as an articulation of why the two "gospels" Derran encountered in Thailand and Brazil stand in such contrast.

God of Mission

The mission of God's people originates in and emanates from the mission of God. This sounds like an obvious truth, but the church, particularly in

---

[1] See Goheen, *Introducing Christian Mission Today*, 73–86, for a more thorough explanation of the terms *mission*, *missions*, *missional*, and *missiology*.

the Global North, has not always approached its theology and practice of missions from this starting point. Thankfully, recent developments in theology and missiology have situated missions and all works of God's people within the concept of *missio Dei*, or the mission of God.

Missio Dei originally referred to the sending of the Son by God the Father and the sending of the Holy Spirit by the Father and the Son. However, by the mid-twentieth century, the term began to encompass the idea that the Father, Son, and Holy Spirit also send the church into the world. This shift prompted a reexamination of the grounding of mission.[2] The church could no longer see itself as the initiator of mission. Instead, mission flows from the very character and activity of the Triune God. While the meaning and usage of *missio Dei* continues to be contested in some circles, the broader understanding of *missio Dei* has helped emphasize the conviction that neither the church nor any other human agent can ever be considered the author or bearer of mission. Mission is, primarily and ultimately, the work of the Triune God—Creator, Redeemer, and Sanctifier—for the sake of the world, a vocation in which the church is privileged to participate. Mission has its origin in the heart of God.[3]

Though churches can and should continue to "do missions," the church itself—its identity, practices, activities, and *missions*—is now more keenly aware that it is a participant in God's mission. God's people engage in ministry as ones sent from God. *Missio Dei* rightfully places the church, its mission, and all its endeavors, including poverty alleviation, within God's purpose and action in the world.

Furthermore, *missio Dei* serves as an anchor for those who are engaged in the challenging and weighty work of holistic mission. The burden of responsibility for the success and effectiveness of such efforts lightens when one realizes that the work is ultimately God's. Though a ministry, project, or enterprise might be painstaking and seemingly fruitless at times, it is not in vain—for the mission belongs to God.

---

[2] See Bevans and Schroeder, *Constants in Context*, 286–95, and Bosch, *Transforming Mission*, 389–93, for detailed accounts of the development of *missio Dei* in missiology.
[3] Bosch, *Transforming Mission*, 392.

The Mission of God

Recognizing that God is the source of mission is a critical first step for all who want to engage in mission. However, this prompts a follow-up question: What is the mission of God? To answer this question, we must turn our attention to Scripture and the work of Christ. But first, let us provide a quick word about our approach to the task of theology.

Theology is never done in a vacuum, and this includes the theology of mission. Every human being who reflects on the nature and activity of God, and any other theological loci, does so from a particular vantage point. We are all shaped by a constellation of influences (culture, time in history, family background, personal experience, etc.) through which we see the world and articulate our understanding of it. This is also true for our perspectives on theological matters. While this might be evident when analyzing different expressions of worship or interpretations of biblical texts across cultures, one might assume that there would be consensus around something as central as naming God's purposes for creation. Surely we can rise above our particular contexts to access and describe the absolute truth about God's mission in the world.

The reality is that no one is free from contextual influences. For too long, Christians in the Global North, particularly White males, have referred to theological works from other cultures and vantage points as contextual theologies. This designation was based upon an assumption, though often subconscious, that White male theologians were the standard bearers. They did theology, while others did *contextual* theology. Thankfully, this trend is changing, and more and more theologians, authors, and pastors recognize that their background and context always shape their theology.

Therefore, we, the authors, acknowledge that our specific social, historical, and religious backgrounds inform our perspective. This, in turn, influences what we say about the theology of mission. We agree with Henning Wrogemann: "Today, mission theology can only be pursued contextually."[4] So, like other attempts at naming the purposes and actions of God, what follows is contextual theology.

---

[4] Wrogemann, *Theologies of Mission*, 384.

With that said, we have intentionally and diligently investigated theologies of mission from disparate perspectives and contexts. We have especially attempted to glean from the rich body of work within the various Christian traditions reflecting on the relationship between God, the church, and mission.[5] We have also sought to incorporate theological voices from around the world, particularly from the Global South, in our understanding, all the while working to increase our awareness of colonial biases that might influence our viewpoint and articulation.[6] This chapter is far too short to touch on the many important facets of this global conversation.[7] What follows is our endeavor to distill the most relevant and applicable concepts for the overall purposes of this book.

God's Love for All Creation

"Now after John was arrested, Jesus came to Galilee, proclaiming the good news of God, and saying, 'The time is fulfilled, and the kingdom of God has come near; repent, and believe in the good news'" (Mark 1:14–15). Jesus shows up on the scene and declares to all within earshot that he has good news. *This good news is that the kingdom of God is at hand.* This proclamation is key to understanding the work of Jesus Christ. But we must first situate Jesus's words within the larger narrative of Scripture. Only then can we begin to understand the significance of the kingdom of God, why it is good news, and how Jesus is inaugurating it.

The biblical story begins with one character performing all the action. God "created the heavens and the earth" (Gen. 1:1). God set out to make something (the physical universe) that was not necessary but was desired—by God. The first domino was the creation and ordering of energy ("Let there be light" [v. 3]), followed by the progressive emergence of the entire

---

[5] Ott, *Mission of the Church*, is a good example of how particular Christian traditions shape mission theology. See also Ross and Walls, *Mission in the 21st Century*.

[6] Isaak, "Mission as Praxis for Peace-Building," 240, describes how postcolonialism creates opportunity for constructive cooperation in doing theology: "Today in the postcolonial era, one should accept diverse theologies that do not necessarily exclude each other; they form a multicoloured mosaic of complementary and mutual enriching as well as mutually challenging frames of reference."

[7] See Wrogemann, *Theologies of Mission*, for an exhaustive historical and systematic analysis of trends in the theology of mission.

material universe (land, water, celestial beings, plants, animals, and much more). Each new feature of creation was good in the eyes of God. God did not stop there, though. God, who is by nature relational, created human beings "in our image, according to our likeness" (Gen. 1:26). God designed humans for relationship, with God and with each other, and tasked them with caring for the material world in a symbiotic and interdependent manner.

However, the purposes of God for creation and humanity were thwarted. Humans succumbed to the powers of sin and death due to their disobedience (Gen. 3:1–24), and creation soon found itself under the bondage of decay. God did not abandon all that was made, though, and God set forth to reclaim and rectify that which was broken and suffering.

The story of God's patient and unyielding pursuit of restoration is the thread that runs through the complex mosaic that is the Hebrew Bible (Old Testament). The people of Israel are birthed because God wants to call out a people through whom "all the families of the earth shall be blessed" (Gen. 12:3). The Israelites are to be a people set apart and formed by their allegiance to Yahweh and Yahweh alone. When God's chosen people find themselves enslaved and oppressed, and they cry out to God, God delivers them. The message God sends them is "I will take you as my people, and I will be your God. You shall know that I am the LORD your God, who has freed you from the burdens of the Egyptians" (Exod. 6:7). Yahweh made a covenant with Israel, and God remains true to that promise.

Upon saving them from bondage, God gives the Law to guide them toward flourishing and demarcate them as God's holy, chosen nation. Unfortunately, Israel is unable to remain faithful, turning to other gods and failing to uphold the Law. The strain of its idolatry, sin, and disobedience produces fractures and brokenness throughout Israel, both individually and collectively. The remainder of Israel's story is a roller-coaster ride of abandoning trust in Yahweh, fidelity and infidelity to the Law, reaping the dire consequences of sin, and repentance. Through it all, God never forsakes these chosen people with whom God made a covenant.

The cycles of obedience, disobedience, punishment, and repentance continue until finally the Israelites find themselves in exile, cut off from their land and wondering if God will deliver them once again. During this time of banishment and desolation, a hope, a longing, an anticipation emerges from within Israel for a time when the Lord will once again deliver them and establish God's reign. Isaiah 65:17–18 captures this hope by imagining the restorative work of Yahweh: "For I am about to create new heavens and a new earth; the former things shall not be remembered or come to mind. But be glad and rejoice forever in what I am creating; for I am about to create Jerusalem as a joy, and its people as a delight." This hope is tied to God sending a Messiah, a king in the line of David, to bring about this restoration. Although God's people eventually find themselves back in the land promised to them, they continue to suffer under the tyranny and oppression of numerous rulers and empires. At the close of the Hebrew Bible, the day God's people long and hope for has yet to come. They continue to wait for God to reign once again.

This is a simplistic retelling of a fascinating and complex story. We have told the story this way to make the following points about the narrative from which Jesus emerges:

1. God created humans with the intention (mission) for them to enjoy being in loving relationships with God and with each other. God also commissioned humans to be co-creators by stewarding the physical world in which they inhabit.
2. Humans disobeyed, and continuously disobeyed, which brought about destruction and brokenness. The consequences of sin penetrated all aspects of human life: mental, emotional, physical, familial, economic, social, cultural, and environmental.
3. God set out (on a mission) to redeem and restore all that was broken. Yahweh chose Israel to be a vessel through which all people would be blessed. God remained faithful to the covenant with Israel.
4. When God saved Israel—most clearly seen in the exodus from Egypt but also in other instances—the result was Israel's deliverance from oppression, suffering, and despair. God called Israel back to worship Yahweh and no other gods (Exod. 20:2–3).
5. However, Israel failed to remain faithful. The power of sin and death continued to wreak destruction, and Israel longed for the

day when all things would be restored and Yahweh would reign once again through a new king, the Messiah.

This summary of the Hebrew Bible illustrates that God's mission is twofold. First, God created the universe and humans as image-bearers for a purpose. Deborah Ajulu explains:

> The mission starts at creation when God makes human beings in his own image and likeness, and assigns them, both male and female, the role of co-workers with him. Creation begins in perfect harmony under the lordship of God, with human beings in relation to their creator as stewards of his creation. This role of stewardship given to human beings (men and women) was a responsibility to care for the whole of creation.[8]

Second, as soon as the first bite was taken from the infamous fruit, God set out to redeem and renew all that was now under the power of sin and death. Yahweh seeks to restore that which is broken and return humans to the joy and responsibility of co-creating. The story of Scripture bears witness to God's fidelity to that mission. Christopher Wright summarizes and amplifies this point.

> The writings that now comprise our Bible are themselves the product of and witness to the ultimate mission of God. The Bible renders to us the story of God's mission through God's people in their engagement with God's world for the sake of the whole of God's creation. The Bible is the drama of this God of purpose engaged in the mission of achieving that purpose universally, embracing past, present and future, Israel and the nations, "life, the universe, and everything," and with its center, focus, climax, and completion in Jesus Christ.[9]

Now that we have set the stage, let's dig deeper into why Jesus Christ is the "center, focus, climax, and completion" of God's purposes.

---

[8] Ajulu, "Development as Holistic Mission," 166–67.
[9] Wright, *Mission of God*, 22.

The Gospel of Jesus Christ

Recall the two stories that began this chapter. Why do these accounts and their expressions of the gospel diverge so radically? We hope it is evident, even before we finish articulating our theology of mission, why the robust ministries in Itu, Brazil, are more congruent with God's holistic work in the world. Why did the man at the night bazaar in Chiang Mai, Thailand, think that telling people they are going to hell is the heart of mission? It is because of a gross misunderstanding of the gospel that stems from taking Jesus out of the overarching mission of God. This type of misunderstanding is far too common. While most people would not be so crass and off the mark as that man, many maintain the same undergirding misconceptions about the meanings of gospel and salvation. We will now address these two interconnected matters and, in the process, illustrate how the gospel of Jesus Christ is the climax of God's overarching mission.

There is a strange phrase used in some Christian traditions: "Obey the gospel." This expression implies that the gospel is some sort of commandment or rule. Other traditions sum up the gospel with a particular doctrine, such as "justification by faith." Yet others suggest it is a set of propositions, most commonly related to a plan of salvation. These conceptions are certainly not unrelated to the gospel, but they miss something fundamental about the good news—specifically, that it is *news*. This critical misstep completely alters the way we understand the gospel, the significance of Jesus, and God's overarching mission.

What if we start with Jesus's own words about the gospel? "The time is fulfilled, and the kingdom of God has come near; repent, and believe in the good news" (Mark 1:15). This is an announcement that something is happening. This is news. A commandment, a doctrine, or a proposition is, by definition, not news. The term *news* necessitates that something has or is occurring. It is an event or a development within a larger story or context. News is decipherable and relevant only when the audience knows the backstory.[10] Misconceptions about the gospel often derive from ignoring that it is news, ripping it from the story of God and God's purposes for the world.

---

[10] See Wright, *Simply Good News*, 1–13, for more on what constitutes news in relation to the gospel.

When Jesus first proclaims the kingdom is at hand, he is emerging from both the desert and the entire narrative of the Hebrew Bible. Jesus makes this announcement to an audience, the Jewish people, who know this story, are in the story, and anticipate the day when God will bring it to completion. They long for God's reign to come so they will be delivered and restored. When Jesus arrives and announces that the time for which they have been waiting is here, it is news indeed.

Furthermore, it is *good* news. The Jews are being crushed under the Roman Empire, one empire in a long line of oppressive empires. Beyond that, humanity as a whole has been under the power of sin and death for so long (Rom. 5:12–21). All those voices are tired of crying out, "How long, O Lord?" (Ps. 13:1). Then, a new song breaks out: "Thanks be to God through Jesus Christ our Lord!" (Rom. 7:25). The awaited Messiah, the King of kings and Lord of lords, has arrived. God is fulfilling the covenant with Abraham. The power of sin and the sting of death have been conquered through Jesus Christ (1 Cor. 15:20–57). The entire created order has now come under "the reign of God that was inaugurated in the life, death, and resurrection of Jesus of Nazareth."[11]

The story of God's creation forever changed upon the crowning of Jesus. Nothing will ever be the same. Of course, not everyone is going to believe this good news. In one sense, who can blame them? The entire gospel hinges on the incarnate Son of God, the anticipated Messiah, dying on a cross. This is foolishness (1 Cor. 1:18)! Yet, at the heart of the gospel is this mystery: "For in him all the fullness of God was pleased to dwell, and through him God was pleased to reconcile to himself all things, whether on earth or in heaven, by making peace through the blood of his cross" (Col. 1:19–20). This is certainly news. Indeed, it is good news.

Salvation

A treasure trove of scholarship has been written in recent years about how the modern church, particularly in the Protestant tradition, has a narrow and distorted view of the salvation found in Jesus Christ.[12] The

---

[11] Abraham, *The Logic of Evangelism*, 17.
[12] Green, *Salvation*, and McKnight, *King Jesus Gospel*, are two accessible works that address this narrow view and offer a more complete account of salvation.

summation of this truncated perspective is that the salvific work of Jesus enables human souls to avoid eternal hell and, instead, spend eternity in heaven. This is most likely the underlying assumption of our night bazaar friend's retort. The biblical notion of salvation, however, is much more robust and, frankly, interesting.

A major problem with such a view of salvation is that it does not flow from the story of Scripture. A careful examination of the Hebrew Bible reveals that "going to heaven" is found nowhere. The intention of Israel's God is not to free souls from their bodies to live in heaven forever. The mission of God is to restore and renew all creation through the chosen people of Israel.

Furthermore, "going to heaven" is not the way Jesus and his disciples understood and proclaimed salvation. A quick look at Luke-Acts will put this into sharp focus. The ministry of Jesus begins in a Nazareth synagogue when he reads from Isaiah 61: "The Spirit of the Lord is upon me, because he has anointed me to bring good news to the poor. He has sent me to proclaim release to the captives and recovery of sight to the blind, to let the oppressed go free, to proclaim the year of the Lord's favor" (Luke 4:18–19). He then declares, "Today this scripture has been fulfilled in your hearing" (Luke 4:21).

Jesus is stating his agenda and purpose. The Savior of the world is liberating those who are being crushed under oppression and injustice. He has come to reorder human relationships. He proceeds to free people from the torment of unclean spirits and heal them of their afflictions (Luke 4:38–41). He forgives people of their sins (Luke 5:17–25). He gives nourishment to those who are hungry (Luke 9:10–17). He completely revolutionizes what it means to love your neighbor, breaking down ethnic lines that divide people (Luke 10:25–37). He frees the rich from their bondage to wealth (Luke 12:13–21) and welcomes those in poverty and on the margins to his table (Luke 14:15–24). We could go on. The point is this: "According to the Gospel of Luke, Jesus understood his sending as a holistic service inextricably linked to his person and unmistakenly [sic] oriented toward the human being as a whole and to the human environment."[13]

---

[13] Wrogemann, *Theologies of Mission*, 305.

With this picture of Luke's Jesus in mind, we will zero in on two particular stories that directly use the term *salvation* (σωτηρία in Greek). Luke 19:1–10 records the story of Jesus encountering Zacchaeus in Jericho. Zacchaeus is "a chief tax collector and was rich." This means two things: (1) He was not liked by other Jews because he was serving the government oppressing them (thus, they referred to him as "a sinner"), and (2) he exploited those in poverty by collecting taxes, often more than was warranted. It takes only a moment in the presence of Jesus for Zacchaeus to repent and exclaim, "Look, half of my possessions, Lord, I will give to the poor; and if I have defrauded anyone of anything, I will pay back four times as much." This is shocking. What might be more shocking, however, is Jesus's reply: "Today salvation has come to this house." There is no mention of heaven here. Zacchaeus does not confess faith in Jesus to avoid hell—he is already in hell. What is happening is the dignity and well-being of those in poverty are being restored. And an unjust man who was enslaved by the love of money is liberated. Zacchaeus is saved.

Luke later recounts the story of Peter and John healing a lame man (Acts 3:1–4:12). After the man is restored to health, Peter tells those in earshot about the good news of Jesus. Because they are in the temple at the time, the Sadducees and other religious leaders hear about this commotion and are unhappy. After arresting Peter and John, they ask them, "By what power or by what name did you do this?" (4:7). Peter replies:

> Rulers of the people and elders, if we are questioned today because of a good deed done to someone who was sick and are asked how this man has been healed, let it be known to all of you, and to all the people of Israel, that this man is standing before you in good health by the name of Jesus Christ of Nazareth, whom you crucified, whom God raised from the dead. . . . There is salvation in no one else, for there is no other name under heaven given among mortals by which we must be saved. (Acts 4:8–12)

This is such a rich story. For our purposes, though, the key is to recognize the context into which Peter claims that salvation is found only in Jesus. It came after healing the lame man. Jesus saves the man—from being lame to being whole. Salvation means more than healing, but it also encompasses it.

This brief examination of Luke-Acts highlights the holistic nature of Christ's salvific work. Salvation, with the exodus story as a precursor, means the deliverance of God's people from all the destructive powers of sin and death. Salvation encompasses life after death, but it also brings life, and life abundantly (John 10:10), to people and communities now. Bob Mitchell summarizes: "The biblical picture invokes the future of communities and of the whole world, and it has strong practical dimensions to it. Too often salvation is passed off as some kind of a theological abstraction concerning concepts about the afterlife. It must speak to the here and now."[14]

The biblical account of salvation is rich, holistic, and awe-inspiring. It goes way beyond the idea of souls going to heaven, and one does not need to examine the whole of Scripture to find the problem with a disembodied view of salvation. The resurrection of Jesus Christ reveals this truth. The resurrected Lord is the "first fruits" of the resurrection awaiting "those who belong to Christ" (1 Cor. 15:23). Jesus was resurrected in the body, and humans will be raised up with imperishable bodies (1 Cor. 15:35–57). Therefore, salvation is not the soul's escape from the body and the created order. Instead, it is an embodied participation in God's restoration of all things. It is to be a "new creation" (2 Cor. 5:17). Salvation is the holistic liberation of creation, in which sin and death are conquered, and, both now and forevermore, nothing "will be able to separate us from the love of God in Christ Jesus our Lord" (Rom. 8:39).

The gospel of Jesus Christ is the climax and culmination of a long story of God's love for the world. This is why the confession "Jesus is Lord" is the most radical proclamation ever made by a human being. It means that God reigns in Christ Jesus, and all the powers and false gods of this world no longer have dominion. Jesus has saved, is saving, and will save all that which is God's. God's mission of restoration and renewal is summed up in this good news. For those of us who confess and embody this gospel—that is, the church—God's mission becomes our mission.

---

[14] Mitchell, *Faith-Based Development*, 38.

What Is (Not) Mission?

According to Christopher Wright, "Mission . . . while it inescapably involves us in planning and action, is not *primarily* a matter of our activity or our initiative. Mission, from the point of view of our human endeavor, means the committed *participation* of God's people in the purposes of God for the redemption of the whole creation."[15] This is a profound statement and a good summary of our argument thus far. But what do we do now? What does all that mean for us as we discern how to participate in the mission of God? Or, put differently, what now constitutes mission?

Stephen Neill famously wrote, "If everything is mission, then nothing is mission."[16] His concern was that mission would lose focus by becoming too broad. While his caution for watering down mission should be heeded, it begins with a false premise. Everything is not mission. Framing mission as a participation in God's mission, as we have expressed it, certainly expands the horizon from conceiving it only as missions. The mission of God, however, is particular, and not everything done in the name of "doing good" aligns with the mission of God. (We will say more about this in the next chapter as it relates to poverty alleviation.) Furthermore, situating mission within *missio Dei* and undeniably widening the scope enables the church to (1) conceive of its identity and all its endeavors as participation in God's purposes for the world, and to (2) evaluate and assess the congruity of the church's practices with God's mission.

Let's take the liturgical practices of the church as an example. Worship is first and foremost an act by and for the community of faith. We affirm that corporate worship is not primarily intended to be an outreach to non-Christians, even though it is an act of proclaiming the gospel, and "outsiders" often encounter the living God when visiting a worship service.[17] Nevertheless, gathering in worship is a participation in the mission of God. The church professes that Jesus is Lord and exalts God as the one true God. The people of God express their gratitude for the salvific and

---

[15] Wright, *Mission of God*, 67.

[16] Neill, *Creative Tension*, 81.

[17] See Hauerwas, "Worship, Evangelism, Ethics," and Chilcote, "The Integral Nature of Worship and Evangelism," for more in-depth analyses of the purpose and outcomes of worship in relation to the community of faith and nonbelievers.

restorative work of Jesus Christ and are formed by the liturgy, through the power of the Holy Spirit, to join in that work for the sake of the world. The community of saints, with all its diversity, gathers around the table as a manifestation and signpost of the inbreaking reign of God. Worship is not *missions*, but it certainly is *mission*.

Another benefit of the church orienting itself toward God's mission is that it can approach its work holistically. Churches too often disregard certain practices and issues—such as racial and gender justice, peacemaking, and environmental stewardship—as outside the purview of the church's domain and purpose. Or, at least, some churches downgrade such concerns to second- or third-tier priorities. A robust theology of mission helps churches be attentive to all concerns that are subsumed in the prayer "Your kingdom come. Your will be done, on earth as it is in heaven" (Matt. 6:10).

Holistic Mission

Now that we have articulated how the church in its entirety participates in the mission of God, there remains a question about the implications for how the church loves and serves the world beyond itself. What is the church to do for the sake of the world? Often, due to a narrow view of the gospel and mission, there is a tendency for people to prioritize certain aspects of mission work and global engagement.[18] This is unfortunate and unnecessary. It is why missiologists and practitioners have labored in recent decades to proffer a framework for connecting the global engagement of the church with God's mission to renew all things. Thus, the term *holistic mission* was birthed.[19] Holistic mission intends to keep *all* of God's purposes for the world, summed up in Jesus Christ, as the landscape for faithful engagement.

---

[18] Tinker, "Servant Solution," 147–67, offers a counterargument to this tendency, specifically in reaction to the tendency to pit evangelism and social action against each other.

[19] Tizon, "Precursors and Tensions in Holistic Mission," details the development of the idea and term *holistic mission*. A similar conversation started, predominantly in Latin America, around the term *integral mission*. See Padilla, "Integral Mission and Its Historical Development," for an overview of the development of "integral mission." Though holistic mission and integral mission have nuanced differences, they share a common call to the church to engage in all facets of God's work in the world.

The challenge with holistic mission is that we can easily become overwhelmed with the vastness of the task and the uncertainty of how we can do it all. Thus, it is critical to remember that this is God's mission and that the church (universal) carries the responsibility for holistic mission. No individual person or congregation can do everything. We each play our part. The key is to approach our particular ministries and enterprises as contributions toward God's restoration of all creation. And we must continually discern how our efforts can expand and adapt to address the world's vast and complex problems and shortcomings. As Emilio Castro implores: "In carrying out God's mission, we *cannot opt permanently* for one aspect of mission or another, be it liberation, development, humanization, or evangelization. These are all essential, integral parts of the mission entrusted to us and cannot be set against one another without becoming, simply, caricatures of what they really are."[20]

Poverty Alleviation and/in Holistic Mission

Holistic mission encompasses a wide swath of ministries, initiatives, and enterprises. While much could be said about the various domains of holistic mission (e.g., church planting, theological education), it is time to turn our attention to the primary focus of this book: poverty alleviation and transformational development.

The mission of God compels God's people to love, care for, and serve our neighbors, local and global, who are in poverty and suffering from injustice, oppression, and mistreatment. Caring for those in poverty is integral to the holistic mission of the church. Relatedly, "the poor" are uniquely dear to the heart of God[21] and hold a special place in the kingdom (Matt. 5:3). Loving and being with those who are suffering is to mysteriously

---

[20] Castro, "Liberation, Evangelism, and Development," 88. Emphasis in the original.

[21] This section is heavily indebted to liberation theologians. It is from this tradition that the phrase "preferential option for the poor" is derived. Though we do not extensively engage with liberation theology in this book, our theology and praxis are significantly shaped by it. There are many important works in this tradition, but if the reader is not familiar with liberation theology, we suggest beginning with Gutiérrez, *A Theology of Liberation*.

encounter Christ himself (Matt. 25:31–46). God's "option for the poor"[22] reminds us that God's love for those living in poverty precedes our call to address poverty. Jon Sobrino beautifully elaborates this perspective:

> The mystery of the poor is prior to the ecclesial mission, and that mission is logically prior to an established Church.... It is not that the Church already existed, and later asked what to do for and with the poor.... But the mystery of God and Christ is being revealed in relationship with the poor of this world, so that by deepening our understanding of the historical figure of the mystery of the poor, we are deepening our understanding of the mystery of God, and vice versa.[23]

Therefore, as we embark on poverty alleviation and transformational development, we must stay conscious of the reality that God's love for those in poverty precedes and funds our engagement. Bob Mitchell helps ground us in two theological commitments: "The first is the conviction that God is the ultimate change agent in the world and that development practitioners are working cooperatively in this God-inspired *agenda*. The second is that development work takes place within God's overarching redemptive metanarrative for all creation."[24]

Although poverty alleviation is only one sphere of holistic mission, it is a large tent (see Chapter Four) and is intricately related to all other domains. This is because poverty is complex and has multiple causes.[25] Poverty does not emerge or occur in isolation from other factors, and engaging it cannot be reduced to one strategy. Thus, addressing poverty calls for a holistic approach itself—an approach for which we use the term *transformational development*.[26]

---

[22] Sobrino, *No Salvation Outside the Poor*, 19–22, makes the case for using the phrase "option for the poor." We have adopted this usage.

[23] Sobrino, 21.

[24] Mitchell, *Faith-Based Development*, 43. Emphasis added.

[25] See Myers, *Walking with the Poor*, 114–44, for a summary of perspectives on the causes of poverty.

[26] At times, we use only the term *development* as shorthand.

DEVELOPMENT IN **MISSION**

Can We Do It All?

We have established that holistic mission is expansive, and within that larger framework, transformational development is broad and extensive. So, oriented toward the mission of God, how do God's people decide which aspects of development to pursue? We recommend two guiding principles as answers to this question.

First, each person, church, and organization should discern what they uniquely bring to transformational development. What gifts has the Spirit given to each person or group of people? Moving people to wholeness and flourishing (*shalom*) is unquestionably the work and desire of the Holy Spirit. Therefore, as God's vessels in the world, disciples of Jesus will make a difference for those suffering from poverty and injustice when they trust in the Spirit working through them. The impact is exponential when those disciples bring their gifts together to work in unity and with shared purpose.

Also, God's people have specific training, skills, spheres of influence, material resources, and expertise. "The shape of one's focus of concern depends heavily on the resources at one's disposal, one's life stage, and one's awareness of global and domestic needs."[27] No one person or organization is equipped to effectively create positive change in all facets of global poverty. A lawyer might be able to address public policy and corruption, but he or she is not prepared to create systems and infrastructure for sanitation in a remote village. A church might be able to provide education for children in its vicinity, but it cannot, on its own, resolve the refugee crisis. A nonprofit organization might have qualified people to counsel victims of trafficking but is unlikely to also have staff who can effectively translate Scripture. Recognizing the tools and resources at one's disposal can clarify which path to pursue in transformational development.

Second, the scope of the vision of an individual, congregation, or organization sets parameters for engagement in transformational development. Let's return one more time to Crescimento Limpo in Itu, Brazil. The mission of CL is to help its neighbors struggling with addiction and homelessness flourish and thrive. Because CL's vision is community-based,

---

[27] Wydick, *Shrewd Samaritan*, 52.

it is able to address various issues and employ numerous strategies. CL provides temporary housing, case management, counseling, and job training/placement. It also fosters community within CL and with the church. Its approach is certainly holistic. CL can provide expansive services and resources because the scope of its work is local and focused on these particular neighbors.

However, transformational development efforts often have a much wider scope. Nonprofit organizations, for example, often focus on a particular issue, or set of issues, on a regional or global scale. There is no way they can effect substantive change in one area if they are also trying to address related tangential problems elsewhere. Although it is especially easy for those who are captivated by God's holistic mission to want to be a part of every global issue, they must clarify their scope based upon their qualifications and resources, and they must set boundaries for their work. As Bruce Wydick cautions, "Rather than embarking on a mission to 'save the world,' those who create boundaries—whether they be individuals, churches, nongovernmental organizations (NGOs), or foundations—develop competencies in core areas that foster their effectiveness along with making their work sustainable."[28]

The reason we bring up scope in this chapter about theology and holistic mission is to encourage churches and Christian nonprofits to pursue their vision and goals as participants in the larger mission of God's restoration of all creation. One church or organization cannot do it all, so each must discern its role and task. Yet it is part of a larger mission and a global church; therefore, it should always be seeking out partnerships and encouraging others in their pursuits. Just as a local body of disciples has many parts (1 Cor. 12:4–26), so does the global church.

A Partial Conclusion

As we wrap up this examination of holistic mission and how poverty alleviation fits within this framework, a few nagging questions remain. Recall the quote from Stephen Neill: "If everything is mission, then nothing is mission." At this point in our argument, we might reword this statement

---

[28] Wydick, *Shrewd Samaritan*, 26.

as a question: "If everything is mission, then what is uniquely *Christian* in mission?" Or, more pointedly, if poverty alleviation is good, and if many non-Christians are eager to engage and have proven effective in various endeavors, then is there anything uniquely "Christian" about Christian development? If so, what makes it distinctly a Christian approach to poverty alleviation? It is to these questions that we now turn.

3

EFFECTIVE CHRISTIAN
POVERTY ALLEVIATION

In 2015, the United Nations released *Transforming Our World: The 2030 Agenda for Sustainable Development*. The agenda lays out a detailed plan, which includes seventeen Sustainable Development Goals (SDGs) and 169 targets and advances a call to make the world better for all: "In these Goals and targets, we are setting out a supremely ambitious and transformational vision. We envisage a world free of poverty, hunger, disease and want, where all life can thrive. We envisage a world free of fear and violence."[1] It is a lofty agenda, and while there is nothing explicitly Christian in the agenda, many of the goals, such as ending poverty, promoting well-being, and stewarding the Earth and its climate, seem to align with God's purposes for the world.

This raises a particularly challenging question for God's people. If the SDGs and many other reputable secular proposals for alleviating poverty share so much in common with the hopes and objectives of Christians engaged in holistic mission, does it matter whether or not humanitarian work is "Christian"? Certainly, some secular approaches to poverty alleviation advance outcomes or practices that do not align with the mission of God. But proposals such as the SDGs appear on the surface to be congruent,

---

[1] UN General Assembly, "Transforming Our World."

the only difference being in name. So, what is unique, if anything, about *Christian* efforts to care for vulnerable populations and mitigate poverty?

We believe emphatically that there is something unique, and ultimate, about Christian, or "gospeled," poverty alleviation.[2] One intention for writing this book is to highlight the latest and best theories and practices related to poverty alleviation, some of which come from those who do not profess Jesus Christ as Lord. We believe this is a fruitful and faithful endeavor that can sharpen faith-based efforts. Yet we also think poverty alleviation, when in service to God's mission in the world, will have a distinct flavor.

What makes Christian engagement distinctly Christian? Building upon our explanation of God's mission from Chapter Two, we argue that Christian poverty alleviation is unique because of its uniquely Christian end and its means to that end.[3] While there may be similarities with secular development in objectives, best practices, and measurements, humanitarianism in the name of Jesus differs in its ultimate aim and the way it seeks to achieve that aim.[4] Those differences make all the difference. Once we articulate that which is unique and distinctly Christian, we can then offer principles for effective poverty alleviation that (1) incorporate the latest research from the wider landscape of global development and (2) emanate from the end and means of the *missio Dei*. Standing on this foundation, Christians and churches can begin to imagine their roles and actions, as explored further in Chapter Five.

---

[2] We use the term *poverty alleviation* in this chapter to compare Christian and non-Christian humanitarian work. Ultimately, however, we prefer to avoid the term *poverty alleviation* and instead use *transformational development* to delineate Christian development and poverty alleviation.

[3] We recognize that not all poverty-alleviation efforts in the name of Jesus share the exact same end and means. Christianity is a diverse landscape. This chapter is our best effort to articulate a biblical theology of the end and means.

[4] Smith, *Awaiting the King*, 82–83, appropriately cautions: "In strange, often unintended ways, the pursuit of 'justice,' shalom, and a 'holistic' gospel can have its own secularizing effect. What begins as a gospel-motivated concern for justice can turn into a naturalized fixation on justice in which God never appears. And when that happens, 'justice' becomes something else altogether—an idol, a way to effectively naturalize the gospel, flattening it to a social amelioration project in which the particularity of Jesus as the revelation of God becomes strangely absent."

The End of Christian Poverty Alleviation

Amartya Sen, the 1998 Nobel laureate in economics, is one of the most influential scholars in the area of poverty alleviation. He has argued that the development of a country and its citizens should not be measured primarily via gross domestic product or the income of the nation's population. Instead, the fundamental measure of well-being should be the freedoms people have to pursue the kind of lives they so choose. Sen advocates for government and investment policies that increase the number of choices people have in deciding where they want to work, live, and engage in leisure activities. In other words, people's increased freedom and capabilities to choose, not material accumulation or a nation's economic growth, are the true gauge of success in development.

Sen offers two helpful comparisons to illustrate the significance of freedom and choice. The first involves two hungry men who both appear and feel similarly.[5] One man is famished due to his lack of income; he is unable to access food to nourish his body. The other man chooses to be hungry because he is fasting for spiritual and emotional growth. Both men are physically hungry, but one man is deprived of almost all choices, to the point of near starvation, while the other man has enough basic needs met that he can afford to voluntarily skip meals.

The second illustration describes a person with moderate wealth and means but who also suffers from paraplegia.[6] This person might have access to goods and financial resources, but that does not necessarily ensure flourishing. If the government has not enacted any laws requiring roads, stores, and buildings to be disability-compliant, then this person would experience severe limitations. This person might experience more hardship and less satisfaction in life compared with a financially poorer yet able person because the government has not ensured freedoms and choices for persons with disabilities.

These two examples help reveal how well-being is not fundamentally about economics. For Sen, quality of life, the ability to choose one's activities, and freedom from oppression and coercion result in lives worthy of living. Sen solidified a foundational principle of poverty-alleviation

---
[5] Sen, *Inequality Reexamined*, 111–12.
[6] Sen, "Equality of What?," 145–46.

work—that is, the importance of investing in activities and structures that increase people's freedoms and capacities, thus enabling people in poverty to flourish.

The church can glean much from Sen's inclusive and holistic approach to well-being. God's people should be grateful for these insights. However, we should think carefully about Sen's project, specifically his aim for global development, before buying it wholesale. For Sen, "Freedom is both the goal and the means to human development."[7] This presents at least two problems. First, people do not always utilize their freedoms to pursue trajectories that lead to flourishing. People can have a multitude of options in life and can ultimately make choices that harm themselves and others. Second, freedom cannot be an ultimate end because people must have something to which they orient their freedom. If freedom is the end, then free people would be at a standstill because they would have nothing upon which to base their choices.[8] Therefore, while Sen's work is extremely incisive and valuable, the church would be wise to reflect on how his ultimate aim, as expressed in his writings, does not fully capture a Christian vision of *shalom*.[9]

This brief overview of Sen's work highlights how churches and Christian organizations can learn and benefit from the theories and practices of non-Christian scholars and practitioners. It equally asserts that the gospel distinctively extends and shapes our aims and methods. We should select the best principles and practices we can find to seek justice and to

---

[7] Myers, *Walking with the Poor*, 30. Admittedly, Sen does not intend to argue for an ultimate end for humanity (i.e., a philosophical or religious account for human existence), only an end for development work. Although it is not expressed, he does, as all people do, have an ultimate telos that informs his argument. Mitchell, *Faith-Based Development*, 45, helpfully points out, "Every organization has a worldview that underpins its work, whether explicitly acknowledged or not."

[8] Cavanaugh, "Unfreedom of the Free Market," 103–28.

[9] Servais Pinckaers describes this contrast as the difference between "freedom for indifference," in which one chooses between two neutral paths, and "freedom for excellence," in which objective goods exist and one is invited to make choices consistent with the kingdom of God. See Pinckaers, *Morality*, 61–74. Global development asserts values in programming—often the donor's—but normative grounds for well-being can be asserted by other participants. Secular conversations about normative ends in global development generally focus on human rights. For more, see Copestake, "Wellbeing in International Development," 577–97.

care for vulnerable communities, but we should tailor these to align with "the will of God—what is good and acceptable and perfect" (Rom. 12:1–2).

The End Is God

For those who profess the Christian faith, and especially those who grew up in the church, an explanation of the aim, or telos, of Christianity might seem unnecessary. It should be obvious and straightforward. Yet Christians can miss the mark. For example, a common view, especially among Evangelicals, is that the ultimate goal of Christians is to go to heaven after they die. One problem with this understanding is that it is often coupled with an assumption that it is only the soul or spirit that will spend eternity there. It is a disembodied eschatology.[10] This is not the biblical account, in which the hope of the gospel is inextricably connected to the resurrection of bodies—beginning with Jesus's body (1 Cor. 15:1–56).

This view also portrays the gospel as being concerned primarily with what happens after a person dies, wherein the physical needs of people on Earth become secondary to the destination of their souls. But the Bible testifies to a more holistic vision of redemption—one of justice for the widow, orphan, and stranger; of welcome for the child; of giving shelter, drink, and food; and of taking on the mind of Christ as we consider others and humble ourselves. These are all part of salvation in ways both practical and mystical.

Furthermore, if heaven is the ultimate goal, then God can easily become the means to our end—the one who saves us—but not the end itself.[11] It is as if God is saving us to heavenly bliss and not to God's self. Subtly, heaven becomes our ultimate desire—that is, an idol. God, however, is not just the one who saves. God is also the one to whom we are saved. God is both the end and the means to that end.

---

[10] See Wright, *Surprised by Hope*, for a thorough critique of disembodied eschatology and how the Bible presents a different vision.

[11] Understanding the Christian telos as "going to heaven" often derives from insufficient views of the atonement, especially certain perspectives of penal substitutionary atonement. For an analysis of various atonement theories and their strengths and weaknesses, see Crisp, *Approaching the Atonement*, and Green and Baker, *Recovering the Scandal of the Cross*.

Asserting that God is the end of the Christian faith is to make two interdependent claims. First, God yearns to be in communion with human beings. This is God's aim, and God will bring it to fruition. God has already fulfilled this purpose in Jesus Christ: "So if anyone is in Christ, there is a new creation: everything old has passed away; see, everything has become new! All this is from God, who reconciled us to [Godself] through Christ, and has given us the ministry of reconciliation" (2 Cor. 5:17–18). God's work of reconciliation is due to God's desire for everlasting communion with the divine image-bearers. This is because God, as three-in-one, is relational in nature. As Mark Heim writes: "The fundamental Christian word about the 'doctrine of God' is therefore that relation is intrinsic to God's character. Salvation as a relation of deep communion with God makes sense because God's nature itself has the character of communion."[12]

Second, God, through the work of Christ and the power of the Holy Spirit, is transforming humans into the likeness of God. God's intention for humans is not just for them to live for eternity, but that they "may become participants of the divine nature" (2 Pet. 1:4).[13] The divine Word became human and conquered death so that humans could "be perfect, therefore, as your heavenly Father is perfect" (Matt. 5:48).[14] Communing with and participating in the nature and character of the Triune God is the end to which humans are headed, which they will enjoy for all eternity.

Framing the telos of Christianity in such a way is vital for understanding the aim of Christian mission in general and transformational development specifically. It both illuminates the direction of the church's mission and clarifies that God's people are called to participate in that end now. Michael Gorman explains, in his work on Pauline theology, "The goal of human existence, for Paul and for those who receive his words as Christian Scripture, is to participate now and forever, individually and corporately, in the very life and character of this cruciform, missional, world-redeeming God of righteousness and restorative justice."[15] The

---

[12] Heim, *Depth of the Riches*, 59.

[13] This idea is heavily emphasized in the writings of early Christians such as Irenaeus and Athanasius. See Crisp, *Approaching the Atonement*, 30–47.

[14] "Perfect" is a translation of the Greek word τέλειος, from which the English word *telos* is derived.

[15] Gorman, *Becoming the Gospel*, 6.

implication for mission, therefore, is that "theosis—Spirit-enabled transformative participation in the life and character of God revealed in the crucified and resurrected Messiah Jesus—is the starting point of mission and is, in fact, its proper theological framework."[16] Keeping this end ever before us reminds us, as we go out into the world, that "God does not so much want something *of* us as want to be *with* us.... Within this non-purposive context, however, purposive action, our action for ends, maintains its proper place. The already replete triune God may not need anything from us, but the world does, especially in so far as it is our very sinful actions that hinder the world's reception of God's gifts."[17]

This articulation of the ultimate aim of Christianity is incomplete, however, because it is too anthropocentric. God's end is not just for humanity but for all of creation. Our end is wrapped up in God's intention for the entire created order. John's apocalyptic vision in Revelation hints at this coming reality.

> Then I saw a new heaven and a new earth; for the first heaven and the first earth had passed away, and the sea was no more. And I saw the holy city, the new Jerusalem, coming down out of heaven from God, prepared as a bride adorned for her husband. And I heard a loud voice from the throne saying, "See, the home of God is among mortals. [God] will dwell with them as their God; they will be [God's] peoples, and God ... will be with them; [God] will wipe every tear from their eyes. Death will be no more; mourning and crying and pain will be no more, for the first things have passed away." And the one who was seated on the throne said, "See, I am making all things new." (Rev. 21:1–5a)

God's end includes making all things new through Christ. God will dwell with the world that God so loves. Sin and death will be vanquished. There will be no more suffering from greed, injustice, hatred, and violence. Chaos in the natural order will disappear. God will reign. God will be all in all (1 Cor. 15:28).

---

[16] Gorman, 4.
[17] Tanner, *Jesus, Humanity and the Trinity*, 68–69.

This end is the culmination of God's purposes for the world, which God will bring to fulfillment. As Wrogemann summarizes: "The aim of God's mission is salvation for the entire planet. By making this possible and by bringing it about, God glorifies himself."[18] God's mission, however, does not stop with saving creation but continues in the sustaining and prospering of it, with humans as participants and beneficiaries of God's loving intention for a renewed creation.

> The care and keeping of creation is our human mission. The human race exists on the planet with a purpose that flows from the creative purpose of God himself. Out of this understanding of our humanity (which is also teleological, like our doctrine of God) flows our ecological responsibility, our economic activity involving work, productivity, exchange and trade, and the whole cultural mandate. To be human is to have a purposeful role in God's creation.[19]

Humanity's participation in the life of the Triune God is inextricably tied to God's renewal and sustaining of creation. This participation is twofold: (1) humans are to enjoy communion and relationship with God as creatures, made holy and blameless (Eph. 1:4), in a cosmos that is as God intends, and (2) humans have the privilege and honor to co-labor with God in stewarding the good gifts God has bestowed upon creation.

Establishing this particular and holistic vision as the Christian end enables those engaged in development to properly orient their efforts.[20] Globally, ministries will work toward specific objectives based upon the contexts and sectors in which they work. Partners might mutually focus on increasing access to quality health care or providing clean water. But those outcomes are penultimate. They are part of and in service to a more

---

[18] Wrogemann, *Theologies of Mission*, 401.

[19] Wright, *Mission of God*, 65.

[20] Mitchell, *Faith-Based Development*, 15, uses the language of the coming kingdom to describe the theological motivation for development work. He writes: "As Christ's disciples orient themselves toward this future vision, they will actively seek God's rule within their communities and the world. Development work is one way to give expression to this Christian hope of a renewed world."

robust Christian end, and Christian churches and organizations must always evaluate whether their efforts align with that vision.[21]

Furthermore, faithfully upholding participation in the life of God as the aim of Christian mission will mitigate the human tendency to elevate other pursuits to the highest priority—that is, to make them idols. Working to increase income levels within a community can readily turn into the worship of money and wealth (Matt. 6:24). Providing quality education could possibly lead to incessant chasing after knowledge (1 Cor. 8:1–3). Advocacy and policy change within governments can alleviate suffering for citizens, but putting too much hope in nations can give rise to the idol of nationalism or displace our trust to chariots and horses rather than in God (Ps. 20:7). The good works of *Christian* poverty alleviation stay on target when they are aimed at the Triune God, the only one worthy of humanity's ultimate hope and desire.

Fulfilling the Christian end, as we have stated it, is fundamentally the work of God through Christ by the power of the Holy Spirit. God's people, however, have the privilege and calling to co-labor with God toward that end.[22] No one person, church, or organization can do it all. Each must discern what role to play in God's work in the world. But in terms of our end, the key is to ensure that one's limited role is aligned with God and God's telos for creation.

The Means to the End

A few years ago, I (Derran) was invited to an event at which a guest speaker was making a case for how God's people can be agents of cultural change. I am not sure why I was there, because the audience consisted primarily of

---

[21] Tearfund recounted its journey in Christian development work, admitting that the organization struggled to articulate the "end" of its labors. Finally, in 2012, "Tearfund had clarified what it saw as the end point of 'transformation.' It defined the outcome that it wanted to see, and this was 'human flourishing.'" Tearfund's desire to constantly reevaluate its alignment with the Christian faith, while also gleaning insights from secular development, is admirable. See Freeman, *Role of Faith in Tearfund's Work*.

[22] In *Jesus, Humanity and the Trinity*, 91, Tanner eloquently writes, "Because the human has become God's own by way of the Word's assumption of it, the triune God achieves God's ends—the fullest possible communication of goods to the creature—by appropriating human powers for that end; God saves in and through the living of a human life."

city council members, business owners, educational leaders, and the like. The speaker began by talking about the kingdom of God and how God desires to reign in all facets of our society. While I would have articulated a few things differently, I was tracking with him at this point. He then pivoted to make his primary appeal to the leaders sitting in the room. He divided up US society into sectors—politics, business, education, entertainment, health care—and claimed that God is calling Christians to pursue positions of power in those spheres of influence to institute "biblical values." The only way for the kingdom to come in "our nation" is through power and dominance.

What struck me as confusing and irreconcilable, other than listening to a speech about biblical values while eating at an exclusive country club, was the absence of Jesus in his proposal. The end, the coming kingdom of God, was somewhat on target, but the means to bring about that end was completely disconnected from the way in which God's reign broke into the world. The speaker was apparently not cognizant of how his call for the church looked nothing like the crucified king who rules that very kingdom.[23]

This anecdote illustrates how God's people can pursue God's desire for the world—or at least an approximation of it—by means that are incongruent with the way God is bringing it about. As Lesslie Newbigin exhorts, "The means by which the good news of salvation is propagated must be congruous with the nature of the salvation itself."[24] Elsewhere, he warns, "When the Church tries to embody the rule of God in the forms of earthly power it may achieve that power, but it is no longer a sign of the kingdom."[25] Humanitarianism in the name of Jesus is no different. Mitigating poverty is an admirable goal and vocation, but if it is to be Christian, it must align with the way of Jesus.

---

[23] The role of Christians in furthering God's kingdom on Earth has been debated at multiple points in history, including in nineteenth-century Scotland and in early twentieth-century missions. See McKay, *The Kirk and the Kingdom*.

[24] Newbigin, *Household of God*, 169.

[25] Newbigin, *Gospel in a Pluralist Society*, 108. For a discussion of power and poverty, see Christian, *God of the Empty-Handed*, 181–223.

The Way of Jesus Is the Means

Paul, the apostle, wrote to the church in Corinth that he "decided to know nothing among you except Jesus Christ, and him crucified" (1 Cor. 2:2). This is an apt summary of Paul's participation in the mission of God. He proclaimed and embodied the gospel by conforming to the cruciform way of Jesus Christ, his Lord. Furthermore, he appealed to his brothers and sisters to follow along the same way (1 Cor. 11:1; Phil. 2:5). So, what is the path of Jesus that Paul and all disciples are to emulate?

One of the clearest and most concise summations of the way of Jesus is found in Philippians 2:6–11, which is often referred to as the "Christ Hymn." At the heart of this passage is Jesus, who was in the form of God, emptying himself. This way of kenosis (from the Greek verb κενόω, which means "to empty") reveals the extent of Christ's love. He does not hold onto equality with God but humbles himself, relinquishing his power and honor, to enter into the brokenness of the world as a human without privilege and authority—that is, a slave. His love does not stop there, though. The second person of the Trinity is willing to be given over to death, "even death on a cross."

The kenotic Christ does not remain in the hands of death, however, because God raises him up and exalts him to the highest place. It is through Jesus's self-sacrificial love that God brings about resurrection, first for Christ and then for all.[26] It is in choosing the way of the cross that the world recognizes and proclaims that "Jesus is Lord." The reign of God emerges from a grave. This is the way of Jesus, and it is the way God's people participate in God's renewal of all things. The church is to be, as René Padilla describes, "the community of cross-bearing people, called to live as Jesus himself lived. . . . The church therefore is called to provide a glimpse, both in its life and in its message, of a new humanity that in anticipation incarnates God's plan."[27]

---

[26] This idea is drawn from Colossians 1:18–20, which reads: "[H]e is the beginning, the firstborn from the dead, so that he might come to have first place in everything. For in him all the fullness of God was pleased to dwell, and through him God was pleased to reconcile to himself all things, whether on earth or in heaven, by making peace through the blood of his cross."

[27] Padilla, "The Biblical Basis for Social Ethics," 199.

Kenosis reveals the character of the God we serve and are to emulate as we engage in holistic mission. Put differently, "the cross of Christ reveals a missional, justifying, justice-making God and creates a missional, justified, justice-making people. Because the cross reveals a missional God, the church saved and shaped by the cross will be a missional people."[28] It is through the cross that we most fully know the Triune God, and it is the way of the cross by which we join God's work in the world. This is another way that Christian poverty alleviation is unique within the larger landscape of humanitarianism. Followers of Christ are called to love those who are in poverty, who are oppressed, and who are suffering through self-sacrifice and the relinquishment of power and control. Kenosis is the means for Christian poverty alleviation.[29]

This does not mean that God's people cannot adopt principles, practices, and even penultimate outcomes from non-Christian theorists and practitioners. There is much to be gained from incorporation and cooperation. Ultimately, however, there should be something distinctive about Christian efforts because Christians make the distinctive claim that they follow a crucified Lord. The implications of such a "gospeled" stance are varied and numerous. For our purposes, reflecting on the humanitarian sector of peacemaking might help illustrate how Christian means are unique.

Creating and sustaining peace is a worthwhile goal shared by many Christians and non-Christians alike. Furthermore, there are common practices and strategies that can be implemented across religious and secular entities.[30] In the face of violent threat or conflict, however, Christians hear Jesus saying to love our enemies (Matt. 5:44). This is a radical claim because love is not an emotion or a disposition for followers of Jesus. Love means to lay down our lives for others—including our enemies—as Jesus Christ laid down his life for us (1 John 3:16). This is possible because Christ

---

[28] Gorman, *Becoming the Gospel*, 9.

[29] Paul describes, in 2 Corinthians 8:9, the kenotic way of Jesus using the language of rich and poor: "For you know the generous act of our Lord Jesus Christ, that though he was rich, yet for your sakes he became poor, so that by his poverty you might become rich."

[30] See Thistlethwaite, *Interfaith Just Peacemaking*, for an example of different religious traditions seeking commonality in peacemaking.

Jesus has conquered death, and now nothing, not even death, can separate us from the love of God (Rom. 8:37-39). Therefore, Christian peacemaking means imitating the nonviolent, kenotic, self-sacrificial love of Jesus.[31] It entails modeling and inviting others to follow the way of Jesus, trusting that God, through the power of the Holy Spirit, will bring peace and life from violence and death.[32]

More broadly, Christians working in the field of poverty alleviation should always seek the kenotic way of relinquishing power and privilege, exemplified by Christ Jesus, for the sake of the other. Unquestionably, churches and Christian organizations should seek out the best practices in the larger development landscape, but they must then filter these practices through a gospel lens. Regarding mission in general, Wrogemann provides a word of caution for US churches: "The pragmatic-activist trait characterizing much of US-American thought completely eclipses the motif of self-emptying, i.e., of kenotic mission. Christian mission is seen as action, planning, and strategy—not as suffering, waiting, or clinging in faith to a reality that is yet to be revealed."[33] For development work specifically, this means that individuals, churches, and organizations should pursue ways to empty themselves and give up power for the sake of those who are vulnerable.

Principles of Effective Transformational Development

Framing poverty alleviation as a facet of God's holistic mission in the world, as well as showing the distinctive end and means of Christian engagement, establishes a foundation upon which we can stack theories and practices from the wider landscape of development. This synthesis is what we call *transformational development*.

In the next chapter, we will survey various sectors of humanitarian work, incorporating insights from Christian and non-Christian practitioners. Chapter Four moves us from thinking broadly about holistic

---

[31] It should be noted that there are appeals to nonviolence from non-Christian voices. This is good news because it provides opportunity for even greater cooperation. See Abu-Nimer, *Nonviolence and Peace Building in Islam*, for a Muslim perspective.

[32] For a detailed discussion of the place of love in Christian ethics, see Pope, "Love in Contemporary Christian Ethics," 167-97.

[33] Wrogemann, *Theologies of Mission*, 223-24.

mission to specific opportunities for engagement in transformational development. Before we embark across that terrain, however, it is important to keep in mind a few general principles of effective transformational development. These principles stem from the most current research in development and are grounded in the end and means of the gospel of Jesus Christ.

These principles and related practices, which emerge from the end and means of Christian engagement, help clarify what is distinctive about Christian poverty alleviation. Holding fast to and being formed by both the means and the end of God's mission creates individuals, churches, and organizations that offer something unique and peculiarly hopeful to the larger world. As Michael Gorman summarizes, "A people characterized by communal *kenosis* for the good of the world is both the means and the goal of God's saving activity here and now."[34]

Principle 1: Cultivate Loving Relationships

Transformational development is fundamentally about relationships. As Bryant Myers writes: "Our work is about people before it is about ideas, about relationships before development programs. Global development workers, who use being good neighbors as their metaphor for working alongside the poor, will be more effective than those who see themselves as problem solvers or answer givers."[35] Creating and growing loving, mutually beneficial relationships is the seedbed for transformation for all involved.

We suggest two ways in which relationships in transformational development can be characterized by kenotic love. First, practitioners should seek solidarity with those who are suffering. This is solidarity not only in cause but also by proximity.[36] The command to "love your neighbor" (Matt. 22:39) must be embodied by living alongside actual people. This move toward solidarity requires us to remove the distance between people, whether due to gaps in power, wealth, or culture,[37] for the sake of forging loving, intentional

---

[34] Gorman, *Inhabiting the Cruciform God*, 38.
[35] Myers, *Walking with the Poor*, 218.
[36] Warren, *The Power of Proximity*.
[37] This does not mean erasing cultural differences; that would be an abuse of power. Recognizing and celebrating differences in culture is essential and ethical. It leads to healthy relationships and effective work. The intention here is to seek understanding

relationships. This is no easy task, and there is no formula. Overcoming relational disparities based on power differentials is complex and requires humility, wisdom, and courage. This is true in all facets of ministry and service, but it is especially challenging in the arena of poverty alleviation. The nature of the endeavor entails an imbalance of power.

Poverty alleviation implies that one party lacks access to fulfilling a need or to enhancing capacity and that the other party has some ability, or at least a perception of ability, to help gain that access. For example, individuals and organizations working to increase income levels for people in abject poverty will most likely have greater financial means. This inevitably produces a power gap.[38] Therefore, development workers who follow the kenotic way of Jesus must evaluate their standard of living. There is no way to completely erase the power differential, but choosing to live simply, reside among, and fellowship with those in poverty and to give and receive hospitality in contextually appropriate ways can help bridge the gap and create meaningful relationships.

Liberation theologian Jon Sobrino observes that the first and often greatest challenge is *wanting* to relinquish power and wealth. Jesus provides the kenotic example and calls us to the same, and many show it is possible.[39] It happens when God's people avail ourselves of the Spirit's transformative power to shape our desires and proclivities. From decades of experience in the Philippines, Viv Grigg writes:

> The missionary who wishes to make disciples must go deep into the soul of the people. A disciple of Christ is one who follows the disciplines of Christ. Many think of these disciplines as the scheduling of set times of prayer, Bible reading, and so on.

---

and immerse oneself in the cultural-linguistic norms of the host culture. See Rowe and Aldred, "Healthy Leadership," 211–23.

[38] See Bonk, *Missions and Money*, 53–67, for an examination of how wealth is an obstacle to building relationships in mission work. Particularly relevant to our point in this section, he cautions: "It is hard to assume the role of a servant when one is rich and powerful, while those whom one ostensibly serves are mired in poverty and powerlessness. In such situations, the word 'service' is usually adapted to mean whatever the powerful condescends to do for the less powerful," 61. Also see Christian, *God of the Empty-Handed*, 212–20.

[39] Sobrino, *Where Is God?*, 37–43.

> But Christ gave little teaching on such things (except to avoid parading them). His are the disciplines of the inner person, the disciplines of the Beatitudes and the Sermon on the Mount—qualities such as humility, meekness, and peacemaking. These involve the transformation of the inner soul of the person.[40]

Through the work of the Holy Spirit, it is possible to move toward solidarity as we follow the way of Christ.

Second, those engaged in development efforts should approach their work and service as an exercise in reciprocity. Because we are all in need, transformational development recognizes that we all will be blessed by giving and receiving. Transformation is available to everyone who enters into such collaborative, mutually edifying relationships.

Kenotic reciprocity begins with the vulnerable population determining its aims and objectives instead of the outside partner dictating goals. From this starting point, all partners can cooperate toward shared outcomes and healthy relationships. Describing a decade-long Christian development effort in Cambodia, Simon Batchelor writes:

> We were not in the business of "alleviating poverty," or "reducing poverty," or "strengthening sustainable livelihoods," or even "mission." We had reflected on our theology and reframed our ideas into terms that everyone could accept and which proved to be a helpful guideline. Our journey together had centered on people thinking through problems, on creativity as a learnable skill and on "loving relationships." . . . Our journey together resulted in change both in the clients and the practitioners; we grew together. Our journey is not finished.[41]

When poverty alleviation entails one party offering resources to another—whether this is an individual caring for a neighbor or an international organization serving thousands—the relationship between the two parties should involve a two-way exchange. Jon Sobrino writes, "The option for

---

[40] Grigg, *Companion to the Poor*, 71.
[41] Batchelor, "Christian and Secular Approaches to Development," 132.

the poor is not just a matter of *giving to* them, but of *receiving from* them."[42] Those in poverty have needs, but they also have much to offer (local knowledge, talents, time, and more).

For example, an organization might be effective at digging wells and providing clean water, but the local community knows how to steward its water resources to enhance sustainability. Development workers or short-term visitors to a location, who often come from societies that waste an exorbitant amount of water, could benefit from learning the habits and behaviors of that community to help conserve this precious commodity. To quote Batchelor once again:

> One of the strengths of this goal was that it did not define people by their lack of something. We did not assume that our clients would be starting from a zero point. They have resources (as we all have resources), they have relationships (as we all have relationships), they have some wisdom (as we all have some wisdom). By avoiding defining people by their poverty, the goal encourages the agency workers to start with a view of the clients as equals, not as beneficiaries receiving something from outsiders who are "better."[43]

Intentionally cultivating reciprocity helps reduce the power gap, thus establishing healthier relationships and increasing the efficacy of collaboration. This will mean a change of mindset from ministering *to* those in poverty to collaborating *with* those in poverty.[44] Identifying and utilizing the resources and talents of neighbors produces benefits for all, and generally, the outsiders are not the ones who know best.[45] When everyone is contributing to the work and the relationship, everyone involved flourishes. This is a glimpse of the renewed humanity God desires.[46]

---

[42] Sobrino, *No Salvation Outside the Poor*, 53.

[43] Batchelor, "Christian and Secular Approaches to Development," 127.

[44] See Bosch, *Transforming Mission*, 368–89, for a survey of this shift that happened across Christian traditions in recent decades.

[45] See Corbett and Fikkert, *When Helping Hurts*, 119–31, for an introduction to the benefits and practice of asset-based community development, which is a practical way to employ this aspect of reciprocity.

[46] See Acts 2:44–45 and 4:32–35 and 2 Corinthians 8:13–14 for examples of the earliest churches seeking to embody this vision through reciprocity and the sharing of goods.

Principle 2: Empower to Sustain

The effectiveness and sustainability of transformational development hinges on the engagement and empowerment of vulnerable communities.[47] Development workers must consciously seek tangible ways to share with and cede leadership to the local community. If collaboration involves the exchange of goods, such as expertise and material resources, individuals and organizations should wisely deploy those goods while being attentive to ways the power imbalance can disempower or create dependency.[48] Sharing or ceding leadership is a type of empowerment that represents a faithful response to the kenotic way of Jesus, and it supports rather than erodes local agency and leadership.[49]

Empowerment such as this means that practitioners, from the outset, surrender ownership and control in how they think about the effort, share in planning and decision-making, and avoid paternalism cloaked as accountability, even at the risk of the demise of the enterprise.[50] This does not mean that the burden of the work should be handed off to unwilling parties. Instead, empowerment must derive from a trusted relationship between partners. Once common goals are established, decisions and responsibilities can be entrusted to those best suited to lead the way forward to continue flourishing for all involved.

While this might sound easy in theory, the call to empower and entrust can be extremely difficult, particularly for large organizations. It takes a

---

[47] Someone once commented: "The Achilles heel of empowerment is that it implies that you don't have power. Subordination is built in." Quoted in Eyben and Napier-Moore, "Choosing Words with Care?," 285–300. We eschew the thinking that development workers have power and local leaders do not, and instead, we affirm that all have gifts and knowledge. Empowerment occurs when partners respect one another and accentuate and contribute to each other's capacities.

[48] Several authors and practitioners warn against creating dependency. Their cautions should be heeded, as well as many of their recommendations for the appropriate sharing of resources. On dependency, see Harries, *Vulnerable Mission*; Reese, *Roots and Remedies*; Schwartz, *When Charity Destroys Dignity*.

[49] Myers, *Walking with the Poor*, 218, captures what we intend by the term *empowerment*. "The essence of empowerment is that there is some kind of process of social change directed by the people themselves by which people—as individuals and groups—are able to shape their own lives in ways that they choose."

[50] There are ways to ensure accountability without a disequilibrium in power. For practical ideas, see Lederleitner, *Cross-Cultural Partnerships*.

high level of competency to implement and operate large projects and systems. The collective resources of an organization can produce substantial positive outcomes for vulnerable populations. The challenge is that an institution of any kind, due to invested resources and an established identity, often makes decisions—consciously and subconsciously—to ensure its own survival. There is seemingly too much to lose if it were to give itself away. The gospel, however, calls all who invoke the name of Jesus, including organizations, to empty themselves for the sake of others. This means even the most "successful" institution will wisely and progressively entrust the direction of its work to local leaders.[51]

Relatedly, long-term and sustained transformation means that Christian partners will invite others to follow the way of kenosis—emptying oneself for the empowerment of others. This is especially important as those in the local community take on the work of alleviating poverty and suffering themselves. There must be intentionality in embedding kenosis in the organizational culture so that self-sacrifice and empowerment of others are inherent in the structures and strategies of the work.

We recognize the potential danger of calling those who have historically been on the receiving end of abuses of power to empty themselves.[52] In one sense, kenosis, or giving up one's power, is a privilege of those with power. Therefore, we must be cautious not to convey that those who have little power in society should continue to be powerless. This would be antithetical to the humble, loving way of Jesus. Though Jesus was willing to be humiliated for the sake of humanity, there is nothing virtuous about suffering in and of itself. The means might include entering into the suffering of others, but the end goal is the cessation of suffering. As Kathryn Tanner writes: "Humiliation is not, therefore, the Son's or ours in perpetuity; it is

---

[51] Mitchell, *Faith-Based Development*, 31, astutely writes: "What participatory processes can guarantee, when undertaken in a genuine way, is treating humans with dignity. For this reason, participatory approaches will appeal to those faith-based development organizations that seek inspiration from the unconditional love of Christ. What participatory approaches cannot guarantee, however, is success."

[52] Feminist theologians have been particularly helpful in elevating this concern. See Coakley, *Powers and Submissions*, 3–39, for a constructive proposal to maintain kenosis as a viable theological framework by keeping vulnerability and empowerment together in tension.

a means to elevation. The Son humbles himself, Jesus humbles himself, to be with us in the lowliness of our suffering and need, in order to save us from it, not to engrave that lowliness into the world as its final good."[53] The aim is to lift up those who are vulnerable. Only once people have been freed from oppression and injustice can they be in a healthy place to give up power on their own accord for the benefit of others. Partners can invite those coming out of poverty and oppression to practice kenosis, but pursuing that path must derive from that population's own agency and through the power of the Holy Spirit.

Principle 3: Give It Time

A few years ago, there was a large construction project at a university in northern Thailand. The workforce, which spent 10–12 hours per day laboring to erect a series of new buildings, primarily consisted of a minority ethnic people from Myanmar (formerly Burma). This community of three hundred or so people had fled Myanmar, where they were not considered full citizens, and had temporary immigration status in Thailand. However, they could legally work in only one designated province. The problem was that many could not find work there because of the abundance of asylum seekers living in that area. Therefore, this community had to risk deportation by securing contractual employment in a nearby province.

These stateless people established a shantytown in the forest adjacent to the construction site. They worked long hours, received minimal pay, and lacked access to affordable and adequate health care. There was no running water in their makeshift village, and the sanitation services were almost nonexistent. On top of all that, they lived in constant fear of deportation. The circumstances surrounding this community were dire, yet they persevered, caring for one another and contributing to the larger society around them.

Poverty and suffering can be complex and all-encompassing. There is no quick fix to situations such as this one. Helping and enabling these communities to flourish will take time, which is often the case when working with any vulnerability or injustice. It is true that there are occasions when

---

[53] Tanner, *Jesus, Humanity and the Trinity*, 76–77.

a fast and temporary response is appropriate. In times of crisis—whether an earthquake affecting thousands or a sudden loss of a job affecting one family—providing immediate relief to those who cannot secure the necessities of life can be the right course of action. In most cases, however, the historical and systemic causes of poverty and suffering are extensive and multilayered, and the remedies have to be similarly comprehensive.[54]

This means that those engaged in compassion work, whether practitioners or supporters, need to make a long-term commitment to a particular work or context. Transformational development, which is the right approach to addressing sustained poverty and suffering, entails assessing the conditions, involving the affected population in planning and implementation, carrying out initiatives, measuring impact, adjusting and adapting strategies, and equipping and empowering others, particularly those at the ground level, to bring forth flourishing. This is accomplished only with an integrated and long-term approach. Transformational development efforts are easily thwarted when workers and organizations are unable or unwilling to stay committed for the long haul. Therefore, counting the cost upfront, securing ongoing funding, creating dependable structures, and practicing self-care are essential for individuals and organizations that answer the call to join God in bringing *shalom* to those who are vulnerable and oppressed.

Principle 4: Attend to Context

One of the challenges of writing about global poverty is that development efforts, like all aspects of holistic mission, vary based upon particular contexts. We can offer general principles and sweeping summaries of development sectors, but there is no universal formula for alleviating poverty or assisting vulnerable communities. The context in which practitioners work will shape the particulars of every facet of the enterprise. It is

---

[54] Corbett and Fikkert, *When Helping Hurts*, 99–109, make the important point that effective poverty alleviation begins with determining the nature of the poverty and matching the correct response. They helpfully describe how some crises call for the temporary responses of relief and rehabilitation, but most situations call for the long-term work of development. Historically, much funding from churches and Christian organizations in the Global North has mismatched relief efforts when development was better suited, resulting in harm.

therefore imperative that individuals and organizations do the hard work of contextualization.[55]

Intentionally and thoroughly contextualizing development is necessary and critical for three reasons. First, contextualization is inevitable. The Christian faith has always transformed and been transformed by a local community's surrounding cultural symbols and practices.[56] There is no contextless expression or embodiment of Christianity. Christian theology and praxis are always contestations of meaning and import between the surrounding cultural material and the local faith community's use of such material in submission to Jesus Christ. As Kathryn Tanner states, "Christian practices are always the practices of others made odd."[57] Poverty alleviation and transformational development are no different. The particular context in which practitioners labor will shape the development practices as well as the meaning and significance of this gospel work in the life of the local community. Therefore, individuals and organizations would be wise to be proactive and intentional in contextualizing their work.

Second, contextualization is ethical. The history of Christian missions has too many examples of the church assuming that one particular expression of the Christian faith, shaped by the context of the sending entity, is normative for Christians in other contexts. This trend is especially disturbing when it manifests in cultural superiority, domination, and oppression.[58] Therefore, contextualization becomes paramount as a means of showing

---

[55] There are various terms that refer to the relationship between mission activities and the local context: *accommodation, indigenization, inculturation,* and *contextualization.* See Wrogemann, *Intercultural Hermeneutics,* 317–18. We choose to use *contextualization* because it captures how the entire context (culture, politics, society, lived experience) is relevant, while the other terms typically focus exclusively on how culture shapes theology and practice. Using the terms *culture* and *inculturation* can be beneficial, assuming the terms are used carefully and holistically. See Arbuckle, *Culture, Inculturation, and Theologians,* for an explanation of the contested use of the word *culture* and for an incisive examination of how cultural anthropology is essential for the work of theology.

[56] See Walls, *Missionary Movement,* 3–54, for a broad examination of this dynamic throughout Christian history.

[57] Tanner, *Theories of Culture,* 112.

[58] This unfortunate reality in Christian missions is particularly visible in colonialism. An examination of this story is beyond the scope of this book, but we agree with many others who exhort the church to repent of this sinful legacy. See Tizon, *Whole and Reconciled,* 37–55, for an overview of the colonial legacy in missions and a call for a postcolonial missiology.

respect and appreciation toward other ways of being—as well as humility toward one's own cultural norms and assumptions. Furthermore, it gives more power and agency to those who call that particular context "home." Contextualization is ultimately the work of those in the host culture. Contextualization in transformational development, then, is a mechanism of empowerment for those in poverty.

Third, contextualization leads to success and sustainability. Importing practices and strategies, without regard for the particularities of the host culture, will lead to failure. If development efforts remain "foreign" in the minds of those served, then those people will most likely abandon the structures and practices associated with the effort once the "outsiders" leave. Even if some of the structures and practices continue for a time, the targeted population may not feel a sense of ownership and empowerment, thus hindering long-term problem-solving options when inevitable challenges emerge. Additionally, adapting systems and processes to the specific context enhances impact and effectiveness because it addresses actual needs in the community, not theoretical or presumptive ones.

This brief explanation of the merits of contextualization in transformational development is intended to encourage practitioners to engage in the challenging and exciting work of learning about and immersing themselves in the cultural realities of vulnerable communities. This will mean seeking proficiency in navigating the linguistic, social, political, and philosophical norms in a particular context. Yet, because we now live in the twenty-first century, it is also critical to recognize that contextualization also means paying attention to the ways in which globalization is a part of every context.[59] Cultures are not bounded, demarcated domains, so other cultures and global trends continually refashion every context. Practitioners must continually keep one eye on the local context and the other on the larger world around them.[60]

---

[59] Van Engen, *Transforming Mission Theology*, 66, helpfully points out that contextualization must also consider voices and practices from the global church. He writes, "This involves an act of theologizing that propels the Christian to active engagement with the cultural, socioeconomic, and political issues extant in the context, in conversation with Christians in all other contexts."

[60] See Myers, *Engaging Globalization*, for an incisive analysis of globalization's impact on mission and poverty alleviation.

Principle 5: Invest in Friendships and Partnerships

As we stated in the previous chapter, the expansiveness of holistic mission and poverty alleviation necessitates establishing partnerships or, at least, friendships. We use the term *friendship* to emphasize the relationship between and among parties, rather than primarily a legal or organizational arrangement—although these can be important elements, too. (However, the *friendship* wording can be awkward, so we will continue to use *partner* and *partnership* language.) The "partnership" can simply be checking with and learning from and knowing other organizations. It does not have to be a shared venture. The important thing is to avoid going it alone. Instead, with the humility of Jesus, learn from others, share the credit, and allow God to be glorified.

There are three types of partnerships that, if managed well, can help enhance the effectiveness of transformational development. We will use the construction workers in northern Thailand mentioned earlier as a case study to describe these partnership models.

First, a coalition of people and organizations on the ground is needed to help these construction workers and their families. The assets and needs of this community are multifaceted. It might be that a nongovernmental organization, or NGO, from the health-care sector is the first entity to engage with this group of migrant workers and their families. The health-care NGO can provide vaccinations, wellness exams, and self-care training. While providing health care is critical for this community, it is not enough to help them flourish. Therefore, the NGO will need to create partnerships with others who can assist with other needs.[61] This might include other nonprofit organizations in the region that specialize in other sectors, such as immigration and advocacy, WASH (water, sanitation, and hygiene), and family services.

The NGO will need to seek help, carefully and wisely, from governmental entities, whether local, federal, or international, to ensure protection and create a path to a more secure immigration status for the workers and their families. It could work with local businesses and organizations, such as the construction company, the university, or a potential new employer,

---

[61] Large NGOs regularly work with local, capable partners who can respond quickly and effectively. Just one example is Start Network's Start Fund.

to establish a living wage and appropriate benefits. And the NGO will want to partner with a local church or churches to surround the workers and their families with the love of Christ. Creating a coalition of partners who can come alongside a population such as this, or merely linking with other organizations who are engaged, is invaluable in transformational development.[62]

In the past, many Christian churches and organizations in the Global North have tended to go it alone, often assuming they are doing pioneering work. They may have been concerned about a compromise in Christian witness or the added challenge of coordinating with another organization. NGOs and governmental organizations, on the other hand, are accustomed to working through partnerships and learning from coalitions, knowing they cannot effectively carry a project every step of the way. Hazards exist here, alongside great benefits, and there are ways to ensure that the values and witness of the Christian effort inform the partnership.[63]

Second, the partners working on the ground will benefit from learning from organizations doing similar work elsewhere. For example, a nonprofit organization doing advocacy work for migrant families in northern Thailand should seek out contacts in organizations doing related work in other regions around the world. Other agencies and congregations might have experience working specifically with stateless people. Potentially, they could provide expertise and resources. Additionally, the nonprofit can seek advice and guidance from refugee resettlement agencies about the possibility of relocating people to a more secure and welcoming environment. These intra-sector partnerships across regions can be mutually beneficial as organizations learn from each other's experiences and share resources, expertise, and best practices.

Third, some of the nonprofits or churches working with this community might receive financial support from nonprofits or churches in other countries. What might initially be a financial agreement could and

---

[62] The UN Sustainable Development Agenda highlights the importance of partnerships by making them one of the seventeen SDGs (Partnerships for the Goals) instead of only a strategy for fulfilling the goals. Note specifically the targets 17.16 and 17.17. UN Department of Economic and Social Affairs, "Goal 17," 17.

[63] For practical tips on integrating Christian witness in a diverse partnership, see Norman and Odotei, "Faith Integration and Christian Witness," 31–43.

should be transformed into an equal, mutually beneficial friendship or partnership.⁶⁴ Reducing the power gap between the two entities—the one providing financial support and the one receiving it—will positively affect the target population because it reduces the likelihood of paternalism. Furthermore, a partnering relationship creates the opportunity for everyone to contribute to the well-being of all involved. For example, a church or nonprofit in the United States can learn a lot about sustainability and simplicity from those caring for this community, as well as from the community members themselves. It will take intentionality and a long-term commitment to create this type of relationship, but it is important and worth it.

Partnerships and friendships characterize Christian engagements in transformational development because they seek more than a financial or contractual transaction of a humanitarian project. They seek transformation for all involved.⁶⁵

Principle 6: Seek Out Insight

In his book *The Tyranny of Experts*, Bill Easterly writes, "The sleight of hand that focuses attention on technical solutions while covering up violations of the rights of real people is the moral tragedy of development today."⁶⁶ Easterly critiques the authoritarian development of autocrats advised by technical experts and instead promotes a form of development that affirms the right of people to choose from "a myriad of spontaneous problem-solvers, rewarding those that solve our problems."⁶⁷

Easterly's support of local self-determination is consistent with the principles we are advocating, as is his warning to avoid placing confidence in development solutions that do not recognize culture and context. But it is the opposite ditch that many churches have veered into by not seeking advice at all. Regrettably, they have failed to appreciate how previous

---

⁶⁴See Lederleitner, *Cross-Cultural Partnerships*, for potential challenges and opportunities in forming partnerships such as this.

⁶⁵For a critique of the commodification of aid, see Freeman and Schuller, "Aid Projects."

⁶⁶Easterly, *Tyranny of Experts*, 6.

⁶⁷Easterly, *Tyranny of Experts*, 7.

experience can provide a bypass around a number of hazards, whether technical or cultural. Seeking out insight from seasoned practitioners, researchers, and local residents demonstrates humility and wisdom—two valuable virtues in transformational development.

Methods and strategies exist that have been rigorously tested, found effective, and continue to work in a number of locations and among various populations. It is lamentable and harms the church's witness when a Christian congregation launches a new ministry based on an approach discarded decades ago. The problems a particular community faces most likely have been encountered elsewhere, and the approach imagined has probably been tried already. Whether in a global pandemic or serving a family next door, we believe it is critical for God's people to learn from, listen to, and seek the insights of those familiar with the path.

Many practitioners in global development are Christians, as are researchers in fields related to development and leaders in government and nonprofit agencies working to address global poverty. Churches are wise to listen to their counsel.[68] There is much to learn from those, whether Christian or not, who possess the education, experience, and expertise to address poverty and related issues of oppression and injustice.

We have already affirmed the necessity of local voices and relationships, so to be clear, we are not suggesting a technocracy.[69] Mere knowledge transfer has limited application in global development, and it is possible for "expert" views to act as veiled imperialism, trampling local realities and practices. What we are advocating for is to listen to and learn from respected experts and experienced practitioners before launching and to continually give attention to the innovative research emerging in the

---

[68] Relatedly, churches should encourage and support their members who have vocational aspirations of addressing global poverty. God has and will continue to use the insights and connections gained from a specialized field to further the kingdom as a whole, often in ways we cannot envision or predict. And when that expertise leads to more effective work and improved conditions within target populations and communities, the witness of God's people, as embodiments of the gospel, will be more credible.

[69] For an example, see Telleria, "Development and Participation."

Principle 7: Assess and Improve

Another critical yet commonly overlooked principle for effective transformational development efforts is to assess and improve. Too often, church-initiated efforts continue for years without anyone conducting a proper evaluation of their effectiveness outside of some anecdotal remarks of positive influence. In a recent survey of around four hundred churches' global well-being initiatives, only three congregations had publicly available assessment data on their work.[70] Although it is possible that more congregations had data but did not post it, many churches consider a budget completely spent and everyone returning home safely to be the only necessary measure of success. But, as we can learn from sporting events, the final buzzer does not tell us how effectively each team played—only that the game is over.

Most congregations are not accustomed to evaluating their efforts. We plant and water, and we leave it to God to give the increase (1 Cor. 3:6). But when it comes to efforts that are intended to improve short- or long-term food security, sanitation practices, education, or income, it is not enough to have good intentions, impressive operations, stirring stories, hordes of activities and volunteers, or the latest approach. If congregations are not assessing their efforts, they cannot gauge their effectiveness or improve them. Evaluation reveals whether we are truly helping others.

Tearfund, a development organization that partners with churches, suggests that evaluation enables congregations to "prove" and "improve"—to be accountable in stewarding resources and evaluating partnerships and to learn lessons so they can enhance current and future transformational development. When the results of evaluations are shared publicly, results will encourage members and observing congregations, and they can lead to learning for all.

Evaluation is an academic field of its own, a combination of art and science. A considerable toolkit of evaluation approaches, procedures, and

---

[70] Lynn, "Congregational Aid."

techniques is available.[71] But congregations need not become evaluation experts—they can partner with organizations that have evaluation expertise or share the evaluation role with a partner. Ideally, discussion of a plan for assessment should occur as the development effort begins. Addressing assessment before starting an initiative helps clarify goals, allows baseline measures to be taken, and provides midstream monitoring so adjustments can be made along the way to enhance effectiveness.

If possible, measures should drill down deeper than outputs. An output is the numeric count of people served, goods distributed, or activities completed. A nonprofit or church running a soup kitchen to address local hunger may count the number of people fed or meals served during a specified period of time. An afterschool ministry may count how many children attended a session. In contrast, an *outcome* is the desired goal for an initiative. For addressing hunger, we might measure whether the initiative increased food security, improved the dietary nutrition of an average family, or positively affected child development (be it physical, mental, emotional, or spiritual). In an afterschool tutoring program, the outcome might be higher reading levels or better grades among the student participants, not the number of sessions conducted or attended.

As with other aspects of transformational development, culture should inform the assessment outcomes and methods chosen, and all partners should be welcomed to participate in the design and implementation. Unintended as well as targeted consequences should be surfaced, and care must be taken to avoid social desirability influencing the outcomes. Finally, evaluation should be appropriate in scale and scope for the effort, not overbearing for staff or an end unto itself. And, always, it should lead to the question "What did we learn, what should we repeat, and what should we change next time?"

Although it is beyond the scope of many congregational efforts, much can be learned from poverty research that utilizes randomized control

---

[71] Blackman, "Partnering with the Local Church," 79–83. Introductions to evaluation include Ebrahim and Rangan, "What Impact?"; Crawford and Pollack, "Hard and Soft Projects"; Social Value UK, "A Guide to Social Return on Investment"; Social Value UK, "Tools by Principle"; Woolnough, "But How Do We Know We Are Making a Difference?"; USAID Learning Lab, "Worksheet: Six Simple Questions."

trials (RCTs). Researchers using RCTs set up field experiments that allow an intervention to be tested and then scaled if found effective. RCTs have been powerful and important tools that have allowed researchers to test the effectiveness of direct cash transfers, bed nets, deworming pills, farmer schools, and other interventions mentioned in Chapter Four in terms of what is or is not working in the poverty-alleviation space; and they show what approaches, among several that might be available, prove most useful in promoting human and community flourishing.[72] Development researcher Esther Duflo is a strong advocate of RCTs, but she cautions that global development is more like plumbing than engineering—it requires tinkering, trial and error, contextualization, and improvement.[73]

Churches and Christian NGOs need to take seriously the task of assessing their development efforts and sharing their findings. New tools frequently become available that enable volunteers and professionals to better understand the challenges facing those living in poverty and often provide practical steps to improve the effectiveness of services provided to people and their communities. We hope this book, and particularly the next chapter, is one of those resources.

---

[72] An excellent introduction to RCTs in poverty alleviation is Banerjee and Duflo, *Poor Economics.*
[73] Duflo, "The Economist as Plumber."

PART TWO

ENHANCING ENGAGEMENT

4

TRANSFORMATIONAL DEVELOPMENT SECTORS

Our aim in the first three chapters was to provide a theological and holistic foundation for participating in God's mission for all creation. We turn now to consider possible avenues for engagement in transformational development. The terrain is expansive, and first steps can be challenging, but it is also fascinating to consider the abundant diversity of interrelated sectors.

This chapter differs from all the others. Although it can be read from beginning to end, most will want to bounce around, investigating areas of interest. Because sectors interlace, some may find themselves following breadcrumbs from one sector to another, enhancing the appreciation for holistic transformational development. Each section addresses a topic and offers an introduction, including theological warrant for some less-known sectors, along with research- and field-based insights and practices. Because congregational missions often differ in approach from faith-based development, many of these insights may be new. In addition to a sectoral description, Appendix B offers a sampling of information sources and possible partners.

While the descriptions are introductory, our hope is that they guide individuals and congregations to courageously engage in transformational development. Knowing the basics of how a given sector operates, ways it interweaves with other concerns, and some of the lessons that have been learned over time can enhance thoughtful and effective engagement. Exploring past and current strategies and gleaning from the wisdom and experience of others opens a treasure trove of wisdom while providing rich resources for churches and individuals who desire to see their efforts achieve significant kingdom benefit.

We have named sectors in positive terms (such as, "food") rather than in deficits (such as, "hunger"), but some of the topics within identify challenges. The sectors we introduce are as follows:

- Children, Youths, and Older Persons
- Creation Care
- Education
- Food
- Freedom and Liberation
- Health
- Income Generation
- Migration and Refuge
- Peacemaking and Peacebuilding
- Relief
- Scripture Translation
- Shelter
- Sport
- Technology
- Water, Sanitation, and Hygiene

While we recognize this list of sectors is not exhaustive, we selected sectors that historically have been popular among churches, along with a few less-commonly explored sectors that are accessible to congregations. Ultimately, our desire is that churches and individuals gain a foothold in one or more sectors so, over time, transformational development practices continue to improve. The dynamic nature of needs and responses means that best practices are ever-emerging and evolving, so we too must continue reflecting, learning, and innovating. We advise churches to partner with individuals and organizations that do the same.

It is prudent to remember that development efforts are holistic and multifaceted, even when a congregation focuses on a single sector or goal. For example, food security is affected by education, household income, gender roles, natural resources and climate, finance, and technology. Similar interconnections can be made with most of the other sectors as well. Identifying drivers and holistic influences can yield insight into important programming variables—a topic we will explore further in Chapter Five.

Some subjects, such as justice, gender equity, and culture, are so pervasive and all-encompassing that they tend to be marbled through every sector. In particular, the circumstances that women and girls face across sectors have resulted in a number of organizations and initiatives focusing exclusively on gendered injustice and mechanisms of support.

Inevitably, individuals and congregations ask, *Where should we engage and how do we know what is most needed, wanted, and effective?* We conclude these introductory comments by offering four recommendations. First, when seeking to engage in a new sector or embark on a new initiative, prioritize listening to those living in vulnerable communities. These communities can offer valuable perspectives and insights into how to prioritize needs and steward assets and resources. Intentional and purposeful listening maintains the dignity of such communities and leads to greater impact.

A second recommendation is to dialogue with implementing partners (or potential partners) and other congregations in the areas of operation. Often, communities have different priorities, and congregations and local partners have different assets and interests. The strengths and gaps among all partners need to be considered when exploring a commitment to a specific sector or approach. We discuss this in more detail in Chapter Five.

Third, one should always consider and evaluate the approach. Development economists often test the effectiveness of initiatives *within* a sector to judge which approach actually enhances the well-being of people. Comparing approaches *across* sectors is more complex and often requires making a large number of assumptions. Yet, these types of evaluations become necessary when clearly one approach is more effective, necessary, or desired than many others.[1] Our approach to presenting these sectors has not included any attempt to rank or order sectors in terms of their importance or reported effectiveness. Instead, we offer critical commentary within each sector and strongly urge those who have identified an approach of interest (or are open to pursuing whatever experts claim to

---

[1] Bruce Wydick offers an evaluation of several interventions in *Shrewd Samaritan*, 102–49. For example, he rates fair trade coffee and shoe, clothing, and laptop donation programs as less effective, and he rates cash transfers, comprehensive poverty graduation programs, international child sponsorships, deworming, and early childhood interventions as generally highly effective.

be the more effective approaches) to include doing this kind of research as part of their due diligence and continual learning.[2]

Last, evaluate an organization's impact. We advise against dismissing or endorsing any potential partner organization without meaningfully investigating the impact of their work. Some organizations are effectively utilizing an approach that has been critiqued; other organizations are employing the latest methods with little or no positive impact. Ask organizations how they measure their impact toward achieving their stated mission and vision, including what data they regularly collect and what reports (internal and external) they produce that document their effectiveness and learnings.

No matter which sectors garner attention, we recommend reflecting on how each sector and approach is shaped by the distinct claims of the gospel and the mission of God. Occasionally we make those connections explicit. We hope it is evident how all our recommendations derive from the principles articulated in Chapter Three.

Children, Youths, and Older Persons

Jesus gave special honor to children during his ministry (Matt. 19:13–15), and Scripture reveals God's heart for orphans and widows who are often marginalized by society (Isa. 1:17; Ps. 68:5; James 1:27). Many have followed this ethic by caring for such individuals and populations. Faith-based humanitarian efforts have included a variety of initiatives over the years, including building and operating Christian schools and orphanages, and offering a variety of support services for families and the aged.

Orphan Care, Mentoring, and Sponsorships

Societies address their vulnerable members and populations through a wide range of formal and informal systems that include traditional kinship, governmental agencies, and nonprofit organizations. In many countries, family members take in orphans and vulnerable children, but this approach

---

[2] Besides Wydick's research, we recommend websites such as GiveWell (https://www.givewell.org/), AidGrade (https://www.aidgrade.org/), Giving What We Can (https://www.givingwhatwecan.org/), and the Bill and Melinda Gates Foundation (https://www.gatesfoundation.org/), each of which provide information on nonprofit organizations.

can be overwhelmed when large numbers of children are in need due to political, economic, ecological, or health crises. Children can be left to fend for themselves and may have limited avenues for growth or income. Formal systems can suffer from inadequate resources or oversight as well.[3]

In 2014, UNICEF estimated that there were 140 million orphans, whom they define as children up to the age of seventeen who have lost one or both parents. An estimated 13 percent of these children were orphaned due to HIV/AIDS.[4] Although orphanages have been a common and sometimes desirable approach for caring for children, this approach to care can have unanticipated consequences. Several organizations that participate in the Faith to Action Initiative encourage caring for orphans within families and communities whenever possible instead of thinking of orphanages as the primary means of care. They argue that Christians should develop partnerships supporting family care whenever possible.[5]

Tatek Abebe notes that currently preferred approaches to orphan care emphasize:

- Strengthening and supporting the capacity of families to protect and care for their children
- Mobilizing and strengthening community-based responses
- Strengthening the capacity of children and young people to meet their own needs
- Ensuring that governments protect the most vulnerable children and provide essential services
- Creating an enabling environment for children and families in poverty[6]

However, kinship care is not immune from hazards and exploitation. Children can receive inadequate care, be treated inequitably within the family, or be abandoned.[7] Family members may take in children to capture

---

[3] Bailey, *Orphan Care*, 7–10.
[4] UNICEF, *Reimagine the Future*, 59.
[5] Faith to Action Initiative, *Continuum of Care for Orphans*; Faith to Action, "Guiding Principles."
[6] Abebe, "Orphanhood, Poverty, and the Challenges for Care," 165; Olson, Knight, and Foster, *From Faith to Action*.
[7] Maundeni, "Care for Children," 19–37.

inheritance or may be unable to care for additional children beyond their own. Children may receive material care but inadequate medical, educational, or psychosocial support.[8] Cases of abuse within family care should be considered carefully.

The Christian Alliance for Orphans (CAFO) attempts to equip church leaders to create local faith-based networks that inspire local Christians to adopt or foster children. To build capacity, CAFO leaders train parents and families in adoption, fostering, parenting, and caring for children struggling with trauma, while also working to bolster church support.[9] Another approach, developed by Craig and Nay Greenfield in Cambodia and employed by Alongsiders International, is to pair young mentors from congregations in the Global South with vulnerable children in the community.[10] Youth mentors follow a three-year curriculum in sharing gospel insights and life skills with their "little brother" or "little sister."

Congregations in the Global North and South occasionally deliver seminars centered on marriage, family, and child-rearing. Contextualization is critical in these since family relations are culturally as well as theologically defined. Short-term missions and "voluntourism" with children have been popular as well. Yet, short-term interactions have been criticized for forming temporary bonds that benefit the visitor much more than the child.[11] Additionally, short-term workers and volunteers often promote superficial notions of poverty and can form unrealistic expectations among children regarding ongoing relationships or opportunities.[12]

Finally, child sponsorships have been a popular approach in supporting families and creating bridges from Christians in the Global South and North. Perhaps best known (and researched) are sponsorship programs by World Vision, Compassion International, and OneChild. These and other programs connect a child with a sponsor who provides financial and emotional support.[13]

---

[8] Maundeni, 25, 29.
[9] Christian Alliance for Orphans.
[10] Alongsiders International.
[11] Freidus, "Unanticipated Outcomes of Voluntourism."
[12] Freidus, "Unanticipated Outcomes of Voluntourism"; Richter and Norman, "AIDS Orphan Tourism."
[13] Compassion International.

Research into Compassion's sponsorship approach shows that sponsored children are more likely to complete their schooling and obtain better employment compared with nonsponsored siblings. Sponsored children and their families benefit from immediate financial support, enabling continued school enrollment, health care, and other benefits.[14] The sponsorship approach is also linked to increased aspirations and hope, which research shows contribute to many aspects of well-being.[15] Not all sponsorships are alike, however, and outcomes may differ between programs. For example, World Vision "flipped the script" on the traditional child sponsorship model and had the children who were to be sponsored select their sponsors.[16]

Widows and Seniors

Although age is honored in many cultures, widows and the elderly can suffer in isolation and poverty. Yet, widows in the Bible are often inspirational figures. Just recall Ruth and Naomi, the widow of Zarephath (1 Kings 17:8–16); Anna (Luke 2:36–38); the widow who gave all she had (Mark 12:41–44); and the widow appealing to an unjust judge (Luke 18:1–8).

A long tradition exists in extending care to children, but attention to widows—or to the aged—can be overlooked. As with children, it generally is optimal for families to care for relatives. Services may be needed to address elder abuse, mental and physical health, food security, income, and other needs of seniors. Churches sometimes have informal programs to support widows, but few Christian organizations currently fill these gaps. Insights can be gleaned from secular organizations such as Age International, the Global Alliance for the Rights of Older People, the Global Ageing Network, and Help Age International.

---

[14] Wydick et al, "Does International Child Sponsorship Work?"; Wydick, *Shrewd Samaritan*, 118–19.
[15] Lybbert and Wydick, "Poverty, Aspirations, and the Economics of Hope"; Barnard, Dercon, and Taffesse, "The Future in Mind."
[16] Weber, "World Vision Flips the Script."

Creation Care

A 2016 survey of Protestant churches engaged in global poverty alleviation found that the most frequently engaged sector was disaster relief and the least engaged was creation care.[17] So, why do most churches respond to natural disasters *after* rather than before they occur? Among the potential reasons are that: (1) Natural disasters frequently are viewed as unpredictable and uncontrollable; (2) a relatively small number of faith-based nonprofits focus on creation issues so few partnership opportunities exist; (3) congregations may seem ill-suited and feel ill-equipped to address such a large and complex issue; (4) there may be a lack of awareness within churches on how creation care impacts people who live in poverty; or (5) congregations may not perceive creation care as part of the church's mission.

The limited presence of creation care among many congregations does not mean that the sector has not been addressed, however.[18] Resilience and sustainability are marbled through many initiatives in secular and faith-based development. Issues of soil deterioration, deforestation, sanitation, conservation, and water are included in many agricultural and water, sanitation, and hygiene programs. Churches have engaged some, but more avenues for potential engagement remain.

Theological perspectives treasuring God's creation have been offered throughout Christian history, yet recent political views have overshadowed this tradition, at least in the United States.[19] A major cause of diminished environmental concern is the false premise that ecological innovation is detrimental to the economy. Eco-justice counters and corrects this mindset. Norman Faramelli explains:

> Eco-justice always includes the "Three Es"—Ecology, Economy and Equity. The term eco-justice covers more than Environmental Justice, although it includes it. Assessing the disproportionate impact of economic activity on various groups is important but, by itself, is insufficient. Eco-justice also entails resistance to false choices. For instance, it is not a choice between whether there will

---

[17] Lynn, "Congregational Aid."

[18] Tsimpo and Wodon, "Faith Affiliation, Religiosity, and Attitudes," 52.

[19] Politics rather than theology may determine environmental commitments among many Christians in the United States. See Arbuckle and Konisky, "Role of Religion."

be jobs at a strip-mining site or a clean environment. Eco-justice states that it is not an "either/or" proposition; it must be "both/and".... Eco-justice forces us to "think outside the box" when there seem to be no alternatives that embrace both Ecology and Economy.[20]

Resisting unfortunate political trends, Christians can affirm the theological tradition that values all of God's creation—land, air, water, animals, and humans. Humans have been given the high call and duty to care for all of God's magnificent handiwork.[21] As Kwok Pui-lan asserts:

> Christian mission has been preoccupied with God's interaction with humanity. Concern for the environment has been rendered secondary or absent. Yet the environmental crisis challenges us to see God's missionary purpose as integrated with environmental concerns and responsibilities.... This means that we need to radically expand our understanding of Christian mission—from an anthropocentric to a cosmological focus.[22]

Creation care is critical in poverty alleviation for a number of reasons. Many in the Global South rely on subsistence and small-scale farming (agriculture) to feed their families and generate an income, making them directly dependent upon local rainfall and soil quality, as well as subject to spikes in global commodity prices. Many of the poorest families have few resources to mitigate or adjust to environmental changes that impact where they live and work. As regional climates change, many are, and more will be, involuntarily displaced while having limited resources to mitigate climate and land impacts or resettle to new locations.

Some in poverty often live close to industrial sites that spew toxic chemicals or release waste into local water supplies. Likewise, millions live in slums or near garbage dumps.[23] These living conditions envelop eco-justice issues as well as pollution. Additionally, conflicts continue to arise over

---

[20] Faramelli, "*Missio Dei*," 151.
[21] For a careful exegesis of groaning creation, see Hunt, Horrell, and Southgate, "Environmental Mantra?"
[22] Pui-lan, "Sustainability," 219.
[23] For more on slums, see the section on Shelter.

scarce natural resources such as land, water, and forests. Christopher Shore of World Vision International highlights four ways that changes in ecosystems affect poverty.

PROBLEM	IMPACT
Disasters	People in economic poverty become more vulnerable after disasters, as they often have no buffer to deal with crop failures or physical damage to their homes. They are less likely to have flood or other disaster insurance.
Cost of Adaptation	People in economic poverty are less likely to have reserve funds to mitigate disaster impacts. If they choose to spend money on preparing for change, they may sacrifice other necessary items, such as food, education, or health care.
Displacement	Migration due to drought or agricultural demise disrupts livelihoods and often affects host and transit countries negatively.
Diminished Resources	A lack of natural resources leads to conflicts over territory and goods.

Table 4.1. Creation Care and Poverty[24]

Added to these are a host of other issues that affect health, security, and livelihoods: land management, water harvesting, pest control, conservation agriculture, renewable energy, and more.[25] Between 2030 and 2050, the World Health Organization estimates that climate change is expected to result in 250,000 additional deaths per year from climate-related malnutrition, malaria, diarrhea, and heat stress. The direct social costs to health care and earning power are estimated to be between $2 billion and $4 billion per year by 2030. Areas with weak health infrastructure will be the least able to prepare and respond.[26]

Most large development organizations are aware of ecosystem issues, and they weave resilience and sustainability into their programming. World Vision, for example, uses integrated approaches to increase the

---

[24] Adapted from Shore, "How Climate Affects the Poor," 29–36.

[25] For a thorough review of links between poverty and ecosystems, see Millennium Ecosystem Assessment, *Ecosystems*.

[26] World Health Organization, "Climate Change and Health."

sustainability of smallholder agriculture.[27] World Vision equips farmers with tools for managing natural resources and mitigating environmental shocks. Australia's Tony Rinaudo advocates Farmer-Managed Natural Resource Regeneration techniques, which have resulted in sizable gains in reclaiming land that had been deforested and subject to erosion. Plant with Purpose is focused on similar goals, employing a holistic and faith-based approach to land and forest reclamation. Likewise, World Neighbors promotes community-based natural resource management.

Many agricultural missionaries receive help from ECHO, a Christian organization that provides farming advice, research, and resources. Its innovative campus in Florida includes a variety of ecosystems where researchers teach and experiment with plants and various agricultural practices and techniques. ECHO also maintains a large collection of tropical seeds for distribution around the world. Tearfund, another faith-based organization, has facilitated tree planting to aid in water management, combat flooding, and support honey production. It addresses climate change by promoting clean energy solutions.

Although climate concerns and renewable energy are often addressed on a global scale, many household-level applications have been developed as well. Biogas, solar, water, and human-powered energy sources have been explored, along with improved cookstoves, which reduce indoor smoke (a cause of major health issues in women and children), and firewood collection. But creation care initiatives entail much more than mere technology transfer. Sustainable tools must be culturally appropriate. Cultural, practical, and financial considerations and tradeoffs can make a seemingly obvious idea infeasible in application. Each setting requires hearing voices in the community and listening to their lived realities.[28]

Beyond agriculture, climate change will continue to affect people living in poverty in many ways. The poorest billion people living in the

---

[27] Smallholders are farmers with small amounts of land to cultivate or small herds to manage.

[28] For insights into economic and cultural obstacles, see Beltramo et al., "Effect of Marketing Messages"; Hanna, Duflo, and Greenstone, "Up in Smoke"; Khandelwal et al., "Why Have Improved Cook-Stove Initiatives"; Soini and Coe, "Principles for Design." For health implications, see Bruce, Perez-Padilla, and Albalak, "Indoor Air Pollution." For energy usage, see Legros et al., "Energy Access."

most fragile parts of the environmental ecosystem bear the greatest brunt when ecosystem changes occur. Advocating for local, national, and global ecosystem protection and wise resource use is an important and faithful expression of Christian love and discipleship.[29] Business owners and corporate leaders have the opportunity, and the responsibility, to implement environmentally friendly policies and practices as a means of neighborly care. Connections between personal lifestyle and God's creation link the notions of "sparing" and "sharing": when we limit expenditures and conserve resources, we become more mindful of others and can share resources. As Pope Francis wrote about creation care efforts in his encyclical *Laudato Si'* (*Praise Be to You*): "We must not think that these efforts are not going to change the world. They benefit society, often unbeknown to us, for they call for a goodness which, albeit unseen, inevitably tends to spread."[30]

Even if a congregation does not directly engage in the creation care sector, it is critical for churches to discuss financial, operational, and natural resource sustainability with partners, as well as with communities who are most directly impacted by climate and ecological issues. Often, when one digs deep enough into the roots of a community's challenges, creation care issues become apparent. Stewarding creation is humanity's vocation, so the church should be cognizant of fulfilling that call in all aspects of its life and service.

Education

Christians have long engaged in educational initiatives as part of their mission. Over the past several centuries, Catholic and Protestant missionaries frequently started schools, and the impacts of their presence have been detectable decades later.[31]

Literacy and Primary and Secondary Schooling

The historical emphasis on supporting primary education and scriptural literacy remains popular among congregations today. Additionally, several

---

[29] Chowdhury, "Religiosity and Voluntary Simplicity."
[30] Francis, *Praise Be to You (Laudato Si')*, 142.
[31] Calvi, Mantovanelli, and Hoehn-Velasco, "The Protestant Legacy."

faith-based institutions of secondary education have arisen in the Global South in recent years.

Secular development efforts have also emphasized education. Following the signing of the Universal Declaration of Human Rights in 1948, interest mushroomed in supporting universal primary education. That effort continued with the global adoption of the United Nations (UN) Millennium Development Goals in 2000, which included a target of universal primary education for boys and girls. By 2015, this goal was met in many countries, but not all.

Some African and Asian countries still have low school enrollments due to poverty, population growth, armed conflicts, and discrimination against children with disabilities. Pervasive gender discrimination (another primary focus of the UN) in some regions results in girls receiving poorer quality or less education than boys. Unfortunately, this discrimination contributes in measurable ways to lifelong inequality and gender disparities. Substantial progress has been made in increased school attendance, especially among girls, but room for improvement remains.[32]

Multiple good reasons exist to invest in education. Basic reading and math literacy have been shown to be related to gains in income, health, nutrition, employment, and other poverty-linked outcomes. When aggregated at a national level, higher reading and math literacy are linked to increases in a country's economic output.[33] Overall, literacy interventions reduce poverty.[34] However, effectiveness and scaling remain issues of concern.

Many have focused on building schools and increasing attendance, however, these initiatives do not equate to improved learning. Measures of what students know and can do show a very different picture from enrollment or attendance figures. Aside from a few notable exceptions, between 50–90 percent of students in the Global South perform below students in countries in the Global North on key educational metrics such as reading, arithmetic, or life skills. In some areas, approximately half of fifth- or

---

[32] MDG Monitor, "MDG 2"; UNICEF, "Gender Equality."
[33] Hanushek and Woessmann, "Do Better Schools."
[34] Kim, Lee, and Zuilkowski, "Impact of Literacy Interventions."

sixth-grade students cannot read.[35] Although high-quality private schools have been built in several countries, the impacts of these institutions do not always scale to the larger population of low-income students.[36]

In a comprehensive review of educational systems in developing countries, Lant Pritchett of the Center for Global Development notes that it is an inadequate goal to focus on school construction instead of on learning outcomes. It is what happens *within* the school that is critical.[37] According to Pritchett, the primary answer to the learning challenges faced by children in poor countries is not more schools, higher enrollment, or advanced grade levels (although these may address other needs), but rather a focus on the pace and effectiveness of learning and tracking dropout rates.[38] Pritchett argues that a focus on expanding inputs (e.g., physical infrastructure of the school and classrooms; school supply inputs such as paper, textbooks, and learning materials; formal teacher qualifications and training; and teacher-to-pupil ratios) is unlikely to be sufficient in improving the rate of learning.[39]

Pritchett's research suggests that faith-based educational initiatives should focus on learning methods, student and teacher supports, and learning outcomes instead of merely tracking inputs or enrollments. Investigating the root causes of student learning challenges and personal barriers to school attendance (e.g., facilitating deworming or providing female hygiene products for girls) can enhance overall school effectiveness.

In his review of educational interventions, Bruce Wydick advocates international child sponsorship, improvements in teacher quality, and conditional cash transfers to pay families to keep their children in school as

---

[35] Measures of literacy performance produce dramatically different results. Pritchett bases his conclusions on international rather than national measures of literacy to enable comparisons across countries and provide robust assessments of learning. See Pritchett, *Rebirth of Education*.

[36] Stambach, *Faith in Schools*; Pritchett, *Rebirth of Education*, 198.

[37] Pritchett, *Rebirth of Education*.

[38] Dropout is influenced by "push" and "pull" factors, such as the need to work to support a family or offers of marriage (pull) and disliking school (push). On the latter, Pritchett says, "It is hard to make children who are not learning, and know they are not learning, stay in school." Pritchett, *Rebirth of Education*, 84.

[39] Pritchett, *Rebirth of Education*, 100.

vastly superior interventions to new school construction or free laptops.[40] Indirect approaches to enhance literacy and learning may be more effective than capital improvement, although again, there is a need and place for wise investments.

Technical and Vocational Training

Vocational education has been a popular service among Christians in building capacity for income generation. Donors from the Global North have shared expertise in sewing, welding, woodwork, computer software, cosmetology, bicycle repair, jewelry making, weaving, beekeeping, and other trades, and they have helped establish training and mentoring programs. Some have targeted youth underemployment, particularly in rural areas or with street kids, just as Made in the Streets has in Kenya. Others have extended opportunities to women and men who are healing from sexual exploitation and provided job training and employment for children at risk for trafficking, as Urban Light, Basha Boutique, and Eden Ministry have in Asia. Programs sometimes include a provision of basic tools to launch a small business, and products and services are sometimes sold in local markets through artisan importers.

What some may not know, however, is that in many locales, informal apprenticeships already are widely available in family-run businesses and that commercial training programs frequently advertise in the newspaper and over the radio. These typically are businesses themselves, offered on a fee-basis to relatives or the general public. They provide lodging and food as well as training for youths who desire to pursue a nonfarm skill.[41] Often, public funding is available for vocational training programs, but programs can be plagued by low enrollment, low graduation and placement rates, poor-quality instruction, and unequal access for women.[42]

Faith-based vocational programs often begin as supply-side initiatives: a tradesperson in the Global North mentors students and possibly provides the basic tools and equipment to start a business. Sometimes, vocational training produces more labor than the market can absorb or

---

[40] Wydick, *Shrewd Samaritan*, 117–22.
[41] Chea and Huijsmans, "Rural Youth."
[42] Blumenfeld and Malik, "Human Capital Formation."

provides training for roles that are not financially sustainable. Faith-based efforts should consider the impact of their programs on existing apprenticeships. They should consider unmet training needs and whether market demand and business development resources can support trained artisans and trades.

Beyond basic vocational training, opportunities may exist to consider what might be missing in the overall market system. For example, consider whether certifications, licensing, co-ops, or networks of reputable tradespersons might raise the quality of services provided, enlarge the market, and enhance the livelihoods of tradespersons. Educators might also look beyond the curriculum to create networks of formal or informal employers and enhance partnerships in internships, resources, and hiring; or they might focus on skills that can be transferred across a variety of occupations or that can be coupled with formal apprenticeships.[43] While vocational programs are designed to equip workers to sustain a livelihood, the programs themselves sometimes struggle due to lack of funding.

Higher Education

A final educational initiative has been the building of colleges, universities, and seminaries. For more than a century, Christians have built higher education institutions around the world. Today, more than one thousand colleges and universities exist with a faith-based identity. Most institutions are small and staffed by dedicated leaders, faculty, and students. A few, such as Baekseok University in South Korea, are sizable. Over time, a few of these institutions have been absorbed by the state, as happened to sixteen Christian colleges in China. Online programs are being offered as well by institutions such as Nations University.[44]

In recent decades, higher education particularly has grown in Africa. In 2010, nearly seven hundred colleges and universities in sub-Saharan Africa enrolled a combined 5.2 million students. Several of these were faith-based, including Daystar University and Africa Nazarene University

---

[43] Biavaschi et al., "Youth Unemployment and Vocational Training"; International Labour Office, "Upgrading Informal Apprenticeships."

[44] Bays and Widmer, *China's Christian Colleges.*

in Kenya, Northrise University in Zambia, Heritage Christian College in Ghana, and African Christian College and Southern Africa Nazarene University in Eswatini.[45] Africa Business Institute offers certificates in business and entrepreneurship. Around 130 Christian universities have been founded outside North America since 1990: 58 in Africa, 30 in Latin America, 22 in Asia, 17 in Europe (mostly in the East), and 2 in Oceania.[46]

Research suggests that higher levels of education per capita are associated with lower levels of poverty and that in many regions, graduates are able to find suitable employment after graduation.[47] In countries and regions where limited employment is available to graduates, educational programs may prepare students for nonexistent jobs. Professionals who are able to do so often emigrate elsewhere, contributing to what is often referred to as "brain drain" from a country's labor force. Seminaries, likewise, can prepare pastors for jobs that pay little or nothing at all and do not yield sustainable livelihoods. The local economy and educated workforce may be something of a chicken-or-egg problem, but job creation, aligning programs with market needs, and accreditations are, in general, worthy considerations for those supporting higher education.

So, what are the takeaways for education? Education contributes to poverty alleviation, but educational institutions and their sponsors need to consider learning effectiveness, student impact, and outcomes rather than merely facilities and resources. This likely requires innovating multiple types of learning methods and being sensitive to local approaches to knowledge attainment and family support, not merely transferring teaching methods and resources from the Global North. It is also important to keep an eye on the local and global job market for graduates. For programs that have the flexibility to adjust, providing educational opportunities that align with sound employment potential for students while grounding the educational curriculum in Christian theology can enhance the effectiveness of education and contribute to transformational development.

---

[45] Carpenter, Glanzer, and Lantinga, *Christian Higher Education*.
[46] Glanzer, "Growing on the Margins."
[47] Gyimah-Brempong, "Education and Economic Development in Africa"; Al-Samarrai and Bennell, "Where Has All the Education Gone."

Food

Famine and food insecurity are woven throughout Scripture. Recall the burden of hunger in the stories of Joseph and Ruth, the widow of Zarephath (1 Kings 17:12), and Paul's allusions to hunger as an apostle (2 Cor. 11:27; Phil. 4:12). Jesus's encouragement to "hunger and thirst for righteousness" (Matt. 5:6) resonated with the masses because they knew both. Indeed, hunger is a motif of human history, affecting individuals and entire societies.[48]

Agriculture, Food Insecurity, and Nutrition

In the decades before 1980, tens of millions of people died annually from starvation. Print and television ads frequently displayed hungry children with bloated stomachs and flies on their faces to solicit sympathy and donations from the Global North. These types of ads offered little dignity to people. The ads came to be labeled as "poverty porn" and, thankfully, have mostly disappeared.

Since 1980, starvation, hunger, and food insecurity have declined considerably around the world, primarily because of increasing household income. With more money, people can purchase larger quantities and more nutritious food to feed their families. Despite these gains, food insecurity still exists for millions, and it has been rising again in recent years, especially in Asia and Africa.[49]

According to the Food and Agriculture Organization of the United Nations, around 800 million people are chronically undernourished, and two billion experience moderate or severe food insecurity during part of the year.[50] *Food security* is an umbrella term that the Rome Declaration on World Food Security defined as occurring when "all people, at all times, have physical, social and economic access to sufficient, safe and nutritious food to meet their dietary needs and food preferences for an active and

---

[48] Other biblical references to famine cite Abraham, Isaac, Joseph, Elimelek and Naomi, David, Elijah, Elisha, Amos, Zedekiah, and Agabus (Gen. 12:10, 26:1–6, 41:54–57; Ruth 1:1–2; 2 Sam. 21:1; 1 Kings 17:1, 18:1; 2 Kings 6:24–29, 8:1–3, 25:1–3; Lam. 4:4–5, 8–10; Amos 4:6–9; Luke 4:25; Acts 7:11–14, 28–30). For a broad historical survey of famine, see Ó Gráda, *Famine*.

[49] Food and Agriculture Organization of the United Nations, *State of Food Insecurity*.

[50] Food and Agriculture Organization of the United Nations, *State of Food Insecurity*, 8.

healthy life."[51] When any one of these conditions is not met, food insecurity occurs. Food insecurity is found in all countries and impacts the physical and mental development of children, especially during their first three years of life.[52]

Complicating the lives of smallholder farmers in the Global South are pressures placed on families to shift production from the traditional food grown for personal or local consumption to cash crops that can be sold in the global marketplace for export. When farmers switch to growing cash crops, they usually have to increase and diversify their agricultural inputs, including purchasing chemical fertilizers and expensive hybrid seeds that can cause poor farmers to go into debt. Sadly, farmers who get into a cycle of perpetual debt are just one bad crop season away from losing their land. Cash crops, enhanced seed, and fertilizer sometimes can work to boost a community's food security. Other times, however, this enhanced approach to farming results in greater vulnerability.[53] With any technology, it is critical to consider the context, weigh the research, and monitor the impact.

An additional factor that severely harms the income potential of large swaths of subsistence farmers in the Global South is governmental farm policy. Debates about agricultural economics can be complex, but there is no doubt that farm policies in the Global North impact smallholders in the Global South. Farmers are prone, and often incentivized by government subsidies, to overproduce in the United States, and they hope for strong prices. If they do not materialize, commodities sometimes are dumped into poorer countries, decimating the livelihoods of local growers.[54]

When rural farmers in the Global South cannot grow enough to eat or sell to feed and sustain their families, family members may choose to immigrate to urban areas.[55] If income is not forthcoming there, some are forced to emigrate to other countries for work, risking their lives and

---

[51] Food and Agriculture Organization, "Rome Declaration on World Food Security," 1.
[52] Thurow, *First 1,000 Days*.
[53] To illustrate how context and consequence matter with agricultural technology, consider Flachs, *Cultivating Knowledge*; Kuma et al., "Cash Crops"; Tankari, "Cash Crops."
[54] For a history of US farm policy and its impacts, see Graddy-Lovelace and Diamond, "From Supply Management."
[55] Beginning in 2008, more than half of the world's people live in urban areas. See UN Population Fund, *State of World Population 2007*.

borrowing heavily to journey to foreign lands that offer a possibility of income. In migrating, some families liquidate household assets or are forced to abandon dependents, including children and the elderly. Migration can lead to illness through malnourishment, dehydration, and/or drinking unsafe water. Mental stress and a sense of loss often accompany migrants.

While increasing a family's income is generally the most effective ladder out of hunger and food insecurity, war, famine, and food price volatility often disrupt lives in ways that lead to communities at home becoming even more food insecure. Climate change exacerbates food insecurity through excessive or erratic rainfall, erosion, volatile temperatures, and financial indebtedness, as mentioned previously.[56] Peaks and troughs in the global demand and supply of various foods, especially cash crops, affect both the price and the availability of food in specific regions. Beneath the choppy surface of these food price and availability waves is persistent poverty that limits the ability of some households to achieve long-term food security.

Famine

Before we explore responses to hunger, we should say a word about famine. Famines are exceptional increases in hunger that affect many people, and they occur for several reasons.[57] Although droughts and other environmental events can negatively influence agriculture in significant ways, these result in famine only after a series of cascading events. If adequate income, backup food systems, and possibly government-led social programs exist, famine can be avoided despite the loss of crops and livestock.

Famines are typically the result of a shortage of income, not a shortage of food, and they do not occur in places where democracy thrives.[58] War or overgrazing can be crucial triggers for famines in the Global South, as can be political actions by leaders that interrupt the ability of people (often marginalized groups) to obtain adequate food. Alex de Waal argues that today, most famines occur because of genocide or war—a consequence

---

[56] Azzarri and Signorelli, "Climate and Poverty."
[57] de Waal, *Mass Starvation*, 17.
[58] Sen, *Poverty and Famines*.

of political rather than natural causes.⁵⁹ So, we should think of famine and hunger (food insecurity) in the modern era not merely as a result of drought, flood, or population growth but, instead, the result of social actions and political decisions. Sophisticated forecast models, such as used by the Famine Early Warning Systems Network, monitor rainfall, food availability, conflicts, and other factors that can trigger famines.⁶⁰ As helpful as these predictions can be, however, aligning funding with warning signs has been challenging. Appeals continue to pair relief financing with pre-disaster planning.⁶¹

Food Aid

When we turn to responses by Christians to food insecurity and famine, we find abundant responses in direct food relief, agricultural/market development, and advocacy. We believe it is useful to go back in time a bit to see how these efforts developed in North America and what the latest research and sound practices suggest.

In response to the millions of hungry people who emerged following both world wars, Canadian and US farmers engaged in direct food relief by donating the crops or income from an acre of their cultivated land to churches for domestic and international hunger relief. These efforts popularly were called the "Lord's Acre" or a "Friendship Acre." After the immediate postwar needs were met, many hunger-fighting faith-based organizations turned from relief to development, equipping or supporting farmers with agricultural inputs and training and, in some cases, helping connect farmers with export markets. The faith-based Canadian Foodgrains Bank shipped wheat to food-insecure recipients.

Originally, foodstuffs were shipped as a gift, but increasingly governmental self-interest played a role. Humanitarianism was combined with the dumping of excess commodities and the advancement of strategic interests.⁶² Supported by shipping lobbyists, the United States continued the practice of sending excess agricultural produce abroad, even when

---

⁵⁹ de Waal, *Mass Starvation*.
⁶⁰ Famine Early Warning Systems Network.
⁶¹ Clarke and Dercon, *Dull Disasters?*, 12.
⁶² Clapp, *Hunger in the Balance*.

many other countries abandoned the practice in favor of financing locally sourced food. (The latter reduces transportation costs, environmental impact, and potential food losses due to shipping, while simultaneously strengthening rather than harming agricultural markets in developing countries and infusing additional cash into regional economies.)

In recent years, the shipping of US food aid has diminished, but some dumping continues. Direct food provision from a donor country may at times be necessary but, in most cases, the development preference is for donors to provide cash vouchers to people experiencing a food crisis. This allows households to select their own food preferences from local or regional farmers while adding an economic boost to those farmers while not distorting local prices.

Sponsorships

Christians and congregations have long supported sponsorships as a tool to address global hunger. One type of sponsorship is to pledge a donation for individuals who walk a certain distance in the CROP Hunger Walk, orchestrated by Church World Service (CWS). Thousands of local walks have been held since the inaugural walk in North Dakota in 1969.

Another type of popular sponsorship is donating animals to families in poverty. The Heifer Project (today's Heifer International) began as a response to the Spanish Civil War of the 1930s. It promoted a sponsorship program whereby donors could provide animals to families in need elsewhere. Heifer International's livestock donation program effectively supplemented household income and nutrition.[63] Historically, Heifer International provided households with pregnant animals and require that, upon the animal giving birth, the household donate the newborn animal to another designated poor household. This "passing on the gift" requirement was intended to offer a sense of responsibility and dignity to the initial household, offering an opportunity to bless a neighbor and their community.

There are some issues to consider when promoting or supporting a livestock sponsorship program. Questions include the potential for

---

[63] Rawlins et al., "Got Milk?"

overgrazing or oversupply (such as too many goats for one region to support); how surplus products, like milk, yogurt, or eggs, are distributed; and whether pastoralists have access to markets for sales. Animals may also adversely impact water contamination and household disease.[64] Finally, animal donations may not be as cost-effective for the impact gained as other potential poverty-alleviation interventions.[65] Animal sponsorship organizations differ in their models and impact, and they should be considered carefully.

Agriculture and Market Development

In many locations, food aid is considered the responsibility of the national government. Unfortunately, not all governments support food security for everyone through adequate or effective policies and infrastructure. Where chronic food insecurity exists, many nonprofit agencies have attempted to support agricultural and market development. These efforts focus on enhancing smallholder farmers' ability to obtain access to needed inputs, such as improved seed, agricultural knowledge, and networks for learning, which helps reduce postharvest losses, avoid crippling debt, market produce, and continue to learn about proper household nutrition. World Vision, Save the Children, and CARE are a few of the organizations that have focused on ultra-poor farming households.[66]

Other agricultural development approaches include farmer schools, demonstration plots, and faith-based sustainable agriculture. One of the earliest approaches to the latter was Brian Oldreive's "Farming God's Way."[67] ECHO, a leading Christian research, education, and seed supply organization in Fort Myers, Florida, trains farmers in sustainable faith-based approaches to agriculture and food. ECHO offers conferences and learning resources on agricultural innovation suitable for the world's poorest

---

[64] Headey and Hirvonen, "Exposure to Poultry."

[65] Wydick, *Shrewd Samaritan*, 132.

[66] Norell and Brand, "Integrating Extremely Poor Producers"; Norell et al., "Value Chain Development."

[67] World Gospel Mission, "Farming God's Way." A complementary Christian farming approach is offered by Evans, Vos, and Wright, *Biblical Holism and Agriculture*. Additionally, Food for the Hungry has produced a manual titled "Redemptive Agriculture."

farmers. Secular organizations such as the World Fish Center offer research on fishing, aquaculture, and permaculture for impoverished communities. Some organizations focus on graduating smallholders into market integration and resilience.[68] Some emphasize creation care through caring for the soil and land, enhancing biodiversity, and reducing carbon emissions.[69]

Advocacy

A third approach to promoting food security and better nutrition is through advocacy. Advocacy attempts to listen to and amplify the voices of those who regularly go hungry, and it strives to mobilize political power to influence governmental food-related bills and policies to assist food-insecure households. Many congregations have steered clear of engaging governments in food security legislation, but thousands of Christians have contributed to food security through the efforts of organizations such as Bread for the World and Food for the Hungry.[70]

Advocacy can help millions of food-insecure people gain access to more and better nutrition through food and agricultural policy in both the Global North and Global South. Because food aid in the United States and Canada can come from a variety of different government agencies, and because the bills and regulations that address aid can be complex and nuanced, it makes sense for congregations that are interested in food aid to work with and through nonprofit organizations that understand policy and know policymakers.

Unhealthy eating in Global North countries is impacted by agricultural policies, supporting an overabundance of nutritionally questionable, low-priced foods. These foods can make their way into the nation's diet, particularly among people living in poverty. National food policy and our own lifestyles can play a role in linking us to global friends. David Baker notes how Scripture supports the notion that "agricultural produce is God's gift to his people, to be shared with all."[71] Thankfully, the prevalence of hunger globally is lower than it once was, but abundant opportunities

---

[68] World Vision, "Farming as Business."
[69] See De Haan, "Production Principles"; Spaling, "Enabling Creation's Praise."
[70] Beckmann, *Exodus from Hunger*.
[71] Baker, *Tight Fists or Open Hands*, 309.

remain for Christians to respond to Jesus's call: "For I was hungry and you gave me food" (Matt. 25:35a).

Freedom and Liberation

As with hunger, the footprints of human slavery crisscross throughout Scripture and history. Despite slavery being condemned (Exod. 21:16; Deut. 24:7), it was practiced by Israel and other ancient societies as kingdoms conquered one another and conscripted people as slaves. Enslaved people were the most frequently traded commodity across borders in the ancient world.[72]

Slavery was a significant part of Jewish identity, constituting one hundred to two hundred years of servitude in Egypt and decades of exile in Assyria, Babylonia, and Persia. (And this does not count hundreds of years of Greek and Roman occupation, centuries of antisemitism, or the Holocaust.) Israel's identity with slavery runs so deep that it is revisited each year in Passover Seders, and it constitutes the ancient basis for justice for strangers: "Remember that you were a slave in Egypt and the LORD your God redeemed you from there" (Deut. 24:18a).

Most ancient societies had a relatively large class of enslaved people who did menial and, sometimes, managerial labor. This may be the reason why Paul and many other ancient Christian writers could not imagine an end to the institution of slavery in societies (1 Cor. 7:21; Col. 3:22; Eph. 6:5).[73]

As Christians, we are willing slaves of Christ (Rom. 6:17–19; 2 Cor. 2:14), but this is not the same thing as human slavery, which fails to recognize the dignity of people made in God's image. We celebrate emancipation milestones—from the Exodus to the late Byzantine Empire to the Thirteenth Amendment of the US Constitution—yet, despite these liberating events, slavery continues underground, as people enslaved today are trafficked, not traded.

Today, the International Labour Organization estimates that about twenty-five million people globally are enslaved in forced labor and sexual

---

[72] Fletcher, *Barbarian Conversion*, 113.
[73] Some interpret Paul as hinting at a change in slavery when he entreats Philemon to consider Onesimus "no longer as a slave but more than a slave, a beloved brother" (Philem. 16a; cf. Gal. 3:28). See Cho, "Subverting Slavery."

exploitation and another fifteen million are trapped in forced marriages, or marriages without consent. Other related abuses include coerced begging, forced organ harvesting, and illegal adoption. The total number of identified victims is on the rise, which may indicate an increase in detection, trafficking, or both.[74] Women and girls represent 71 percent of all enslaved people today.[75] Christians have responded, but we can do more, and we can do better.

Forced Labor and Trafficking

It may be surprising to learn that forced labor, rather than sex trafficking, constitutes the largest share of slavery today. Forced laborers work in many of the supply chains of the Global North, yet they have received relatively little attention among Christians. Forced laborers can be found in every region of the world, including the United States, but they are most prevalent in Asia, the Pacific, and Europe.

Because of debt and intimidation, individuals are forced to work in mines, factories, restaurants, construction, agriculture, cleaning, brickmaking, and other sectors, raising the profits of enslavers since the cost of labor is minimal. Workers can become indebted to a lender, often through deceit. When they cannot escape accumulating interest charges that grow faster than their earnings, workers find themselves permanently indebted and subject to the demands of their owners. If a debt is unpaid, bondage can often be transferred to another family member or to the laborer's children.

Although the majority of people enslaved for labor remain in their country of origin, some are transported across borders. When that occurs, traffickers sometimes utilize a complex chain of global entities, making it difficult for anyone to detect the trafficked workers. Traffickers innovate, utilizing loopholes, circumventing detection, and partnering with corrupt officials. Vulnerable workers can lose some of their wages because they do not have legal status or political agency, but they often lose all of their

---

[74] UN Office on Drugs and Crime, *Global Report on Trafficking in Persons 2018*, 7.
[75] International Labour Organization, "Global Estimates of Modern Slavery," 26–27.

wages or, in some cases, are deported if they complain. They often have a limited voice or ability to escape their plight.[76]

About one-quarter of enslaved laborers are children. Many are required to work ten- to twelve-hour days, seven days a week, in mining, fishing, agriculture, and other industries that contribute to the supply of goods to Global North consumers. Others are conscripted for forced begging, child soldiering, and coerced criminal activity.[77] In some regions, boys are vulnerable to being conscripted as porters and then soldiers, similar to what occurs in the drug trade. According to a 2011 United Nations report:

> Children are often desired as recruits because they can be easily intimidated and indoctrinated. They lack the mental maturity and judgment to express consent or to fully understand the implications of their actions. In some cases, they are forced to consume alcohol and drug[s] and are pushed by their adult commanders into perpetrating atrocities, such as killing, torturing, and looting—sometimes against their own families and communities.[78]

Debate continues about whether children can be held responsible for human rights abuses committed under the age of fifteen or eighteen. One perspective is that if they are too young to legally fight, then they are too young to be held responsible for their actions. But this same perspective also makes them attractive candidates to commit heinous war crimes so adults maintain impunity. Many who are conscripted as child soldiers struggle to reintegrate into society.[79]

Sexual Exploitation and Trafficking

Sexual exploitation includes sex slavery and trafficking (forms of forced labor), along with forced marriages, which are most prevalent in Africa.

---

[76] For recent legal developments in labor abuse and trafficking, see UN General Assembly, "Trafficking in Persons."

[77] International Labour Organization, "Global Estimates of Modern Slavery," 22–23.

[78] Office of the Special Representative of the Secretary-General for Children and Armed Conflict, "Children and Justice," 10.

[79] Allen et al., "What Happened to Children?"

Many of today's fifteen million forced marriages involve girls under the age of fifteen.[80]

In *The Locust Effect*, Gary Haugen, founder of International Justice Mission, and Victor Boutros detail how sex slavery occurs. Commonly, malevolent perpetrators target vulnerable people just as swarms of locusts consume fields of grain, preventing them from thriving.[81] Unfortunately, in many economically poor countries, judicial systems and law-enforcement agencies do not serve the needs of all people. Haugen and Boutros suggest this occurs because the colonial system that was in place before these countries achieved independence designed law enforcement to protect the rulers, not the masses.

In the absence of properly functioning judicial and law-enforcement systems, the rich and powerful use money and influence to protect themselves with private hires and bribery, while vulnerable people lack the resources to hire assistance in their fight against injustice. Once entrenched, it is challenging to redirect these systems toward justice for the vulnerable. Anti-trafficking laws exist in most countries, but many have gaps (such as not requiring protection for victims), and some are never enforced. The most vulnerable people in a society often find public systems corrupt, ineffective, untrustworthy, or dangerous and to be feared—that is, if vulnerable people can even figure out how to navigate the bureaucratic systems in place.

Other forces are also at work, in addition to law enforcement. On the supply side, poverty and conflict make families and individuals vulnerable to enticing but deceptive offers of marriage, income, help with migrating to a new country (especially when immigration laws are restrictive, which is often the case in wealthier countries), or professional athletics. On the demand side, there is human sexual desire, distorted through sin, and the opportunity to maximize profits in prostitution and pornography by eliminating labor costs through slavery. Siddharth Kara suggests that when people try to intervene in slavery or trafficking, often they have not taken

---

[80] International Labour Organization, "Global Estimates of Modern Slavery," 22–23.
[81] Haugen and Boutros, *Locust Effect*.

the time to understand how it works. He and others provide heartbreaking details of how these systems operate.[82]

Trafficking exploded with the expansion of globalization in the 1990s. Many well-meaning and courageous individuals, when they became aware of it, attempted bold rescues. These efforts generally were ineffective and naïve, and some made conditions worse for those who were enslaved. Some populations, such as boys enslaved in sex work, were initially overlooked. Many efforts did not have the funding or mission to focus on long-term flourishing.[83] Thankfully, many organizations in the nonprofit sector have learned a great deal and have developed more effective approaches to help guide those who are able to exit slavery into greater freedom and resilience.

Several experienced voices have called for ensuring that human rights, media, public health, and medical issues be included in programming, rather than exclusively focusing on legal issues. Several nonprofits now focus on pathways toward social inclusion, psychological healing, and economic support. Many organizations still need to focus on improving outcomes in long-term flourishing for clients and in program evaluation.

Gender-Based Violence

Gender-based violence (GBV) is defined as follows:

> Any harmful act that is perpetrated against a person's will and that is based on socially ascribed (i.e. gender) differences between males and females. It includes acts that inflict physical, sexual or mental harms or suffering, threats of such acts, coercion, and other deprivations of liberty. These acts can occur in public or in private.[84]

Unfortunately, in many countries around the world, violence occurs against girls and women, and (to a lesser degree) against boys and men. The 2014 Global Summit to End Sexual Violence in Conflict represented a significant

---

[82] Kara, *Sex Trafficking*; Shelley, *Human Trafficking*.
[83] For a constructive critique of Christian responses to sex trafficking, see Greenfield, "Can We Talk about the Anti-Trafficking Industry?"
[84] Inter-Agency Standing Committee, *Guidelines for Integrating Gender-Based Violence Interventions in Humanitarian Action*.

gathering of global leaders to address gender-based violence during wars and conflicts when perpetrators use gender-based violence to subdue others. Although mostly a government-level attempt to address sexual violence during wars and conflicts, the summit stated:

> Good laws and international agreements in themselves are not enough if attitudes don't change. In this respect, faith groups have a key role to play, including in their role providing care, treatment and support for survivors. Through their networks, they often have access and influence with local communities that no other actor has. As such, they are uniquely placed to change hearts and minds, and challenge cultural and social norms, including notions of masculine identity as it affects sexual violence. The Summit recognised the need to engage faith-based organisations as active partners in the fight against sexual violence, both in helping to formulate strategy and in providing front-line support to survivors.[85]

Inequalities often fuel violence. In some cultures, hierarchical views of gender have been manipulated to condone violence against women.[86] Churches can work to correct mistaken understandings of household and social authority, love others sacrificially (Eph. 5:25), and protect vulnerable community members.

Combatting Exploitation and Trafficking

Sex and labor trafficking have attracted considerable attention, activity, and research, yet much remains to be done.[87] If one wants to fight this scourge, a good place to begin is to become familiar with the drivers and details of

---

[85] UK Foreign and Commonwealth Office, "Chair's Summary."
[86] Petersen, "Working with Religious Leaders."
[87] Foot, Toff, and Cesare, "Developments in Anti-Trafficking." Target 8.7 of the UN Sustainable Development Goals reads, "Take immediate and effective measures to eradicate forced labour, end modern slavery and human trafficking and secure the prohibition and elimination of the worst forms of child labour, including recruitment and use of child soldiers, and by 2025 end child labour in all its forms." See UN Department of Economic and Social Affairs, "Sustainable Development Goal 8." For faith leaders, see "Joint Declaration of Religious Leaders against Modern Slavery."

slavery and trafficking and with reputable organizations working in this sector. Reports of multilateral agencies and efforts, such as the United Nations Office on Drugs and Crime's *Global Report on Trafficking in Persons*, provide background information.[88] Broad efforts, such as with the UN Sustainable Development Goals and among faith-based organizations (see Appendix B), also provide context. The Polaris Project's National Human Trafficking Hotline provides links to additional national information, such as reporting trafficking within one's community.

The initiatives of most serious faith-based organizations fit within the Palermo Protocol "3P" foci of prevention, protection, and prosecution (and a fourth—partnership—that was added later), or within the less legally oriented staging of prevention, intervention, rehabilitation, and reintegration. Some NGOs raise community awareness or advocate for enhanced government policy, legislation, and enforcement targeting labor and sex trafficking. Many engage in survivor support. Among faith-based NGOs, International Justice Mission is widely recognized as an important leader on this issue; other smaller nonprofits provide safety nets on a more moderate scale and with different approaches. For each, utilizing effective practices and achieving credible outcomes is important.[89]

Jim Martin offers an excellent action plan for congregations in *The Just Church*.[90] For Christians engaging in advocacy, the Interfaith Center on Corporate Responsibility continues to advocate for US government attention on slavery in corporate supply chains. From an indirect angle, supporting income generation and poverty reduction initiatives can provide economic options for families, making them more resilient against slavery and trafficking. Christians and others have engaged in slave redemption—whereby one purchases an enslaved person's freedom—but

---

[88] UN Office on Drugs and Crime, *Global Report on Trafficking in Persons 2018*.

[89] According to the Global Modern Slavery Directory (https://www.globalmodernslavery.org/), nearly three thousand NGOs work against slavery and trafficking globally. Impact measures provide insight on what works, such as Bryant and Landman, "Combatting Human Trafficking." Finally, for general justice representation, Administer Justice (https://www.administerjustice.org/) operates several offices in the United States and is staffed by Christian attorneys who represent vulnerable people on a variety of justice issues. For more information, see Strom, *Gospel Justice*.

[90] Martin, *Just Church*. Good advice is also provided by Miles and Crawford, *Stopping the Traffick*, and Crawford et al., *Finding Our Way*.

this achieves only a temporary gain. It leaves unaddressed the originating factors that lead to enslavement. Poverty reduction is an attempt to get at the root.

Locally, Christians may also resist slavery by opposing structural racism and high-interest financial services that entrap people in poverty. Churches can use their consumer power to advocate that businesses use their influence and resources to ensure that their supply chains are free of trafficked and enslaved people.

Incarceration

A final issue in this sector is justice systems and the incarcerated. Prisons and jails may call to mind the guilty, but counted among the incarcerated were Joseph, Sampson, Jeremiah, John the Baptist, Paul, Peter, Jesus, and the early Christians, plus many more. Some of the scriptures and literature we hold dear were written in prison cells. Most pointedly, Jesus begins his ministry by proclaiming freedom for captives and the oppressed (Luke 4:18) and later commends disciples who visit those in prison (Matt. 25:36). Engaging this issue is a way for God's people to heed the call to "Remember those who are in prison, as though you were in prison with them" (Heb. 13:3).

An estimated three million people globally are currently being detained without the benefit of a trial. Many others suffer from unjust convictions.[91] Regrettably, few Christian or secular organizations work in this sector. (Justice Defenders is one, highlighted in Appendix B.) Those that do engage typically advocate for fair laws and just procedures, provide legal or educational services for the incarcerated, and/or support prisoners and their families.

Churches and individuals also can advocate for the cessation of capital punishment. This work entails engaging the complexities of political and legal structures, but skilled organizations can assist. Despite the challenges, this is a way disciples of Jesus can embody the prayer: "Let the groans of the prisoners come before you; according to your great power preserve those doomed to die" (Ps. 79:11). And as Pope Francis's declares in his encyclical

---

[91] Injustice in judicial and prison systems also includes discriminatory practices against specific populations. In the United States, this is clearly seen in a disproportionate number of African Americans incarcerated. See Alexander, *New Jim Crow*.

Fratelli Tutti: "The firm rejection of the death penalty shows to what extent it is possible to recognize the inalienable dignity of every human being and to accept that he or she has a place in the universe. If I do not deny that dignity to the worst of criminals, I will not deny it to anyone."[92]

Health

Disease, healing, and health figure prominently in Scripture and in the ministry of Jesus, making it appropriate that health and medical care have had a long history among his followers. Modern medical missions expanded in the late eighteenth century, paralleling the development of Western medicine. Two early medical missionaries were Englishman John Thomas (1757–1801), who worked in India beginning in 1783, and American Peter Parker (1804–88), who practiced in China beginning in 1834. Although other healers preceded him, Parker is considered by many to be the father of modern medical missions.[93]

Medical missions can be a hazardous undertaking.[94] Many physicians and nurses have died due to epidemics and limited access to medical care for themselves. Historian T. F. Davey highlights the challenges of nineteenth-century British medical missionaries.

> Many scarcely knew what they were going to. Few realized on their departure that it would fall to their lot to introduce scientific medicine over wide tracts of land where it was hitherto unknown, and be responsible for the development of medical services that have become a vital part of national life in country after country, but so it was. Many made the supreme sacrifice. Many suffered extraordinary privations; not a few had to return, broken in health, overwhelmed by the mass of human need around them against which they were lonely pioneers. Some had to face suspicions and misunderstanding, regarded as interfering in the status quo that reactionary forces wanted to preserve.[95]

---

[92] Francis, *Fratelli Tutti*.
[93] Chesterman, *In the Service of Suffering*, 15.
[94] A modern reminder of this is the story of Kent Brantly, a physician who contracted Ebola in Liberia in 2014. For the story, see Brantly and Brantly, *Called for Life*.
[95] Davey, "Introduction," 15.

Early modern efforts to establish clinics, hospitals, medical training, and community health initiatives are the seeds of many regional health-care systems today throughout the Global South. History has enshrined the work of pioneers such as David Livingstone, Florence Nightingale, Albert Schweitzer, and Mother Teresa.[96] History also reminds us of the need to be sensitive to cultural influences in medical and health-care practices.[97]

Evolving Faith-Based Health Care

Health care is a major and popular sector of transformational development. Knowing how faith-based approaches have improved and grown over the years can deepen the effectiveness of future medical interventions. David Van Reken catalogs this progression as follows:[98]

- The doing phase—In the nineteenth century, missionary doctors and nurses delivered primary health care and established clinics and hospitals.
- The training phase—In the early twentieth century, Christians turned their focus to building nursing and medical schools to train additional medical personnel.
- The empowering phase—By the mid-twentieth century, oversight of health care began to be transferred to local medical personnel. This includes professionals and community-based health delivery approaches.
- The partnership phase—Medical personnel from the twenty-first-century Global North work alongside host country medical teams.

This is obviously just part of the story; not every initiative is at the same stage of development. But the general cycle suggests that health care in

---

[96] Davey, "Introduction," 9; Browne et al., *Heralds of Health*.

[97] Another tension is the possibility of Western medicine being a veiled form of imperialism. Critics warn that despite the advantages of modern medicine, global health practices need to recognize and appreciate local cultural and spiritual insights into medicine and health, considering their contribution to healing. For critical perspectives, see Halvorson, *Conversionary Sites*; Klassen, *Spirits of Protestantism*.

[98] Van Reken, *Mission and Ministry*.

the Global South has changed over time and that many lessons have been learned. We will attempt to describe some of that story.

By the 1960s, the World Council of Churches recognized that faith-based health delivery institutions in the Global South were becoming obsolete and not meeting the needs of people who could benefit from preventive care and community health. The World Council of Churches set up the Christian Medical Commission in 1968 and issued a report called *The Healing Church*, which advocated for local agency in determining health-care priorities and an increasing focus on community health. The Christian Medical Commission promoted several creative initiatives, but some lost inertia when it was dissolved in the 1990s.[99] The World Health Organization (WHO), however, continued emphasizing primary health care, underscored by the Alma-Ata Declaration in 1978 and reaffirmed by the WHO Declaration of Astana in 2018.[100]

Global Health

Today, health care and missions often divide into specialties such as humanitarian and emergency medical care, provided by organizations such as the International Committee of the Red Cross (ICRC) and Médecins Sans Frontières (MSF or Doctors Without Borders); primary care delivered by trained medical providers; health systems, which include networks of ambulances, clinics, labs, hospitals, and supply chains; public health, which addresses infectious disease and disease prevention; mental health; disability; and health-care education and training.

While practitioners may specialize in one of these, it is important to see the global aspects of health and interconnections in health care. Susan Holman says of Christian views on health, "It is about health *globally*, that is, not just in 'other countries' but encompassing a concept that embraces together all countries and regions, including our own backyard."[101] Dr. Peter Hotez of the Baylor College of Medicine agrees and calls for broadening views on global health and seeing health connections between all

---

[99] Litsios, "Christian Medical Commission."
[100] Galea and Kruk, "Forty Years after Alma-Ata."
[101] Holman, *Beholden*, 73.

regions of the world.[102] A global perspective shifts the goal of medical missions from a transfer of knowledge, human resources, and technology to a deeper appreciation of connections in health.

Health-Care Needs and Funding

Public funding for health care is often grossly inadequate in low-income countries, especially in sub-Saharan Africa and parts of Asia.[103] According to a study of countries by income level, low-income countries spend three cents for every dollar spent in high-income countries on medical care.[104] By 2040, only one of thirty-four low-income countries and about a third of middle-income countries are expected to reach the Chatham House goal of having 5 percent of gross domestic product devoted to government health spending.[105]

While most people in sub-Saharan Africa reside within two hours of a hospital, many health-care facilities suffer from inadequate supplies and training, suggesting that coverage and capacity are much lower than these numbers suggest.[106] The Lancet Commission on Global Surgery concluded that "65% of the world population currently lack access to safe, timely and affordable surgical and anesthesia care and there is an unmet need for 143 million additional surgical procedures each year."[107] And WHO predicts a global deficit of approximately 12.9 million skilled health professionals, such as midwives, nurses, and physicians, by 2035.[108] Despite celebratory gains in health-care delivery, many needs remain.

NGOs and foundations currently provide about a quarter of health financing (about $10 billion) to the Global South. They typically provide a larger share of health-care funding than the US government or the United Nations. Substantial portions of these funds go toward fighting HIV/AIDS

---

[102] Hotez, *Blue Marble Health*.
[103] Chang et al., "Past, Present, and Future."
[104] Country-by-country spending on health is tracked by the World Health Organization's (WHO) Global Health Expenditure Database. See World Health Organization, "Global Health Expenditure Database."
[105] Dieleman et al., "Development Assistance for Health."
[106] Juran et al., "Geospatial Mapping."
[107] Meara et al., "Global Surgery 2030."
[108] Campbell et al., *Universal Truth*.

and bolstering child health and maternal health.[109] Although a wide range of estimates has been reported, a 2013 study estimated that NGOs and foundations flowed $1.53 billion of funding to faith-based (mostly Christian) NGOs in the Global South.[110] Private donations and congregational efforts provide additional global health-care funds.

Globally, substantial gains have been made in reducing maternal, neonatal, and childhood mortality rates, in deworming, and in reducing the incidence of malaria. However, less progress has been made with noncommunicable diseases, suicide, and violence.[111] In many areas, mental health, adolescent health, and palliative care have lagged as priorities.[112] While national and international averages are informative, it is important to consider the particular health status of regions or population segments, as frequently there are special needs at the regional and local level.

Social and Environmental Considerations

Social and environmental factors need to be considered when addressing the disease burden in a region. This recognition is widely known among health-care practitioners but frequently is beyond the view of congregationally sponsored short-term medical missions trips. A recognition of social and environmental impacts on health underscores the interconnected nature of transformation development sectors.

A WHO report suggested that investments in education, social protection, urban development, housing, and transportation infrastructure can have sizable health payoffs.[113] According to Dr. Paul Farmer, to practice medicine and consider structural causes means "first, to seek the root causes of the problem; [and] second, to elicit the experiences and views of poor people and to incorporate these views and all observations, judgments, and actions."[114] An appreciation of social and environmental

---

[109] Institute for Health Metrics and Evaluation, "Financing Global Health."
[110] Haakenstad et al., "Estimating Development Assistance."
[111] Lozano et al., "Measuring Progress."
[112] Krakauer and Rajagopal, "End-of-Life Care"; Li et al., "Global Development Assistance."
[113] For more, see World Health Organization, *Economics of Social Determinants*.
[114] Farmer, "Health, Healing, and Social Justice," 45.

factors underscores the importance of viewing health in broad rather than narrow terms.

Dr. Daniel Fountain has been a leading voice in medical missions for many years. His work with Vanga Medical Mission in the Democratic Republic of the Congo provided evidence that medical missions needed to focus increasingly on community health.[115] According to James Cochrane, former director of the International Religious Health Assets Programme:

> It is a . . . mistake to look only at what happens inside the doors of the clinic or the hospital, into which people come only briefly in their journeys to find and maintain health. What happens before someone enters that door, and again after they leave, is crucial both to their health and to the ability of the formal health system to support their health. . . . To meet that aim, one has to go outside the doors and into communities. But we still find that . . . most formal healthcare facilities . . . [remain] systemically blind to the widespread community-based health organisations, groups and activities that surround them.[116]

Health is clearly linked with climate, food, water, sanitation, hygiene, household air pollution, nutrition, and drug and alcohol use.[117] Health-care providers benefit from considering these interconnected contributors in any transformational development initiative.

Mental Health Care

Because mental health resources are limited in many areas, individuals with needs are often cared for by family members, the latter of whom may carry the financial, social, and emotional burdens of caregiving.[118] The incidence of mental health needs rises after trauma and tends to accompany natural disasters, migration, violent crime, and war. Income loss can contribute to mental health issues, and likewise, people who experience mental illness often encounter challenges in maintaining their economic

---

[115] Fountain, *Health for All.*
[116] Cochrane, "Trustworthy Intermediaries," 152.
[117] Stanaway et al., "Global, Regional, and National."
[118] Ae-Ngibise et al., "Experience of Caregivers."

livelihoods.[119] Economic stress and poverty are taxing on cognitive capacities and exasperate a host of mental health challenges.[120]

Generally, when emergency water, food, and medical care are being delivered, psychosocial care is needed as well. The WHO reports that nearly a quarter of persons living in a conflict-ridden area are estimated to have depression, anxiety, post-traumatic stress disorder, bipolar disorder, or schizophrenia. The tolls endure, too. Civilians and soldiers who have lived through intense conflict carry the scars of their experience; an estimated 9 percent have moderate or severe mental illness years later.[121]

In some cultures, people seek mental health care from traditional medicine or faith healers.[122] With the dearth of national facilities and specialists, nonspecialist health workers have at times been trained to provide basic support and lay counseling.[123] BasicNeeds, a secular UK-headquartered organization, offers support and education to families and individuals suffering from mental disability or epilepsy. Generally, however, many mental health needs go unaddressed in the Global South.

Christian Responses

So how might congregations engage in the health-care sector faithfully and effectively? Churches have several available options.[124]

Considering the breadth of possible engagements, the Salvation Army discerned their niche by prioritizing health practices that benefit from ongoing relationships. Among these services are providing treatment for people with addictions, diabetes, disabilities, vision impairment, the dying, HIV/AIDS, hypertension, infectious disease, maternal and child health, malnutrition, and mental health.[125] This led Salvationists in East Africa to engage local churches in primary care, health promotion, and public health. This discernment highlights one denomination's prioritization of what it does distinctively and best.

---

[119] Ridley et al., "Poverty, Depression, and Anxiety."
[120] Mullainathan and Shafir, *Scarcity*, 147–63.
[121] Charlson et al., "New WHO Prevalence Estimates."
[122] See Ae-Ngibise et al., "Whether You Like It or Not."
[123] Singla et al., "Psychological Treatments."
[124] Magezi, "Church-Driven Primary Health Care."
[125] Pallant, *Keeping Faith*, 164.

Several faith-based organizations provide services that support persons with intellectual and/or physical disabilities, including wheelchairs, bikes, home-based rehabilitation, eyeglasses, deaf education and translation, accessible toilets, prosthetics, and other needs.[126] Congregations and their partners may also target social and environmental contributors to disease and discrimination. Action on Disability and Development (ADD), a secular UK organization, focuses on addressing the one billion people worldwide who live with a disability. ADD works to enhance inclusion and access to services, assisting persons with disabilities to gain protection from violence and pursue vocations and jobs.[127] Persons with disabilities have knowledge, skills, and labor, and are not only recipients of transformational development; they contribute as well, assisting with planning and ministry.[128]

In some areas, congregations partner with community organizations in providing health and medical services, such as HIV/AIDS education, emotional and family counseling, advocacy, working with addictions, and assisting with transportation to health facilities. Sometimes, Christian Health Associations, which are faith-based networks of health providers, act as intermediaries between community-based organizations and other stakeholders. Additionally, congregational members can be trained to deliver health information.[129] Community health workers, such as advocated by Dr. Paul Farmer's Partners in Health, can provide accessible and culturally competent services such as health education and provision of supplies.[130] Community Health Evangelism (CHE) blends community development, health promotion, and evangelism, empowering communities to determine their health priorities and deploy their own resources to meet their needs.[131]

---

[126] World Health Organization, "Disability and Health."
[127] ADD International.
[128] Inter-Agency Standing Committee, "Inclusion of Persons."
[129] Tazelaar and Newhof, "Empowering toward Shalom."
[130] Scott et al., "What Do We Know," 39. India has more than eight hundred thousand accredited social health activists (ASHAs). South African faith-based organizations developed a Practical Approach to Care Kit (PACK), which equips health workers with knowledge to deliver primary care. See "PACK—Practical Approach to Care Kit"; Palazuelos, Farmer, and Mukherjee, "Community Health."
[131] Global CHE Network.

Tragically, in many countries, drug and alcohol dependency has a significant negative impact on household well-being, draining income, labor, hope, initiative, and capacity.[132] In too many countries, children who live on the streets suffer from drug addiction, such as sniffing glue.[133] These are other areas where churches can engage.[134] If a country does not have enforced standards of quality of care in addiction treatment, it is advisable for churches to adopt operational standards from trusted leaders.[135] Faith-based drug rehabilitation centers often emphasize different etiologies and treatments, which may or may not be effective. Faith-based organizations sometimes rely on spiritual healing while ignoring evidence-based causes and treatments. This may worsen the vulnerability of those seeking treatment.[136]

A final response is perhaps the most common, and that is short-term medical missions. These might include a dentist from the Global North performing extractions for a week in a low-income country, or a physician performing outpatient surgeries. Although trips such as these provide needed medical care, they also have been subject to critique regarding their cost-effectiveness, long-term impact on community health and the health-care delivery system, and the potential marginalization of local health providers.[137] Most critics do not dismiss short-term medical missions outright but suggest that their effectiveness could be enhanced.[138]

Greg Seager provides an in-depth review of short-term medical missions, wherein he highlights five unintended consequences:

---

[132] Levine and Sida, "Multi-Year Humanitarian Funding."

[133] Dabir and Athale, *From Street to Hope*. A useful guide for working with street-connected children is the Consortium for Street Children, "Advocacy and Action Guide."

[134] Tumwesigye et al., "Religion and Religiosity."

[135] Dickson-Gómez, "Substance Abuse Disorders Treatment"; Dickson-Gómez et al., "With God's Help."

[136] Garcia et al., "Vulnerable Salvation."

[137] For critiques, see Seager, *When Healthcare Hurts*; Lasker, *Hoping to Help*. Dr. Kevin Sykes of the University of Kansas Medical Center reviewed sixty-seven studies of short-term medical missions. Their impact is difficult to assess because most of the studies report outputs rather than outcomes—activities rather than impact. For example, the number of surgeries performed is reported, but no short- or long-term health outcomes are indicated. See Sykes, "Short-Term Medical Service Trips."

[138] DeCamp et al., "Ethical Obligations"; Farquhar, Nduati, and Wasserheit, "Ethical Obligations."

- Harm to patients
- Diminished confidence in local health-care systems and providers
- Paternalistic, offering relief rather than development
- Economic harm to providers and health systems
- Focused on volunteers rather than the recipients of care[139]

Seager admonishes medical providers to consider patient safety, health-care system integration and collaboration, development over relief, and community empowerment.[140] Complementing Seager's observations, Judith Lasker recommends nine practices to enhance the efficacy of short-term medical missions:

- Foster mutuality between sponsor organizations and host-country partners at every stage.
- Maintain continuity of programming.
- Conduct a substantive needs assessment with host-community involvement.
- Evaluate process and outcomes, and incorporate the results into improvements.
- Focus on prevention.
- Integrate diverse types of health services.
- Build local capacity.
- Strengthen volunteer preparation.
- Have volunteers stay longer.[141]

Global settings pose unique challenges to patient safety in short-term medical missions. Pharmaceuticals require careful management, and evidence-based, quality-improvement protocols are needed. Pre-field training should address cultural competence, global health-care delivery and systems, and health education and counseling. Participatory stakeholder collaboration, documentation of care, and monitoring and evaluation are all recommended.[142]

---

[139] Seager, *When Healthcare Hurts*, 252.
[140] Seager, *When Healthcare Hurts*, xxii.
[141] Lasker, *Hoping to Help*, 162.
[142] A tool for assessing medical short-term missions is available. It combines an evaluation of six major and thirty minor factors. See Maki et al., "Health Impact

Two alternatives to traditional short-term medical care are to train and compensate local health-care providers to perform medical procedures instead of transporting medical personnel from the Global North. Alternatively, medical personnel who can remain on-site for six months to a year can avoid some of the limitations of short-term trips.[143] Generally, there is room for several approaches, but that does not mean we cannot improve delivery and increase effectiveness in congregational efforts.

In the Global North, several efforts have been made to network and coordinate health professionals and resources. In terms of learning and staffing, the Christian Medical & Dental Associations provide resources, networking opportunities, education, and a public voice for Christian health-care professionals and students.[144] Likewise, multiple faith-based health networks collaborate in sharing learning, information, and resources across the Global South.[145] Collaboration with governmental programs brings unique opportunities and conditions. These include shipping medical supplies via the US Denton Agreement and the Global Health Service Partnership, which sends Peace Corps nurse and physician educators to resource-constrained countries to train local medical personnel.[146]

Broadening the view of health care to systems rather than merely procedures is also an opportunity. One example of focusing on health system strengthening is advocated by Partners in Health and PIVOT—two organizations affiliated with Drs. Paul Farmer and Matthew Bond at Harvard Medical School. These organizations work to strengthen preventive care and health-care delivery by linking communities, health centers, and hospitals. This collaboration addresses a variety of key success factors, including networking ambulances, providing infrastructure, enhancing medical and non-medical equipment and laboratory capacity, staffing and training, monitoring and improving effectiveness, ensuring adequate supplies, and reducing costs.[147]

Assessment," 121.

[143] ReSurge, a secular NGO, practices a training approach.

[144] Christian Medical and Dental Associations, "About Us."

[145] African Christian Health Associations Platform; Dimmock, Olivier, and Wodon, "Half a Century Young."

[146] Stuart-Shor et al., "Global Health Service Partnership," 174.

[147] Garchitorena et al., "Early Changes in Intervention."

Cultural and Ethical Considerations

A final note, concerning cultural and ethical aspects of global health and medicine.

Global health exchanges cannot avoid engaging different understandings of health and medicine. Increasingly, complementary medicine is being recognized, with healing approaches from the Global South being combined with those from the Global North. One way in which shifting perceptions are being considering is in terms of *healthworlds*, which are socially constructed notions of illness, health, and medicine.[148]

Healthworlds acknowledge that the boundaries between different cultural conceptualizations of health and medicine are not as clear as many assume. Christians, for example, hold a mix of dynamic beliefs about science, God, healing, nutrition, and medicine.[149] Similarly, healthworlds suggest that medical practitioners from the Global North consider cultural insights that are relevant to health, medicine, and healing.

Medical missionary Dr. Daniel Fountain writes a great deal about the melding of medicine and culture in his book *Health for All*. He likens encountering "Western" medicine from other cultural perspectives to a palimpsest—a manuscript that has been written on multiple times, with layers of faded texts. Health providers need to be aware of the ways local stories and understandings blend with the practitioner's stories, and with God's story.[150]

In addition to recognizing cultural aspects of health understandings, medical care providers face abundant ethical issues, including selecting patients for treatment, postoperative support, behavioral issues regarding medications, and practicing with limited specialty medical expertise, among others.[151] Contraception and family planning pose additional challenges. Health-care practitioners must consider ethical issues in light of Scripture, culture, law, religion, and their medical or health training and standards.

---

[148] Germond and Cochrane, "Healthworlds."
[149] Germond and Cochrane, "Healthworlds," 320.
[150] Fountain, *Health for All*.
[151] Thiagarajan, Scheurer, and Salvin, "Great Need, Scarce Resources."

Income Generation

In recent years, some congregations have warmed to the idea of incorporating income generation and poverty reduction into their transformational development efforts.[152] This realization acknowledges the spillover effect that increased income can have on so many other aspects of well-being. Creating or improving income for people and families in poverty can shift a ministry from directly meeting needs through relief or handouts to an enabling approach that provides for immediate and long-term needs.

In a survey by Afrobarometer, residents of thirty-four African countries ranked their top three national problems as unemployment (40 percent), management of the economy (21 percent), and poverty/destitution (20 percent). All three are income- and employment-related, yet often, responses target other sectors, leaving residents to wonder if anyone is listening.[153] Results like these are supported by the Millennium Development Goals, which ended in 2015 and generally were considered a grand success but failed to result in widespread job and economic growth.[154] While most macroeconomic issues are best addressed by congregations through political advocacy toward their own governments and through lifestyle and consumer advocacy discussed elsewhere in this book, several avenues exist for churches to further income and business development at a grassroots level. For many in the Global South—and particularly in rural areas—a job with a contract, regular paycheck, and benefits is a fantasy. Frequently, income is collected from multiple sources and from various family members. Income fluctuates day-to-day and season-to-season. As with other sectors, it is important to view economic issues both globally and holistically, rather than as disconnected from the Global North or solvable through a simple solution such as entrepreneurship or agricultural innovation alone. Income is generated within a matrix of cultural expectations, gender roles, governmental regulations, regional and global economics, infrastructure, trade regulation, education, and other factors, including having to navigate fluctuating variables of local corruption prevalent in many informal economies. It is advisable to learn about the local

---

[152] Lynn, "Congregational Aid."
[153] Afrobarometer; Leo, "Is Anyone Listening?"
[154] Barbier and Burgess, "Sustainable Development Goal Indicators."

culture and economy and how people finance their households on a daily basis instead of seeing income generation as merely a transfer of skills and technology.[155]

Business Development Services

Included among approaches in job and income generation are the establishment of technical and vocational education and training programs, described in the Education section of this chapter. In these, students are occasionally equipped with small business training and access to capital or other resources required for launching an enterprise. Likewise, collegiate and seminary education sometimes includes training in entrepreneurship and connections to sources of capital.

Some churches offer short-term business training to equip entrepreneurs. This approach is attractive from a demand side because it allows a person with business skills to share valuable skills in a short-term program. Unfortunately, research suggests that minimal improvements occur in knowledge, sales, or profit following such business training, in part because of their short duration and an absence of follow-up, but also because visiting instructors do not understand the local business institutional or cultural environment.[156]

Modifications to traditional training may yield improved results. These include:

- Providing training for targeted populations—Women, youths, and the disabled face unique challenges that can be addressed in specialized training; issues such as household and business demands, appropriate sectors, negotiation, capitalization, and stereotypes might be addressed.
- Offering specialized training—Lean and continuous improvement strategies or social media marketing approaches might be highlighted, for example.

---

[155] A helpful resource for understanding how people in poverty manage their household financial resources is Collins et al., *Portfolios of the Poor*. See also Mullainathan and Shafir, *Scarcity*.

[156] Anderson and McKenzie, "Improving Business Practices."

- Peer mentoring—Peers can supplement formal training beyond the training period.
- Heuristics and rules of thumb—Simple training can emphasize guidelines such as selling what the market will buy or inventory turnover, and simple tools can be shared to calculate breakeven or avoid stockouts.[157]
- Using psychology and creativity to develop entrepreneurial skills—Cultivate a proactive, problem-solving, creative, entrepreneurial mindset.
- Using electronic technologies for training and mentoring—Larger groups may be reached, and more resources may be made accessible; continued support may be offered as well.[158]
- Training high-potential firms—Be selective in identifying firms that will benefit the most from training and can create more jobs locally.

Facilitating business creation or expansion through mentoring is a related approach. Congregational partners may catalyze startups, offer micro-franchises, support midsize firms, or develop bottom-of-the-pyramid businesses. Individuals or organizations can provide capital, mentoring, training, and other resources, or encourage growing firms to hire newly-trained employees.[159]

Two organizations offering services such as this are HOPE International and Partners Worldwide. Each views income generation as a hand-up rather than a handout, but they use different models to promote enterprise development.[160] HOPE International provides capital by way of loans or through savings groups, and it adds training and coaching to support microenterprise development. Partners Worldwide creates partnerships with local community institutions and international business volunteers. These partnerships provide mentoring, training, capital, and advocacy,

---

[157] Gibson and Gibson, *Where There Are No Jobs*; Gibson and Huntsman, *Where There Are No Jobs*.

[158] Much of the material in this section is from McKenzie, "Small Business Training."

[159] Anderson and McKenzie, "Improving Business Practices."

[160] Although not faith-based, Making Cents International offers resources focused on youth entrepreneurship.

catalyzing entrepreneurs and job creators. They celebrate business as a holy calling to do God's work. Secular organizations, such as Sinapis and Upaya Social Ventures, assist entrepreneurs in launching or growing small businesses.

Loans and Savings

A variety of small group loan and savings innovations have developed over the past several decades to provide capital to small business owners and entrepreneurs. Practitioners in the microfinance industry have learned a lot, and researchers have developed considerable insight on what works and why.[161]

Microfinance involves extending credit via small loans and facilitating savings groups in which individuals encourage one another to regularly contribute a small amount of funds and then withdraw those funds once amassed for family or business use. Access to affordable capital through credit-led microfinance can help smooth business or family budgets but carries its own hazards of potentially mounting debt and substantial interest paid. On the other hand, savings groups—such as those advocated by the Chalmers Center—pay out in several ways, including in improved food security, business investments, and savings.[162]

Many organizations offering business development services also provide loans or facilitate savings groups. Other microfinance organizations only provide capital through short-term loans. Some providers are for-profit and others are nonprofit. It is prudent to inquire with individual organizations about their overall approach and explore their overall impact on poverty. Some faith-based microfinance institutions are listed in Appendix B.

Artisan Importing

Artisan importers also encourage small-scale enterprise development, but they do it by connecting local artisans with export markets. Organizations

---

[161] Banerjee, Karlan, and Zinman, "Six Randomized Evaluations of Microcredit."

[162] An excellent church-centered introduction to microfinance is Fikkert and Mask, *From Dependence to Dignity*; on the impact of savings groups, see Steinert et al., "Saving Promotion Interventions."

such as Ten Thousand Villages, SERRV, and Eternal Threads import commodities such as coffee, chocolate, and crafts from producers in the Global South and sell these goods in higher-income markets.

An artisan importing approach sometimes overlaps with fair-trade interests because an enhanced return to the artisan or grower is often an aim. As with microfinance, this is a complex endeavor involving product development, logistics, and the careful matching of supply and demand.

A general critique levied at the artisan importing model has been that it is an expensive approach to poverty alleviation and that it makes local artisans dependent on somewhat precarious external markets. Shipping costs add considerably to the cost of many imports, substantially raising the price of the goods. For the artisans that benefit and the consumers who purchase their goods, mutual benefit is exchanged and connections are felt.

Business as Mission

Business as Mission (BAM) is yet another approach. BAM represents a broad rubric under which businesses are affirmed as expressions of God-given creativity and institutions are called to embody the gospel by offering places of work and contributing to the betterment of society. BAM organizations commonly value triple outcomes in "profit, people, and planet": maintaining a profitable business, emphasizing employment opportunities and sharing the gospel in word and deed with people (especially employees), and operating in an environmentally sustainable way.[163] Examples might include a coffee shop, restaurant, or farm as a means of generating income or identifying connections with others.

Maintaining a profitable business is challenging, however, and some BAM operators are content to subsidize the business and use it as a portal for relationships to a ministry. Some evaluations suggest that some so-called BAM enterprises are driven more by an appealing narrative than by a commitment to a robust triple-bottom-line enterprise.[164] Despite these

---

[163] Gort and Tunehag, *BAM Global Movement*.
[164] Bronkema and Brown, "Business as Mission"; Van Duzer, *Why Business Matters to God*.

challenges, some BAM businesses are committed to a triple bottom-line and are contributing to transformational development.[165]

Cash Transfers

One innovation that has received considerable acclaim in poverty alleviation circles but less attention within the faith-based community is cash transfers. Conditional cash transfers (CCTs) provide income as long as, for example, a family keeps their children in school, or as long as prenatal medical care is maintained. Unconditional cash transfers (UCTs), such as those offered by Give Directly, provide income without any conditions on behavior.

In high-income countries, cash transfers might be viewed as mere handouts. But in the Global South, where few income sources exist, giving families money has been shown to result in meaningful reductions in poverty. In his book *Shrewd Samaritan*, Bruce Wydick evaluates cash transfers as a highly effective economic intervention.[166]

Researchers continue to evaluate the impact of giving cash, but several short- and medium-term indicators in health, nutrition, and other development measures are encouraging. Recipients tend to use cash in ways that enhance education, health, and well-being.[167]

The ethical case for unconditional cash transfers, as many see it, is that it changes giving from being an exercise of power, in which the giver dictates the issues and solutions, and transfers the choice of how to apply the funds, to the recipients. Indeed, the benefit of cash transfers to people in poverty is that it enables those most in need to decide for themselves and their families which of the interventions (education, shelter, income generation, or something else) are the most prudent for addressing their immediate or long-term needs.

Research suggests that most cash transfers are not spent on income-generating activities but instead are used by people to reduce their expenses. Infrastructure challenges and volume limitations often result in people

---

[165] For example, see Gort and Tunehag, *BAM Global Movement*; Johnson, *Business as Mission*; Russell, *Missional Entrepreneur*.

[166] Wydick, *Shrewd Samaritan*, 113–15.

[167] Loeser, Özler, and Premand, "What Have We Learned?"; Pega et al., "Unconditional Cash Transfers"; Innovations for Poverty Action, "Impact of Maternal Cash Transfers."

who live in economic poverty having to pay significantly more for services (water, fuel, electricity) than wealthier people have to pay per unit, even in the same region/country. Thus, helping people in poverty reduce their expenses for basic necessities can have a significant financial impact on households.

As an example, a poor family receiving a significant unconditional cash transfer might purchase a tin roof for their home that can last ten to fifteen years. Not only does the roof immediately improve their living conditions; over the length of time, having such a roof saves the expense and labor involved in maintaining a grass roof. Increasingly, experts are advocating to prioritize cash transfers in disaster situations (rather than food handouts, as cash also can help kick-start local economies) and, to some degree, in areas of extreme poverty.

As a potential downside, long-term cash transfers can be more expensive to sustain compared to other economic development programs that can generate revenue, or more easily and efficiently scale to reach more people. In some cases, a multifaceted approach that includes cash, education, technical skills training, and other resources may be effective in elevating people from poverty.[168]

These represent several but not all of the approaches congregations can employ to target income generation and poverty alleviation. The approach must be pro-poor—that is, it must achieve tangible long-term benefits for those in poverty rather than merely add to regional development or merely be a means for evangelism. Additionally, initiatives need to be approaches that the local community values, not something a congregation in the Global North desires.

Each endeavor, as well, must consider local realities in how goods and income are shared and what happens to assets during times of famine or conflict. One Kenyan farmer who achieved a 300 percent increase in his maize yield by utilizing nontraditional agricultural techniques returned to his old methods the following season. He explained that the increased yield disrupted many of his social relationships. Advocates for income

---

[168] Innovations for Poverty Action, "Graduating the Ultra Poor."

generation and poverty reduction must consider how such efforts and outcomes are interpreted in local communities.

Migration and Refuge

Jesus was a migrant—and, more precisely, he was an asylum seeker. He traveled as an infant with his family to Egypt to escape threatened violence. And he is not alone in the biblical record. Adam and Eve, Abraham, Hagar and Ishmael, Esau, Moses, Esther, the Israelites wandering in the wilderness and suffering in exile, Mary and Joseph, and others in Scripture include "migrant" in their life stories and identity.

First-century Christian churches were filled with immigrants. The members of the church at Rome mentioned in Romans 16 included Aquila, a Jew from Ponto who left Rome due to imperial persecution (Acts 18:1–4); other Jews such as Mary, Andronicus, Junia, and Herodion; and Gentiles such as Phoebe, Narcissus, Ampliatus, and Urbanus. This reality informed Paul's instruction to "welcome one another, therefore, just as Christ has welcomed you, for the glory of God" (Rom. 15:7) and to show hospitality across lines of ethnicity and nationality (Gal. 3:28).[169]

Throughout the biblical record, the instruction to care for migrants and strangers is clear.[170]

> You shall not wrong or oppress a resident alien, for you were aliens in the land of Egypt. (Exod. 22:21)

> When an alien resides with you in your land, you shall not oppress the alien. The alien who resides with you shall be to you as the citizen among you; you shall love the alien as yourself, for you were aliens in the land of Egypt: I am the LORD your God. (Lev. 19:33–34)

> For the LORD your God is God of gods and Lord of lords, the great God, mighty and awesome, who is not partial and takes no bribe, who executes justice for the orphan and the widow, and

---

[169] Escobar, "Refugees."

[170] For additional biblical mention of refugees, see Hamilton, *Jesus, King of Strangers*; Wright and Măcelaru, "The Refugee Crisis."

> who loves the strangers, providing them food and clothing. You shall also love the stranger, for you were strangers in the land of Egypt. (Deut. 10:17–19)

> Then the king will say to those at his right hand, "Come, you that are blessed by my Father, inherit the kingdom prepared for you from the foundation of the world; for I was hungry and you gave me food, I was thirsty and you gave me something to drink, I was a stranger and you welcomed me, I was naked and you gave me clothing, I was sick and you took care of me, I was in prison and you visited me." (Matt. 25:34–36)

> Do not neglect to show hospitality to strangers, for by doing that some have entertained angels without knowing it. (Heb. 13:2)

Sadly, migrants are often subject to scorn and anger; yet our calling is the biblical imperative to love and care for them.

Migrants and Displaced Persons

A helpful step in engaging migration is to understand various groups and their circumstances. Generally speaking, *migrant* is an umbrella term commonly used to refer to any person who has left his or her home. Within this group, however, it is important to distinguish between voluntary and involuntary, or forced, migration.[171] Voluntary migrants exhibit at least some level of agency in choosing to emigrate.[172] We use the term *migrant* to refer to these populations.

Involuntary migrants, or displaced persons, are those who are forced to leave their homes due to a variety of causes. The United Nations High Commissioner for Refugees (UNHCR) defines four types of displaced populations:

---

[171] UNHCR, "UNHCR Viewpoint," specifically calls for not using the term *migrant* in reference to refugees because it causes confusion and does not serve either population well.

[172] See Ottonelli and Torresi, "When Is Migration Voluntary?," for an analysis of how the term *voluntary* is too undefined and a proposal for how better definitions can lead to better outcomes.

- Asylum Seeker—When people flee their own country and seek sanctuary in another country, they apply for asylum—the right to be recognized as a refugee and receive legal protection and material assistance. An asylum seeker must demonstrate that his or her fear of persecution in his or her home country is well-founded.
- Internally Displaced Person—An internally displaced person is someone who has been forced to flee their home but never cross an international border.
- Refugee—A refugee is someone who has been forced to flee his or her country because of persecution, war or violence. A refugee has a well-founded fear of persecution for reasons of race, religion, nationality, political opinion or membership in a particular social group.
- The Stateless—A stateless person is someone who is not a citizen of any country.[173]

Forced migration is a critical global issue in the twenty-first century. Millions of people are displaced each year due to war, conflicts, poverty, climate change, and persecution. About 40 percent of those displaced are children. According to the UNHCR, almost half of all displaced persons are internally displaced, relocating within their country of residence. But, for those who leave their home country or are externally displaced, many will never be able to return. And 80 percent of these displaced persons will relocate to a low-income country, typically near their home country. Receiving countries often are struggling economically, politically, and socially, leaving little hope or opportunity for new arrivals. Only a small percentage of displaced persons are able to journey far enough to reach a high-income country, where often they find life incredibly challenging.[174]

Currently, data suggest about half of global migrants and displaced persons are Christians.[175] Too seldom do these followers of Jesus receive

---

[173] These definitions can be found at UNHCR, "What Is a Refugee?" We would also classify victims of trafficking as displaced persons. See the earlier section in this chapter on "Freedom and Liberation."

[174] UNHCR, "Global Trends."

[175] Data and Resources, Pew Research Center, "Religious Affiliation of International Migrants." For an interpretation, see Kivisto, *Religion and Immigration*.

care from churches. Barnabé Anzuruni Msabah, a Congolese refugee turned university professor, writes:

> I must confess, in all my wanderings as a refugee, for those many years, I was never assisted by the church (apart from faith-based organisations . . . and individual Christians). The only assistance I have ever received from any church directly or indirectly is spiritual accommodation—a shelter for my soul . . . without regard for the other aspects that constitute my holistic self.[176]

Churches are called to respond to migrants and displaced persons with compassion, providing refuge, rather than with apathy or animosity.[177]

Congregational Responses

So, what can congregations do? One pathway for engagement is to partner with relocation and resettlement agencies in supporting refugees. While resettlement and support services vary between countries, there are opportunities for congregations to welcome and serve refugees and immigrants.[178] World Relief and Catholic Charities USA are two of the faith-based organizations that facilitate congregations and parishes supporting refugees in North America and abroad. The International Rescue Committee, a nonreligious resettlement agency, also provides opportunities for churches to support refugees. Individuals and congregations can begin with whichever agency is active in their local communities.

Although refugees are responsible for much of their own support, resettlement agencies assist with securing housing, job placement and training, cultural orientation, and general transition support. Churches can partner with these agencies to provide welcome essentials, teach English, and serve in other ways that invite relationship and embody hospitality.[179]

Congregations also can serve migrants and displaced populations beyond their own communities. NGOs and local churches provide support

---

[176] Msabah, "Greatest of These Is Hope," 118.
[177] See Kaemingk, *Christian Hospitality and Muslim Immigration*.
[178] Santos, "Diaspora Missions."
[179] For additional background and actions, see Bauman, Soerens, and Smeir, *Seeking Refuge*; Das and Hamoud, *Strangers in the Kingdom*; Soerens and Yang, *Welcoming the Stranger*.

services and engage in community development for refugees who have not been resettled, many of whom spend years, even decades, in refugee camps.[180] Asylum seekers and stateless persons find themselves vulnerable to hegemonic states, and the church can partner with organizations that can promote well-being and protection of rights for these people.

Additionally, churches can take a stand against injustices that generate or harm migrants and displaced persons. One way to do this is by supporting advocacy efforts that provide a prophetic voice for the sake of migrants. Faith-based organizations speaking up for others include the Christian Community Development Association, the Evangelical Immigration Table, and World Relief, among others. When thousands write and call elected officials and stakeholders at critical times, legislation can be influenced toward justice and compassion. Advocacy also can be engaged at the local level. Churches can work with local municipalities, businesses, and NGOs to ensure that migrants and displaced persons are welcomed and supported in the community.[181]

In Hebrews 11:3–16, those who live by faith are described as immigrants seeking a home. Followers of Jesus are "aliens and exiles" (1 Pet. 2:11), and ultimately our citizenship does not belong to the nations of this world (Phil. 3:20). Our love for and solidarity with people is not determined by the temporary borders made by humans but by the image of God that each human being bears. Transformational development with migrants and displaced persons recognizes that *they* are *us*.

Peacemaking and Peacebuilding

The Bible refers to the Father as the God of peace,[182] Jesus as the prince of peace,[183] the Holy Spirit as the harbinger of peace,[184] and Jesus blesses those who act as peacemakers (Matt. 5:9). Yet, peacemaking as a purposeful initiative is largely unknown among many churches. God's children must

---

[180] Less than 1 percent of the world's refugees are resettled to a third country. See UNHCR, "Resettlement."

[181] Oliver et al., "Innovative Strategies."

[182] Rom. 15:33, 16:20; 2 Cor. 13:11; Phil. 4:9; 1 Thess. 5:23; Heb. 13:20–21.

[183] Isa. 9:6–7; Zech. 9:9–10.

[184] Rom. 8:6; Gal. 5:22; Eph. 4:1–3.

pick up the mantle, pursuing peace with everyone.[185] Theologian Doug Heidebrecht summarizes scriptures on peace by saying that

> peace is never an optional concern, but imperative to God's work within the world because it reflects his nature and characterizes the relationships he seeks to have with people and creation. Those who have been reconciled with God have peace with him and are now called to imitate the character of God within their own lives (Eph 5:1).[186]

Peace is at the heart of the mission of God—a reconciliation of people and the world to God. Called to walk in the way of Jesus, brothers and sisters love one another and love others in ways that affirm, create, and sustain peace. Conflict, division, and injustice are ever-present and originate from a variety of causes (James 4:1–3). A lack of peace can fester between groups of people who differ from one another because of race, ethnicity, history, culture, religion, or other factors, and it can exist between or within states, regions, and communities.

Thankfully, Christian theology and practice offer rich and unique resources for the work of peacemaking.[187] In a world that mistakenly thinks death can be weaponized to stop death and that violence can halt violence, we follow a nonviolent, kenotic Christ who frees us from the slavery of the fear of death (Heb. 2:15).

Scripture teaches that we participate in God's peace in several ways, one of which is by proclaiming Jesus the source of peace.[188] Jesus reconciles us to God, inviting us into new life: "So if anyone is in Christ, there is a new creation: everything old has passed away; see, everything has become new!" (2 Cor. 5:17). Another way of participating in peace is to follow the crucified Christ in confronting hate, violence, and evil through self-sacrificial

---

[185] Heb. 12:14; 1 Pet. 3:11.

[186] Heidebrecht, "Mennonite Brethren Peace Theology." Our discussion is informed by Heidebrecht's cogent exegesis.

[187] See Cahill, "A Theology for Peacebuilding"; DuBois and Hunter-Bowman, "Intersection of Christian Theology and Peacebuilding." See also Accad, *Sacred Misinterpretation*, 1–17, for a theological framework to engage in interreligious dialogue and peacemaking, which he calls "kerygmatic peacebuilding."

[188] 2 Cor. 5:14–21; Eph. 2:13–18; Col. 1:19–20.

and nonviolent action.[189] Additionally, we can love one another within the body of Christ (locally and globally), as well as others outside the church, across dividing lines that tend to separate people.[190] Often called "righteousness" in Scripture, love prompts us to intercede with special concern for vulnerable and oppressed people in ways that extend *shalom*.

Working toward Peace

Creating peace goes beyond negotiating and implementing a ceasefire or peace agreement. It includes *peacemaking*, which utilizes diverse strategies to end existing or burgeoning conflicts, and *peacebuilding*, which seeks to create conditions in a community or nation where conflict can be prevented and peace is sustained by addressing root causes of potential conflict and strife.

While peacemaking and peacebuilding are fundamentally relational endeavors, peacebuilding necessarily integrates other development sectors to bolster vulnerable populations. One clear connection is with displaced persons. Peacebuilding can be a preventative intervention in volatile regions to address the root causes of displacement.

It is also important to understand that peacebuilding must involve justice for it to be effective. Scott Appleby explains:

> The correction is derived from a model of peacebuilding that insists on the priority of peace with justice (a "justpeace") and which offers concrete strategies for building the kind of robust multiethnic, multi-religious, cross-generational relationships and partnerships capable of transforming conflict, over the long term, toward a condition of justpeace. Peacebuilding that is relational, comprehensive, and strategic in this way cannot and does not wait upon the cessation of violent conflict, the restoration of order, or a return to "normalcy"; rather, it challenges the very desirability of a return to the pre-violence status quo or some facsimile thereof, and it sees the just (and therefore more

---

[189] Matt. 5:38–4; Matt. 26:52; Rom. 12:14–21.
[190] Matt. 5:43–45; Mark 9:50; Luke 10:27; Rom. 13:9–10, 14:17; 2 Cor. 13:11; Gal. 3:28, 5:14.

effective) provision of "law and order" as possible only alongside and concurrent with the striving toward "positive peace."[191]

Mennonites, Brethren, and Quakers have learned much and have much to share about peacemaking approaches from a Christian perspective.[192] Some focus on representing and reconciling differences between national, religious, or ethnic groups, such as Israelis and Palestinians. Some engage in nonviolent confrontation, speaking truth to power. As Glen Stassen writes, "pacifist" does not signify a passive but an active maker of peace.[193]

Christian Peacemaker Teams has a long history in global peacemaking.[194] Likewise, Christian International Peace Service (CHIPS) assembles small teams of individuals who represent all sides of a conflict yet are committed to peace.[195] The group works over the long term to understand one another and move toward peace.

In recent years, an emphasis on local and participatory approaches to peacemaking and peacebuilding has emerged. Building upon John Paul Lederach's "elicitive model," Scott Appleby explains, "By building on and critically assessing 'local knowledge,' and by disembedding and articulating previously unexamined communal values, it aims to deepen and transform the participation of local actors in the development (or peacebuilding) process."[196]

Examples of participatory approaches include Musalaha, a nonprofit organization in Jerusalem that brings Jewish, Muslim, and Christian youths together to share their faith and life stories, as well as facilitating reconciliation between Palestinian and Israeli followers of Jesus. A similar approach has been adopted by the Institute of Middle East Studies at Arab Baptist Theological Seminary in Beirut, Lebanon, where Muslim and Christian youths and leaders gather, share deeply about life and faith, and

---

[191] Appleby, "The New Name for Peace?," 190.
[192] See Schirch, *Little Book of Strategic Peacebuilding*, for a primer on peacebuilding from a Christian perspective.
[193] Stassen, *Just Peacemaking*, 89.
[194] Kern, *In Harm's Way*.
[195] Christian International Peace Service; Calvocoressi, "Leadership in Peacemaking."
[196] Appleby, "New Name for Peace?," 193. See also Lederach, *Preparing for Peace*, and Lederach, *Building Peace*.

engage in service and advocacy. Partnering with organizations like these is one way of participating in peacemaking. Additionally, congregations in the Global North can follow a similar approach and make peace across political, racial, ethnic, and religious divides in their own communities.

Religious Persecution

Related to peacemaking is the issue of religious persecution. Religious restrictions have been viewed by some as the "canary in the coal mine"—a leading indicator of conflict, persecution, and violence. Thus, some argue that working toward the freedom for all religious practice will have long-term benefits.[197] But others argue that religious freedom is never implemented in law as simply as that. It carries with it a host of issues of power, privilege, and culture and can create new flare-ups of conflict.[198] Religious freedom and persecution is a delicate domain characterized by compelling and competing narratives that deserve special consideration, especially regarding the potential perils of action or inaction.[199]

Three Christian organizations that have been voices against religious persecution are Voice of the Martyrs, Open Doors, and International Christian Concern. Related in their efforts, each pursues its mission with unique structures and operations. Open Doors was founded by Brother Andrew (Andrew van der Bijl), a Dutch Christian who smuggled Bibles into Poland and other countries that restricted proselytization. Open Doors delivers Bibles and other materials personally, quietly supporting persecuted Christians. In contrast, Voice of the Martyrs—founded by former victim of torture Richard Wurmbrand—focuses on generating awareness of persecuted Christians around the world. International Christian Concern is the youngest of the three. It operates in the United States and focuses on advocacy, assistance, and awareness.

---

[197] Finke, "Origins and Consequences of Religious Freedoms."

[198] Sullivan et al., *Politics of Religious Freedom*.

[199] Additionally, some scholars count nearly a million Christian martyrs during the past decade, but this number also has been contested. See Johnson et al., "Christianity 2018."

Relief

The Bible is filled with examples of natural disasters impacting people. Earthquakes, floods, fire, famine, landslides, eruptions, and other events are recorded, along with their impacts on people.[200] Today, the story is similar. News of global disasters is often accompanied by a groundswell of action or, at least, a response of sympathy. Because crises are both plentiful and evocative, we have learned a lot about their impact and about ways to respond effectively. But before exploring those, let's consider the prevalence of disasters.

Natural Disasters

During the first two decades of the twenty-first century, global disasters declined in number, which is good news; but the number of people affected has remained relatively steady due to population growth in disaster-prone regions.[201] The impact of earthquakes, storms, and epidemics varies year to year, but these three types of calamities typically tally the most annual disaster-related deaths due to the scale of the events and the number of people affected. Combined, around four hundred complex humanitarian emergencies requiring international assistance occur annually, an average of more than one per day.

Disasters tend to reoccur in regions due to meteorological patterns, fault lines in the Earth's crust, and other physical characteristics. Scientists project that climate change will introduce volatility in the frequency, type of disaster, and number of people affected. Likewise, epidemics, such as COVID-19, Ebola, and others, may flourish if viruses and superbugs develop in places of new and abundant human-animal interaction. As

---

[200] For earthquakes, see Exod. 14:21; Josh. 3:16; Judg. 5:4–5; 1 Sam. 14:12–15; 2 Sam. 22:7–8; 1 Kings 19:11–12; Ps. 18:6–7; Amos 1:1, 3:15, 6:11; Hab. 3:6; Zech. 14:4–5; Matt. 24:7; Luke 21:11; Rom. 8:22; Rev. 6:12, 8:5, 11:13, 19, 16:18. An earthquake shook the prison that held Paul and Silas in Acts 16:25–28 and 32–34. Matthew reports an earthquake at the time Jesus died. Volcanoes are not as predominant in Scripture, but it is possible that Mount Sinai was an active volcano. See also the language in Micah 1:4–5. Regarding floods, see Genesis 6–8 and 9:11. For a complete survey, see White, *Who Is to Blame?*

[201] For the latest research, see International Disaster Database.

a result, migration may spike if these lead to increased regional and cross-national conflicts.[202] All of these factors portend an increase in the number of people impacted by natural disasters.

Although natural disasters occur in the Global North, wealthier nations generally have the resources to mitigate their impact through infrastructure, building codes, insurance, health care, and other resources. Thus, while about a third of natural disasters occur in high-income countries, in recent history, more than 90 percent of natural disaster-related deaths have occurred in low-income countries.[203]

Not all low-income countries, however, are prone to hazards, and not all are unprepared for disaster. Massive loss of life and of property tends to occur where disaster-prone areas overlap with a high incidence of poverty and a lack of disaster preparedness. At present, high on this list are South Asian countries such as Bangladesh, Nepal, and Pakistan; Central African countries, including the Democratic Republic of the Congo, Tanzania, Ethiopia, and Nigeria; and the island nations of Haiti and Madagascar.[204]

A small number of Asian nations have borne the heaviest impacts of natural disasters because of the conditions mentioned and their sizable and regionally dense populations. Asia, for example, endured 40 percent of the disasters over the past decade, but it accounts for 80 percent of the total number of people affected by natural calamities.[205]

Professor Robert White of Cambridge University argues that the "link between poverty and vulnerability to disasters is a moral and ethical issue for those of us who live in high-income countries."[206] While governments are responsible for their citizens and residents, they do not always have adequate resources to prepare for, mitigate, or respond to emergencies. When unprepared, international aid is often the only available answer, yet such aid often generates a complex response that can be confusing and even unhelpful.

---

[202] Shepherd et al., "Geography of Poverty."
[203] White, *Who Is to Blame?*, 22.
[204] Shepherd et al., "Geography of Poverty."
[205] International Federation of Red Cross and Red Crescent Societies, "World Disasters Report 2018."
[206] White, "Sustainability," 88.

Emergency Aid

The beginning of modern relief is often traced to Henry Dunant, a Swiss Christian businessman who came across an Italian battlefield in 1859. Few first responders were available to care for wounded soldiers and local towns and villages were overwhelmed in attempting to provide care. Dunant's book, *A Memory of Solferino*, took Europe by storm and led to the founding of today's International Red Cross and Red Crescent societies.[207]

Countless people have helped others in times of need, and several relief organizations have responded with assistance during times of tragedy. Dunant was not the first or last good Samaritan, but he represents a mobilization of effort in voluntary societies beyond what governments directly provide.

For the Christian church, there are ways to respond to disasters that are effective and sustainable, and there are ways to respond that worsen recovery. Responses may be considered across five stages of relief:

1. Mitigation and preparation
2. Coordination
3. Effective aid
4. Commitment
5. Evaluation

We will address each of these in turn.

Mitigation and preparation. Mitigation and preparation are helpful for both predictable and unpredictable disasters. Surprisingly, and unfortunately, mitigation efforts tend to occur *after* rather than before disaster events because that is when funding becomes available.

Technology allows us to anticipate and therefore help mitigate some climatological, geological, and famine-related disasters, while some diseases can be treated or quelled before they become epidemics. But too often calls for help or mitigating action go unheeded, and early responses and resources do not appear. Likewise, artificial disasters—that is, those created due to poor construction, inadequate building codes, hazardous locations, or specific actions taken by governments, such as with war

---

[207] Dunant was awarded the first Nobel Peace Prize in 1901 for his efforts.

or conflict—can be averted, but inertia and lack of political will lead us into the crevasse. After a disaster, global funding often is directed toward rebuilding homes and buildings that were not built to be disaster-resistant.[208]

Only 3 percent of global aid currently goes to resilience, risk reduction, and mitigation, and 1 percent goes to preparedness. A relatively small percentage of US foundation philanthropy funding supports disaster preparation in the Global South. The majority of disaster preparation funding is directed to the United States. Only 4 percent is channeled to Africa; 7 percent to Asia, the Middle East, and the Pacific; 16 percent to Mexico and Latin America; and 5 percent to the Caribbean.[209] Considering this, Christian groups that opt to build schools or homes in other world regions could save lives and relief funds over time by focusing on building disaster-resistant buildings from the start, as well as helping with relocating families out of harm's way or renovating existing buildings against anticipated disasters common to the region.

Coordination. Coordination is a key component in preparing for and responding to disasters. Networks often form during times of calm, but when a significant crisis occurs, it is not uncommon for communities to be overrun by too many actors arriving on the scene, many of whom are unacquainted with the location and its institutions and customs. These new arrivals often lack logistical expertise in delivering aid or working within a cooperative coordination system—both of which are essential in most disaster situations.

Effective aid. Stories abound of well-intentioned donors who ship goods to disaster areas at considerable financial and environmental costs. Too often, new or used supplies are not suitable or practical for the location; the items imported into the area decimate local or nearby markets, causing long-term harm to the community one is trying to help; or hard-to-reach areas go without aid and accessible areas receive too much. Too often,

---

[208] Patton, "Philanthropic Grantmaking for Disasters."
[209] Candid and the Center for Disaster Philanthropy, "Measuring the State of Disaster Philanthropy, 2020."

donors decide what is given, and the people receiving the aid have to figure out how best to use what arrives.[210]

Sometimes donations are sold by recipient families (often at a significant loss from market value) so they can acquire the cash necessary to purchase needed items for survival and recovery. Additionally, when free or cheap relief goods—whether they are pharmaceuticals, clothing, food, or other supplies—flood a region, the local market gets distorted and can put local farmers, shop owners, tailors, and others at least temporarily out of business and potentially harm the long-term recovery of the whole region.

Special care should be taken when shipping goods to the Global South. While it seems wasteful to discard surplus goods rather than share them with others in need, there can be issues with the upkeep and maintenance of gifts such as medical or agricultural equipment. Additionally, when the shipping costs are added to the "gift," it lowers the cost-effectiveness of this approach for relief and development.[211] Whenever possible, relief agencies should rely on the carrying capacity of the local economy, either giving cash directly or purchasing what is needed as close to the distribution point as possible and using local providers when viable to help deliver goods and services in the crisis.[212]

The fungibility of cash means distributing cash gifts shifts the power for determining a household's greatest need from the donor to the recipient. Additionally, cash can strengthen the local economy. Cash turns donations into economic sparks, instantly multiplying people's choices regarding trading partners (what they want to purchase and from whom).

---

[210] Forecast-based financing has been proposed to anticipate and mitigate the impact of disasters; however, it has been challenging to get international funders to commit to this idea. The UK-based Start Fund is one organization that is preemptively attempting to address localized disasters. See International Federation of Red Cross and Red Crescent Societies, "World Disasters Report 2018," 196; Start Network, "Start Fund."

[211] The USAID Denton Program allows private goods to be shipped on military aircraft. See recommended gifts-in-kind standards and procedures in Accord Network, "Principles of Excellence in Integral Mission."

[212] For more perspective on this issue, see the discussion of Cash Transfers in the Income and Poverty Alleviation section of this chapter.

Additionally, increased cash flow within the community smooths economic transactions between people and enhances economic growth in the region.

Commitment. Commitment to an area impacted by a disaster is crucial for short-term relief and long-term recovery. More than one-third of giving toward disaster relief occurs in the first month. By the end of the second month, nearly two-thirds of the total funds will have been given. Giving stops almost completely after six months.[213] This reality produces a spike of funding that trails off even if not all the needs in the area have been met.

Organizations and congregations that contribute to relief efforts may wish to consider the progress made in recovery and rehabilitation, and continue checking on efforts after the initial response. Although attention is often focused on immediate safety, shelter, and food needs, relief settings frequently require sources of fresh water, psychosocial support to deal with trauma and loss, economic rebuilding, and other needs that may not immediately come to mind. Patient and sustained recovery considers long-term social, economic, and physical needs, not just immediate disaster relief. People affected by disasters seek to understand or find meaning in loss, and many turn to God. Some rely on the grace of God in the tragedy, and others see God's vengeful hand.[214] Relief workers and organizations need to recognize and be prepared for the spiritual and psychosocial needs within a traumatized community.

Evaluation. Finally, post-relief evaluation is important, even if done informally. If one hopes to continue to improve ways of helping, one must keep learning and reflecting on what was done well and what could be improved.[215]

As an example of post-relief evaluation, the global response to the 2010 Haiti earthquake drew intense criticism largely because too many uncoordinated actors delivered goods to people who did not need them. Sometimes the challenge in coordination is not with other humanitarian

---

[213] Patton, "Philanthropic Grantmaking for Disasters," 8.

[214] Clarke and Parris, "Understanding Disasters."

[215] The UN site ReliefWeb collects major relief effort evaluations and documents disasters as they occur. See ReliefWeb, "Disasters."

agencies but with federal or local governments, communicating with recipients about available aid (especially in local languages), and planning an exit strategy.

Due to the complexity of most disaster situations, the default response by congregations should be to cooperate with experienced organizations that have a track record of responding effectively within a network of actors, preferably within the region where the disaster occurred. Generally, partner organizations should be avoided if they lack capacity, do not have a presence or experience in the disaster-affected location, and do not possess clear linkages to credible coordinators.[216]

Neglected Disasters

Some disasters are unseen and receive minimal attention. The 2018 *World Disaster Report*, produced by the International Committee of the Red Cross (ICRC), called attention to a few of these.[217]

One example of a neglected disaster is people affected by urban violence. Some Latin American countries currently experience among the highest violent death rates in the world.[218] The ICRC recommends governmental action combined with community-centered partnerships between local humanitarian organizations and residents to plan for and mitigate disasters of natural and human origin. Local congregations may be well-positioned to collaborate in addressing an unseen disaster at the community level. This reality also represents another example of how relief is not completely separate from development—the two overlap when long-term relief needs are addressed through development planning and mitigation.[219]

Relief Principles

In terms of principles that guide relief efforts, many organizations subscribe to the *Code of Conduct for the International Red Cross and Red*

---

[216] Patton, "Philanthropic Grantmaking for Disasters."
[217] International Federation of Red Cross and Red Crescent Societies, "World Disasters Report 2018."
[218] Small Arms Survey, "Global Violent Deaths."
[219] International Federation of Red Cross and Red Crescent Societies, "World Disasters Report 2018," 20.

Crescent Movement and NGOs in Disaster Relief.[220] These principles convey values and practices important throughout the relief sector, and congregations wanting to engage in relief efforts should be familiar with them. We believe they are all worthy of inclusion here:

1. *The humanitarian imperative comes first.* The right to receive humanitarian assistance, and to offer it, is a fundamental humanitarian principle which should be enjoyed by all citizens of all countries. . . . The prime motivation of our response to disaster is to alleviate human suffering amongst those least able to withstand the stress caused by disaster.
2. *Aid is given regardless of the race, creed or nationality of the recipients and without adverse distinction of any kind.* Aid priorities are calculated on the basis of need alone. . . . Our provision of aid will reflect the degree of suffering it seeks to alleviate.
3. *Aid will not be used to further a particular political or religious standpoint.* Humanitarian aid will be given according to the need of individuals, families and communities. . . . We will not tie the promise, delivery or distribution of assistance to the embracing or acceptance of a particular political or religious creed.
4. *We shall endeavor not to act as instruments of government foreign policy.* We therefore formulate our own policies and implementation strategies and do not seek to implement the policy of any government, except in so far as it coincides with our own independent policy. . . . We will use the assistance we receive to respond to needs and this assistance should not be driven by the need to dispose of donor commodity surpluses, nor by the political interest of any particular donor.
5. *We shall respect culture and custom.* We will endeavor to respect the culture, structures and customs of the communities and countries we are working in.
6. *We shall attempt to build disaster response on local capacities.* All people and communities—even in disaster—possess capacities as

---

[220] International Federation of Red Cross and Red Crescent Societies and the ICRC, "The Code of Conduct."

well as vulnerabilities. Where possible, we will strengthen these capacities by employing local staff, purchasing local materials and trading with local companies. Where possible, we will work through local . . . partners in planning and implementation, and cooperate with local government structures where appropriate. We will place a high priority on the proper co-ordination of our emergency responses. This is best done within the countries concerned by those most directly involved in the relief operations, and should include representatives of the relevant UN bodies.

7. *Ways shall be found to involve program beneficiaries in the management of relief aid.* Disaster response assistance should never be imposed upon the beneficiaries. Effective relief and lasting rehabilitation can best be achieved where the intended beneficiaries are involved in the design, management and implementation of the assistance program. We will strive to achieve full community participation in our relief and rehabilitation programs.

8. *Relief aid must strive to reduce future vulnerabilities to disaster as well as meeting basic needs.* All relief actions affect the prospects for long-term development, either in a positive or a negative fashion. Recognizing this, we will strive to implement relief programs which actively reduce the beneficiaries' vulnerability to future disasters and help create sustainable lifestyles.

9. *We hold ourselves accountable to both those we seek to assist and those from whom we accept resources.* All our dealings with donors and beneficiaries shall reflect an attitude of openness and transparency. . . . We will also seek to report, in an open fashion, upon the impact of our work, and the factors limiting or enhancing that impact. Our programs will be based upon high standards of professionalism and expertise in order to minimize the wasting of valuable resources.

10. *In our information, publicity and advertising activities, we shall recognize disaster victims as dignified humans, not hopeless objects.* Respect for the disaster victim as an equal partner in action should never be lost. In our public information we shall portray an objective image of the disaster situation where the capacities

and aspirations of disaster victims are highlighted, and not just their vulnerabilities and fears. While we will cooperate with the media in order to enhance public response, we will not allow external or internal demands for publicity to take precedence over the principle of maximizing overall relief assistance.

Local Responses

Although much of this sector has focused on hierarchical responses to disaster, churches, local faith-based organizations, and neighbors are often frontline actors in disaster response, recovery, mitigation, and preparedness.[221] Within the global development sector, local organizations increasingly are being recognized as trustworthy partners that have good relationships with at-risk populations on the ground. They often know and can quickly reach people whom international aid organizations have difficulty reaching. Increasing attention has been given to community-based disaster preparedness programs and collaborative aid networks working in concert with governments and humanitarian organizations.[222]

If a church wants to respond to a disaster or crisis, consider transferring cash directly through experienced relief organizations, some of whom work through local networks. These include World Relief, Samaritan's Purse, World Vision, Mennonite Disaster Service, Lutheran Disaster Response, Nazarene Disaster Response, and others. Additionally, consider the role of mitigation, preparedness, and advocacy. The Humanitarian Disaster Institute at Wheaton College offers timely and helpful information and training resources in this regard.

Scripture Translation

Bible translation is not typically included in poverty alleviation. However, Christians believe that an encounter with God in Scripture can enhance flourishing in multiple areas of life. Indeed, individual regeneration as an

---

[221] Aten and Boan, *Disaster Ministry Handbook*; McLaughlin, "What Have Religious Groups Done after 3.11?"

[222] Bealt and Mansouri, "From Disaster to Development."

approach to global development has been historically dominant among Evangelicals, although it is not without critique.[223]

Bible translation is an attempt, whether implicitly or explicitly, to contextualize theology.[224] Translating the Bible into regional languages stretches back to at least the third century BC, when Hebrew and Aramaic Old Testament scrolls were translated into Koine Greek. Translations of the biblical text into Latin, Syriac, Ethiopic, Coptic, Gothic, Chinese, Slavonic, and Arabic followed before the tenth century AD so speakers of those languages could hear Scripture in their language. In the face of considerable opposition, John Wycliffe and William Tyndale translated the scriptures into English, and Martin Luther translated them into German. A flowering of many other languages began in 1804 with the advent of the Bible society era, making the Bible the most translated book in history.[225] Along the way, Christians also produced many grammars and dictionaries of global languages, which have enhanced cultural preservation and focused on improving literacy in a number of communities.[226]

According to William Smalley, Bible translation was sometimes "an outgrowth of mission activity, [and] sometimes the entering wedge."[227] Missions were not always conducted in local languages, but efforts by missionaries, such as William Cameron Townsend and Eugene Nida, encouraged making the scriptures available in vernacular languages.

Townsend discovered that many of the Indigenous people in southern Mexico could not read Spanish Bibles because they spoke Kaqchikel. This language gap formed a barrier to effectively communicating the gospel. Townsend devoted the next several years to learning the Kaqchikel language, and he and others translated the New Testament into it. He then founded a summer training program in linguistics to aid other missionaries in learning local languages. This camp grew into the Summer Institute of Linguistics (SIL) in 1934 and, subsequently, Wycliffe Bible Translators in 1942.

---

[223] For more detail and a critique, see the "Spirit First" approach in Chapter Five.
[224] Maxey, *From Orality to Orality*, 20.
[225] For a history, see Orlinsky and Bratcher, *History of Bible Translation*; Smalley, *Translation as Mission*.
[226] Sanneh, *Whose Religion Is Christianity?*, 69.
[227] Smalley, *Translation as Mission*, 21.

Eugene Nida's approach was to utilize native speakers when translating and combine language translation with anthropology and linguistics. Nida influenced the "dynamic equivalence" approach to translation, expressing ideas naturally in the local language instead of following a word-for-word translation. Nida "aimed at making the 'truths' of the biblical culture relevant in the indigenous culture, and to remove as much as possible the European/American cultural influence."[228]

According to Kwame Bediako, "Whenever Western missionaries or a missionary society made the Scriptures available to an African people in that people's own language, they weakened any Western bias in their presentation of the Gospel," resulting in an awareness that "God speaks our language too."[229] This realization was a catalyst for attempting to translate the Bible into all languages, including languages without a written alphabet. It awakened Western Christians to the thought, as missiologists James Scherer and Stephen Bevans put it, that "the gospel must be neither captive to local culture nor alienated from it."[230]

Despite translators' sensitivities to language and culture, translating the scriptures remains quite challenging. The Bible was composed in a context itself, and each translator is influenced by age, status, gender, technology, and culture.[231] James Maxey describes the tensions that remain in translation and mission efforts:

> A critical difference between a translation model and an anthropological model of inculturation is based upon the starting point. As indicated above, the translation model starts with Scripture in order to exegete the message to be translated into the culture. With the anthropological method, the starting point is the culture, to understand the "web of meaning" within the host culture. Another way of articulating the difference is that the translation model intends to *bring* God's good news to the culture; the anthropological model seeks to *discover* God's good

---

[228] Stine, *Let the Words Be Written*, 171.
[229] Bediako, *Jesus and the Gospel in Africa*, 57–58.
[230] Scherer and Bevans, "Introduction," 12.
[231] Berneking, "Sociology of Translation"; Maxey, *From Orality to Orality*; Sanneh, *Translating the Message*.

news within the culture. Such a distinction reveals each mode's view of culture: corrupted by sin (translation model), reflection of God's image (anthropological model). Each model has its strengths and weaknesses.[232]

Lamin Sanneh argues for the flowering of linguistic and cultural expressions and the indigenization of Christianity.[233] Translation is a first step toward inculturation of the gospel. Thus, it is helpful to see translation as more than a technical exercise and, instead, consider it through theological eyes.[234] Additionally, research in India suggests that a long-term association exists between nineteenth-century Protestant missions and literacy, given that missionaries stressed education and the reading of Scripture.[235] Continuing this tradition, the Wycliffe Global Alliance Vision 2025 aims to have a Bible translation project in progress for every living language that does not yet have a translated Bible.[236] According to the Wycliffe Global Alliance:

- At least 1.5 billion people do not have the full Bible in their first language.
- More than 2,600 languages across 170 countries have translation projects underway.
- Approximately 2,000 languages still need a Bible translation project to begin.[237]

Paralleling written translation efforts are efforts to communicate the message of Scripture orally, particularly in oral cultures. The International Orality Network (ION), affiliated with the Lausanne Committee for World Evangelism, is exploring and promoting this approach. *The Jesus Film* is an example of sharing the gospel in visual story form rather than written form. ION emphasizes assessing communities for their level of literacy and communicating in ways that speak appropriately to oral communicators.

---

[232] Maxey, *From Orality to Orality*, 29.
[233] Sanneh, *Translating the Message*.
[234] Maxey, *From Orality to Orality*, 37.
[235] Calvi, Mantovanelli, and Hoehn-Velasco, "The Protestant Legacy."
[236] See Cornelius and Niemandt, "Vision 2025."
[237] Wycliffe Global Alliance, "Scripture & Language Statistics 2018."

Shelter

Shelter is a basic human need, and God's people should show care and concern for those who lack it. Recall Isaiah's words about the fruits of true fasting: "Is not this the fast that I choose: to loose the bonds of injustice . . . and bring the homeless poor into your house . . . ?" (Isa. 58:6–7). While many individuals, churches, and organizations in the Global North have addressed this sector with effective approaches in their own national contexts, engagement in the Global South has not always seen such positive impact. However, there are constructive approaches that can lead to more fruit.

Short-Term Missions

With construction projects being relatively short-term in duration and suited to a large number of nonspecialist volunteers, they have been attractive short-term mission activities. But are these efforts effective? One insightful study was completed by Kurt Ver Beek after Hurricane Mitch, which passed through Central America in 1998.[238] Ver Beek surveyed 162 short-term missions (STM) participants who traveled to Honduras to assist in house construction, as well as thirty families that moved into newly built houses. Ver Beek found that STM participants reported being impacted by their experience, but their giving did not increase after returning home; Hondurans did not seem to care who built their house—North Americans or Hondurans; and most strikingly, the cost of building a house with STM volunteers was significantly higher than with local labor.

The average cost of an STM-constructed house was $30,000, while the average cost of a house built by local Christians was $2,000. Beyond cost, researchers warn of additional concerns, including imposing on local decision-making, low-quality construction, disrupting local economies, reinforcing stereotypes of people and poverty, and instigating cultural changes.[239] Added to these concerns are questions about whether housing or labor was needed in the first place.

---

[238] Ver Beek, "Impact of Short-Term Missions."
[239] Guttentag, "Possible Negative Impacts of Volunteer Tourism."

Assisted Self-Recovery and Slums

Is it possible to meet housing needs without harming others? The answer is yes, and it happens through supporting local efforts, a pattern evidenced in other sectors as well. In *assisted* self-recovery, residents help one another to complete post-disaster reconstruction projects. An example is provided by CARE Philippines in 2013. Following Typhoon Haiyan, CARE Philippines provided a modest amount of cash and building materials to affected residents. Local carpenters were employed to provide training for "build back better" (BBB) approaches and techniques to reduce future disaster risk.[240] Mixed-gender teams rotated through the community, providing additional labor support.[241] In the years since Haiyan, multiple agencies are experimenting with assisted self-recovery as post-disaster response to rebuilding.

A similar supported local approach has been used by some cities for shelter construction generally. UN-Habitat estimates that 1.6 billion people currently live in inadequate and unsafe housing.[242] As people continue to pour into urban and peri-urban areas in search of work, and as people flee disaster and displacement, families increasingly gather whatever materials are available and cobble together their own shelter.[243]

Persons and families living in shelters such as these often meet the United Nations' definition of a slum household, which is a group of individuals living under the same roof in an urban area who lack one or more of the following:

- durable housing
- sufficient living space
- access to improved drinking water
- access to improved sanitation
- secure tenure[244]

---

[240] For insights into BBB, see Kennedy et al., "Meaning of 'Build Back Better.'"
[241] CARE and World Habitat, "Soaring High."
[242] UN-Habitat, "The Strategic Plan 2020–2023."
[243] For an overview of several challenges accompanying urbanization, see Zhang, "Trends, Promises and Challenges of Urbanisation."
[244] UN-Habitat, "Slums of the World." Although slums appropriately raise concerns about health, safety, income, and shelter, it often is important to consider slums as functioning communities.

Municipal governments gravitate toward one of several approaches in addressing informal housing settlements: they ignore them, uproot and displace them, implement top-down urban management strategies, or engage in participatory building and slum upgrading.

Although considerable challenges arise in participatory slum upgrading,[245] the size and ongoing growth of urban settlements and slums have encouraged some cities to try community-based approaches. Self-help housing engages various voices in creating improved, low-threshold building codes and approval processes that encourage safer construction, construction blueprints, methods, and materials, as well as the development of community spaces and services.[246] Other approaches to address shelter in slums include advocating for land rights and offering subsidized housing.[247]

Several Christians have provided an alternative, inside view of slums—one that highlights the life and dynamics within them.[248] These authors do not ignore the need for positive change, but they accentuate the relationships, community, economy, and self-determination that regularly occurs within them. As in other sectors, any interest in slum-upgrading should heed the voice of the community.

Homelessness

Another shelter-related issue is homelessness. Suzanne Speak reminds us that conceptualizations of homelessness from a Global North perspective often do not fit elsewhere.[249] Although the political, economic, and social drivers of homelessness may be similar worldwide, how homelessness is experienced and what it means can vary greatly between Global North

---

[245] Bardhan et al., "Mumbai Slums since Independence"; Das, "Slum Upgrading."

[246] For an insightful history, see Bredenoord and van Lindert, "Pro-Poor Housing Policies." For an update, see UN-Habitat, "Participatory Slum Upgrading." For a US example, see Mukhija, "Value of Incremental Development and Design."

[247] Landesa; Lizarralde, "Stakeholder Participation." Theology can be applied in land rights, such as in community land trusts, which have been applied in some development settings. See Salsich, "Toward a Property Ethic of Stewardship"; World Habitat, "Let Innovation Thrive."

[248] For examples, see Smith, *Slums Reimagined*; Greenfield, *The Urban Halo*; Jack, *The Sound of Worlds Colliding*.

[249] Speak, "'Values' as a Tool." See also Busch-Geertsema, Culhane, and Fitzpatrick, "Developing a Global Framework."

and Global South contexts. Regardless, people experiencing homelessness are usually vulnerable and often have had a significant crisis, or crises, in their lives.

Few reliable censuses exist of homelessness in the Global South, but undoubtedly, the numbers are in the millions.[250] The majority of homeless people are temporarily homeless due to migration, war, eviction, economic disruption, and natural disasters. Those who chronically are without shelter often have experienced additional influences. It can be helpful to identify and note what is distinctive about particular groups of people who are homeless so appropriate responses can be developed.

Children who work or spend time on the street frequently maintain ties with relatives. A smaller number have lost all family ties and live every day on the streets, caught in poverty and, sometimes, addiction. Many of these most vulnerable children are regularly subject to violence and exploitation and face significant health issues. Interventions with street children often include comprehensive programs focused on education and developing life and work skills, such as those used by Made in the Streets in Nairobi, Kenya.

Research and experiences with the causes and prevention of child homelessness should be considered in any effort. UN-Habitat suggests multiple strategies, including addressing housing stock, land rights, capacity building, economic development, and women's and youth employment.

Refugee Camps

An important final consideration regarding shelter is refugee camps. Although the intent of camps is to provide temporary protection for people fleeing from conflict, violence, or persecution, refugee camps are far from anyone's notion of an ideal or long-term response to shelter.

Globally, an estimated 2.6 million people live in refugee camps. Millions of other refugees live in informal shelters not managed by a nonprofit, UN agency, or host government. People living in these informal settlements are subject to violence, the natural elements, and possible eviction or arrest by authorities. Often, residents in camps and in informal

---

[250] In this section, we utilize UN-Habitat, "Strategies to Combat Homelessness."

settlements officially are restricted from work or any social services available to citizens.

Refugee camps are the result of national locked doors and/or an inability to repatriate to one's country of origin, integrate in a second country, or resettle to a third. Typically, countries do not want to host large numbers of refugees, whether in a camp or in informal settlements. Most governments restrict the movement of people out of camps. Thus, a large camp can function like a microeconomy and society, with small hamlets emerging to do business within a large, informal economy.

Many refugees have lost not only their homes and been separated from their families, but they may also be stateless, rejected by both their home country and their current one and denied entrance to another country for a fresh start. For many, camps represent perpetual limbo and a far cry from any sort of sanctuary.[251]

Some refugees find stability, identity, and solidarity in their historic faith—a faith that sometimes resists secular camp oversight.[252] Missionaries and faith-based NGOs are active in some camps around the world. Christian humanitarian initiatives must carefully consider the fragility and uniqueness of people when attempting to help.[253]

Sport

Sport, which can include play, recreation, dance, and casual and competitive sports and games, has been advocated for in development settings for a variety of desirable outcomes. It has been revived by the United Nations under the rubric of *sport for development and peace* with anticipated contributions in health, social inclusion, gender empowerment, and peace.[254]

Sports programs frequently have been vehicles for character development and social reconciliation following conflict.[255] Laureus Sport for Good is a prominent example from South Africa.[256] Cross Cultures, a

---

[251] For insights into camp life, see Goudeau, *After the Last Border*; Rawlence, *City of Thorns*.

[252] Mim, "Religion at the Margins."

[253] For a case study, see Fiddian-Qasmiyeh, "Pragmatics of Performance."

[254] Although now dated, a brief history is provided in Kidd, "New Social Movement."

[255] Coalter, "Sport-for-Development"; Blom et al., "Sport for Development and Peace."

[256] Laureus Sport, "Using the Power of Sport."

secular organization, used soccer as a means of bringing children and adults together after civil strife in Bosnia and Herzegovina.[257] Musalaha is a faith-based organization that brings Christian, Muslim, and Jewish youths together in peacebuilding through treks to the desert, complete with a camel ride with a peer from a different background.[258]

Perhaps more widely known are sports ministries with an evangelism focus. These engagements teach and mentor youths in the Christian faith. Such organizations may have differing emphases and approaches. Examples include Sports Outreach, Missionary Athletes International, and SCORE International. Adherents to this approach must be careful to avoid neocolonial tendencies, though. Participants in one study of sport practitioners expressed sentiments of coming to help others and doing so by training locals and "giving them our expectations," with no apparent place for the voices of others to be heard. Experienced sports leaders, thankfully, soften language like this.[259]

Many sports programs have yet to be assessed for their impact. Douglas Hartmann and Christina Kwauk counsel that "sport-based interventions may be able to help marginalized communities do better in society, but they do little to change the institutions, policies, practices, and more fundamental conditions that have helped to produce and maintain the marginality of the oppressed." "As a result," they argue, "the majority of marginalized youths and young people continue to be subordinated and disempowered."[260]

Sport can be a popular approach in Global South mission efforts, but their goals and impact should be clear. Initiatives in other sectors will be required if broad poverty alleviation is included in the aim.

Technology

Technological responses to poverty alleviation are appealing. Generally, however, they cannot stand alone but should be considered within a larger response that incorporates local cultures and larger systems.

---

[257] Cross Cultures.
[258] Musalaha.
[259] Welty Peachey et al., "Interrogating the Motivations of Sport for Development."
[260] Hartmann and Kwauk, "Sport and Development."

In the past, many have assumed that transferring technologies such as radio, television, computers, roads and bridges, Internet access, drones, 3D printers, and telemedicine would alone reduce poverty, but to be effective, technologies must be evaluated from the perspective of the adopter rather than the provider. While we have separated technology as a sector, we have done so only because many churches have viewed it as such. In reality, the application of technologies is most effective when supporting broader initiatives in other sectors. Relatedly, transformational development is not equivalent to modernization.

Appropriate technology was one of the earliest applications of technology in poverty alleviation. Appropriate technologies are simple labor- and resource-saving tools that can be used to lighten the load of daily activities, such as obtaining firewood or water, transporting people, or improving farm practices.[261] Many of these tools were developed by people locally, and some were borrowed from others. Whether simple or complex, however, no one passively accepts a new technology. Each one is influenced by culture, norms, knowledge, and other contextual conditions.[262]

While telemedicine would appear to provide rural access to urban medical specialists, electricity and broadband may be unreliable or cost-prohibitive. It may be more effective to pay a person to carry a thumb drive containing radiology scans to a central city. Excessive dust, monopolized intermediaries, or the absence of parts and skilled technicians when things break down can all contribute to the undoing of computer networks, despite the promise of computerization dispelling poverty.

On the other hand, cell phones have had a large impact on the lives of people in poverty in much of the Global South. Many countries leapfrogged land lines to install cell-based communication, and nearly everyone lives within range of a cellular signal.[263] Cell technology has helped improve the ease and cost of communication and, in many parts of the world, the ability to transfer money between urban and rural areas and within rural

---

[261] Carr and Hartl, *Lightening the Load*.

[262] An example mentioned in the Ecosystem sector is improved cookstoves. Despite their apparent advantages, adoption has been poor due to cultural rather than technological issues.

[263] "Measuring the Information Society Report 2018."

communities. Insecticide-treated nets and curtains have yielded massive reductions in malaria.[264] And Zipline, a US company operating in Rwanda, has experienced some initial success in delivering blood and medical supplies to clinics via drones.[265]

Just as in the Global North, technologies diffuse differently within segments of the population. Their adoption can widen the gap between the haves and have-nots and other times help narrow it. Technology adoption must have a decidedly pro-poor aim and be evaluated for impact, if poverty alleviation is to be achieved. The entire application and its ongoing cost must be considered. Drones in rescue operations or medical supply deliveries, advances in the design and deployment of bed nets, computerization, and the construction of road, sanitation, or water infrastructure all need to be evaluated within the cultures in which they are adopted.

Some technological initiatives occur at commercial, large-scale levels. One faith-based organization assisting infrastructure development is Engineering Ministries International (EMI USA). EMI provides engineering and design consultation in bridge, hospital, and building construction; in earthquake response; and in other projects requiring engineering. Water Mission, also a faith-based organization, focuses on the construction of water and sanitation facilities. PATH, a secular health-focused firm, is advancing many culturally sensitive technologies in the health-care arena.

Water, Sanitation, and Hygiene

In Scripture, righteous people are often described as thirsting (Ps. 42:2, 63:1, 143:6; Matt. 5:6), and God is described as quenching physical and spiritual thirst (Isa. 44:3, 48:21, 49:10, 55:1; John 4:13–14). This metaphor spoke to people throughout the ancient Levant because everyone knew of the experience of being parched and longing for water on a long journey, dotted by wells. Clean water is no less essential today to good health.

The Millennium Development Goals of 2015 and the Sustainable Development Goals of 2030 highlight water and sanitation, targeting universal access to improved water supply and treatment, along with basic

---

[264] Some research is showing resistance to chemicals and lessening their effectiveness. See Pryce, Richardson, and Lengeler, "Insecticide-Treated Nets for Preventing Malaria."
[265] Ackerman and Strickland, "Medical Delivery Drones Take Flight in East Africa."

sanitation and hygiene services. Funding these services in rural and low-income urban areas, however, is challenging.[266] Despite encouraging movement, a considerable number and percentage of people in sub-Saharan Africa, Asia, and Oceania do not yet have access to an improved water source. Additionally, improved sanitation is lagging water availability.[267]

Water, sanitation, and hygiene—often called "WASH"—are bound together in a system. Open defecation pollutes water sources, and clean water often is achievable only if community sanitation is practiced. Inadequate handwashing, menstrual hygiene, and food hygiene can convey diseases, just as water can convey waterborne diseases such as cholera. As in other sectors, the social and technical aspects of WASH affect one another. Water requires a community management system, mechanical and well repairs, hygiene education, and other social supports to be sustained.

Water

Well construction varies across a range of geological settings. Many wells have failed due to inappropriate design and poor construction, or because of the high cost of and need for expertise in maintenance. Different treatment approaches exist as well, such as adding chlorine to water or filtering water through sand or membranes. Rainwater harvesting, which captures rain from roofs, is feasible and cost-effective in some areas but is less effective in others.[268] Each approach has its strengths and drawbacks, and refinement of these systems is ongoing.

Like all mechanical devices, wells and piping break down. Some are better designed or utilize more easily accessible and exchangeable parts than do others. Likewise, some are better maintained than others. Unfortunately, after installation and initial operation, relatively high rates of abandonment and breakdowns have been reported.[269]

---

[266] Franceys, Cavill, and Trevett, "Who Really Pays?"
[267] WHO and UNICEF, "Progress on Sanitation and Drinking Water."
[268] Thomas, "Limitations of Roofwater Harvesting."
[269] This is focused mostly on recommendations for improved measures. See Carter and Ross, "Beyond 'Functionality' of Handpump-Supplied Rural Water Services."

Communities also must have a system to maintain and manage available water so it is not wasted or accessible only by a few residents. The location of a borehole can favor one group over another. All these considerations suggest that engineering, construction, water and land management, and cultural knowledge all play an important role in improved water sources. Clean water requires more than a well and a purification system.

Sanitation and Hygiene

Social traditions in sanitation and hygiene differ from place to place. Sanitation typically is viewed as a community issue given that one household's practices affect the health of other households. Because broad adoption of practices (e.g., handwashing and eliminating open defecation) is important for improved health, a large part of the community must buy in, understand the implications of sanitation practices on health, and own the issue.[270] Thus, the marketing and advertising of sound hygienic practices are as important as sanitation facilities themselves, and cultural change may be required to achieve public health improvements. In some cases, microfinance initiatives have been paired with sanitation, and broad community development efforts have incorporated WASH goals.[271]

In addition to behavioral innovations, the Bill and Melinda Gates Foundation has invested in toilet and waste-treatment technologies, inviting universities to explore technologies that promote hygiene while generating energy and saving water. Messiah University's Collaboratory has engaged engineering and business students in researching toilets that serve people with disabilities in the Global South.

WASH Responses

Churches have supported aspects of WASH for several years, but many originally focused mostly on well drilling. Frequently, they partner with small or large WASH organizations, such as Living Water International (see Appendix B). Several large WASH-related organizations employ a district-level approach to manage water access and usage in a region rather than focusing on a single community or well. Smaller organizations

---

[270] Carter, "Sanitation and Hygiene Programmes."
[271] Water.org, "Microfinancing Toolkits."

may use a congregational or funding-based approach for single efforts or household-level water purification solutions.

Multiple WASH methodologies and technologies have been developed and are worthy of exploring. Participatory Hygiene and Sanitation Transformation and Child Hygiene and Sanitation Training are promoted by the World Health Organization. Community-Led Total Sanitation, School-Led Total Sanitation, and Sanitation Marketing encourage households to take charge of community and household sanitation facilities and practices. WASH technologies include household and community biodigesters and wastewater treatment.[272] Methodologies and technologies vary in their effectiveness and their fit with demographic, cultural, and other local considerations. A host of factors need to be considered, suggesting the advantage of partnering with those who have deep and broad experience.

---

[272] Wheaton College, WASTE. See also Greenberg et al., "Small-Scale Waste-Stabilization Ponds."

PART THREE

MOVING
FORWARD

5

WHAT CHURCHES CAN DO

A missionary once told a story about her first time back in the United States after living in Zimbabwe for four years. It came time for her to head to the grocery store, but she was dreading it. She knew it would overwhelm her due to the innumerable choices available to her. Sure enough, when selecting a box of cereal, instead of the two to three choices she had had in Harare, the capital of Zimbabwe, she confronted a seemingly eternal aisle of cereal options.

After finally selecting a brand of cereal for her family, her work was not finished. From one brand, she now had to choose between specific flavors, dietary options, and sizes of boxes, to ensure that she received the best value to stretch her limited missionary salary. In Zimbabwe, the whole family would rejoice if they discovered just one cereal box of their liking. Now, among so many options, she worried that the choice she made might not be the best available to her and, subsequently, that her family might be disappointed in her efforts.

She finally retrieved everything on her list. As she moved her haul from the shopping cart to the clerk's conveyor belt, she sighed with relief and privately congratulated herself for being able to make it through this monumental task without breaking down or crying. She was grateful to be finished with all these anxiety-inducing decisions.

Unfortunately, she had let down her guard too fast. Her eyes filled with tears as soon as the cashier asked, "Cash or credit?"

The bagger added, "And would you prefer paper or plastic?"

Beginning the Journey

After reading about holistic mission, principles of transformational development, and especially the wide range of sectors surveyed in the previous chapter, it is easy to feel like our missionary friend from Zimbabwe. Congregations or individuals wanting to engage in global mission have much to consider and a multitude of available paths. The task ahead can leave us unsure of how to take a step forward. This is a good time to heed Thomas Merton's words: "You do not need to know precisely what is happening, or exactly where it is all going. What you need is to recognize the possibilities and challenges offered by the present moment, and to embrace them with courage, faith and hope."[1]

The journey that lies ahead for those who seek to join God in the work of transformational development can be both thrilling and overwhelming. The work of renewing creation is beyond our capabilities. Yet, we are encouraged: "For mortals it is impossible, but for God all things are possible" (Matt. 19:26b). The assurance of God's faithfulness propels us to discern how we might fit into God's activity throughout the world and then boldly step out in faith.

In this chapter, we provide perspectives and tools that can help the people of God faithfully engage in holistic mission and, more specifically, transformational development. The recommendations we make are most directly applicable to congregations in the Global North, though we pray that individuals, parachurch organizations, and churches in the Global South can distill relevant elements for their contexts. With that primary audience in mind, we recognize that, depending on the size of the congregation, there may be varying levels of engagement among members. Our counsel, at times, may be applicable for the entire body, while at other times it may be more relevant to subgroups, such as church leaders, mission boards, or ministry teams, that lead the church's global engagement.

---

[1]Merton, *Confessions of a Guilty Bystander*, 206.

Regardless, the steps outlined here are intended to be not a formula for success but, instead, suggested mindsets and practices that will help churches discern and engage faithfully while also maturing as disciples and co-laborers in God's mission in the world.

Prayer and Self-Reflection

Missio Dei centers God as the initiator and primary mover in mission. God has been, is, and will be present and active among those who are vulnerable (Matt. 25:31–46). Any effort we make to address the immense suffering and brokenness in the world must begin with that conviction. As Jim Martin declares:

> The places of violent oppression and abuse that may seem utterly God-forsaken are in fact the places where we have most deeply experienced the presence and power of God. The call to the work of justice is therefore not God sending his church *out* to a place where God cannot be found. Rather, God is inviting us *into* the place where he is already at work.[2]

Understanding our role as followers of Christ in God's mission means that we must begin by discerning—attuning our hearts and minds—where God is at work and where God is inviting our particular community to offer its humble efforts. Therefore, the first act of transformational development is prayer. Even though a church may have a noble conviction to jump right into the fray, it is crucial for the community of faith to take time to pray together—and pray a lot. Prayer is the beginning of discernment and should wash over all subsequent practices and activities within the process. We advise churches to engage in various forms of prayer, paying special attention to ways in which the community establishes a posture of openness and listening.[3] Practicing silence and praying the words of Scripture (*lectio divina*) can open our ears to God's voice.

We also encourage churches to devote themselves to intercessory prayer. Specific to the purpose of discerning a path toward transformational

---

[2] Martin, *Just Church*, xx–xxi.
[3] See Calhoun, *Spiritual Disciplines Handbook*, 231–90, for a description of various types of prayer in the Christian tradition.

development, we suggest lifting up regions of the world and sectors of development to God in prayer. During the discernment period, which we recommend should span months, members of the community could spend a week praying for a particular nation, vulnerable population, or global issue. These specific prayers may present trajectories toward which the Holy Spirit is pointing.

The discernment period is also an opportunity to engage in other spiritual disciplines, particularly those that foster attentiveness to God's activity and leading, such as gratitude, journaling, and fasting. Practicing Sabbath is especially beneficial during this stage because it is an embodied recognition that we are not saviors; there is only one Savior. Resting in the presence of God helps alleviate inclinations to be the hero and lifts the burden of believing we are in control of outcomes.

By devoting time and space for prayer and spiritual disciplines, the community is more prepared to discern pathways to engage in transformational development. These practices also serve to surface two key self-reflections at the beginning of the discernment process. First, hopefully, the church will become more aware of its motivation for pursuing work among vulnerable populations. Global engagement can often stem from self-gratification, so the church should be sure its deepest desires are to love and care for others and to form mutually beneficial partnerships and friendships.[4]

Second, the community of faith will need to determine its level of commitment to transformational development. As described in Chapter Three, effective poverty alleviation and development generally requires extensive time. Therefore, it is wise to discern, from the outset, whether the congregation is devoted to this type of work for the long haul. If the church is not willing or able to pursue a long-term vision, then it would be wise to focus its energy on discovering proven organizations doing effective work. Providing financial support to such efforts can be a faithful way

---

[4] Cho, *Overrated*, 97–98. Cho suggests that a common motivation of global mission engagements is how it makes the volunteer feel, rather than its impact.

to participate in global development if the circumstances do not allow for more holistic and long-term engagement.[5]

However, if the church desires to dive deep into transformational development, it is especially critical that leadership take a self-inventory and count the cost. How high of a priority is global engagement in relation to other ministries and initiatives? If difficult decisions arise because of a decrease in giving, are church members willing to make sacrifices to ensure the work among vulnerable populations will not suffer? Clearly stating the church's commitment to a long-term vision from the outset is extremely illuminating and liberating for the discernment process because it enables the congregation to wholeheartedly pursue the best path toward effective engagement.

These self-reflections, along with the foundation established by prayer, orient the church to start thinking more concretely about how its particular community can join God in the work of transformational development. As congregations move deeper into discernment, we encourage members to approach the process with open minds to new possibilities. God is always doing new things, and God is clearly moving throughout the world, particularly in the Global South and among vulnerable populations. Therefore, churches should dream broadly and divergently. Trust that the Holy Spirit is at work and is moving in surprising ways. This should empower communities of faithful disciples to be bold and imaginative as they seek to join God in bringing *shalom* throughout the world and within their own midst.

Congregational Fit

The areas in which a congregation's commitment, calling, capability, and context overlap represent potentially fruitful areas for engagement (see Figure 5.1).[6] The congregation's *commitment* represents its mission and history. Discerning engagement in transformational development typically emerges from a congregation's overall mission and vision. For most churches, that mission does not exist in a vacuum but continues a

---

[5] Wydick, *Shrewd Samaritan*, 153–63, 166–71, provides helpful counsel on how to be a faithful giver and recommends organizations whose work has been evaluated and is effective.

[6] This model was inspired by Dale, *Development Planning*, 18.

congregation's story in seeking first the kingdom of God.[7] Knowing the church's history of local and global ministries illuminates potential opportunities for expansion and revitalization. Has the church sent out missionaries and church planters in the past? If so, where did they serve, and what is the current state of the work? Does the congregation have relationships with churches in the Global South that could become hubs for engagement? Is there a history of giving to or partnering with humanitarian organizations? These historical markers and the current vision can serve as directional light posts along the pathway toward more robust and effective global engagement.[8]

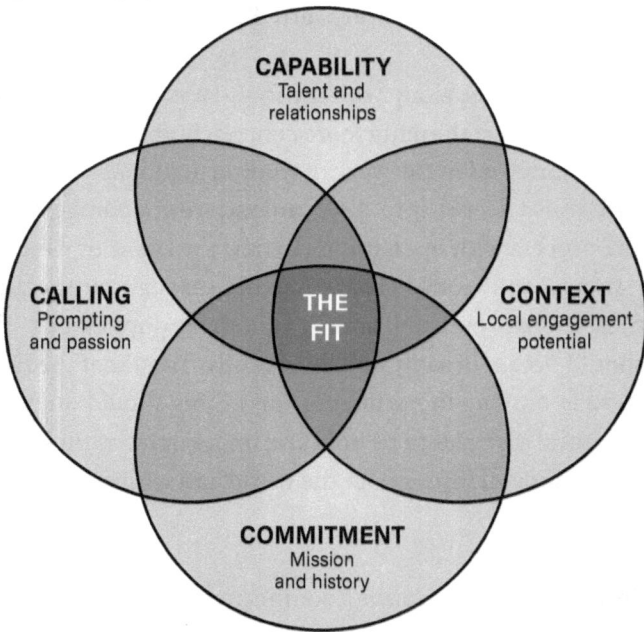

Figure 5.1. Congregational Fit

---

[7] See Martin, *Just Church*, 139–84, for a helpful guide on how a church can discern its unique role and capacity for engaging injustice.

[8] We suggest articulating guiding values for global engagement that flow from the church's overall mission. These broad principles can inform discernment and provide a framework for evaluating outcomes. Stated values can be reassessed and adjusted as experience expands. The Accord Network provides an example of this for faith-based organizations, which can be adapted for congregations. See their "Principles of Excellence in Integral Mission."

Calling includes the Spirit's prompting and members' passions. Church leaders would be wise to pay attention to sectors, contexts, and global issues near to the hearts of its members. Related is a congregation's *capability*, which encompasses the gifts, talents, and expertise found among church members and those outside the church with whom they have relationships. Are there members of the congregation who have specific cultural and linguistic proficiencies? Do any have training or experience in fields related to the sectors presented in Chapter Four? Does the church have existing relationships with potential partners or networks? Building on the church body's passions, gifts, backgrounds, and relationships, instead of charting new, unknown territory, can create a sense of momentum as plans emerge.

There is also immense benefit in connecting potential global efforts to a church's local ministries. This is the congregation's *context*. Areas of overlap often offer resources that provide traction for new transformational development initiatives and partnerships. If a church currently addresses food insecurity within its city or region, it might consider engaging in that sector internationally. Or a church might want to focus on extending hospitality to refugees or economic immigrants within its community, and its global efforts could concentrate on their nations of origin. These connections between local and global efforts can be synergistic, enhancing the church's knowledge, expertise, and effectiveness on both fronts. Additionally, they provide an opportunity for global partners to support and interact with the work in the church's local context, mentoring the local church and thus increasing the mutuality and reciprocity of a partnership.

Discerning Sectors and Regions

After taking ample time to discern possibilities that God may be laying before the church and thoroughly evaluating their congregation's fit, mission leaders might turn to considering sectors and regions of the world for engagement. With Chapter Four as a springboard, exploring a sector will provide a deeper understanding of needs, approaches, and potential partners operating effectively in those areas. Exploration can deepen communal discussions about how or where the church might engage. Listening to multiple voices within the congregation allows for various perspectives and insights as well. While this might slow the discernment process, it will likely increase the sense of ownership throughout the entire body.

As exploration proceeds, mission leaders should listen to vulnerable populations, potential partners, and seasoned practitioners. Investigating current scholarship will be useful, too. History suggests that congregations too often pursue global ministries in isolation, missing valuable insights from experience. Gleaning from networks, conferences, writings, congregations, practitioners, and missionaries will increasingly inform and enhance engagement.

Narrowing down options can be messy and necessitates prayer and humility from all involved. While it may take time, the church will need to identify a clear direction. Depending on the size of the congregation and the resources at its disposal, the way forward might include one or multiple sectors and regions. We advise against pursuing too many divergent trajectories. While there are some pros to developing a large portfolio of ministries in diverse contexts, there are at least three substantial challenges to this course of action. First, because developing and sustaining initiatives and partnerships takes intentionality, time, and effort, having too many ministries can hinder effectiveness and the growth of deep relationships. Second, members of the congregation will most likely have only a superficial understanding of the various partnerships and efforts. Third, effectively assessing and evaluating numerous endeavors would most likely be untenable for a church. Therefore, when it comes to engaging in transformational development as a congregation, less is more. A church cannot do everything, so it is advisable to do one or a small number of initiatives well.

Tools for Discerning Engagement

Once one or more sectors are identified, three tools may be useful in discerning how and with whom to engage: mental models, root causes, and theories of change. These tools are particularly helpful at the discernment stage, but a church might find it beneficial to return to them periodically over the course of its transformational development efforts.

Mental Models

The first approach to thinking broadly about engagement is to consider mental models. We all have assumptions about poverty alleviation and what is primary in creating change, and it can be helpful to recognize and name those assumptions. James Copestake of the University of Bath suggests a taxonomy of assumptions, or mental models, which we have adjusted for congregations (Figure 5.2).[9] Each of the models can operate separately and independently, but most congregations have a combination at work within their diverse memberships.

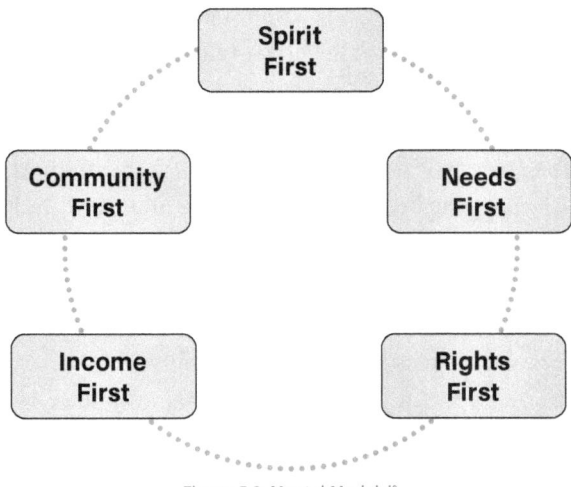

Figure 5.2. Mental Models[10]

"Spirit First" assumptions traditionally have been common in Christian missions. This approach assumes that transformation begins with personal conversion and formation in Christ: if the heart is good, our desires, attitudes, and behaviors will fall into place. Without faith in Christ and a virtuous trajectory, vulnerable communities will not flourish, no matter the level of access to income or support services.[11]

There is wisdom to this approach, but "Spirit First" alone is insufficient to address the complex drivers of poverty, many of which reside outside

---

[9] Copestake, "Wellbeing in International Development."
[10] Adapted from Copestake, "Well-Being in Development."
[11] For an insightful discussion of this point, see Fikkert and Kapic, *Becoming Whole*.

an individual and within systems of injustice. Additionally, this approach misses the mark if it assumes that Christians are somehow immune to ongoing personal challenge—that embracing Christ resolves any need for mutual aid. Following Christ is a path of mutual support, bearing one another's burdens (Gal. 6:2).

A second model begins with needs: if the basics of life, such as water, food, health care, and education, are not met, individuals will not flourish. Once children have adequate food and security, they can learn; once people are healthy and nourished, they can work; and so on. Scripture explains that it was a response to basic needs that prompted the early Christians to share: "All who believed were together and had all things in common; they would sell their possessions and goods and distribute the proceeds to all, as any had need" (Acts 2:44–45).

Though the "Needs First" model has merit, repeatedly responding to needs can be challenging because needs can be unending and exceed available resources. Dependency can be a concern as well when approaching vulnerable populations through a lens of deficiency. With a "Needs First" approach, it is important to differentiate between relief and development so as to preserve dignity and enable sustainability.[12]

A third approach to transformational development is to view human rights as central and necessary. Without human rights, individuals and communities will be denied opportunities for choice or development. This "Rights First" approach is particularly relevant in situations of oppression, such as with those vulnerable to trafficking or persecution. This approach does not imply an in-your-face protest for rights but, instead, is an appeal for fair and just treatment, as Jesus and the Old Testament prophets assert. One must be careful, though, as a "Rights First" approach can veer toward individualism devoid of communal attachments or cultural considerations.

An "Income First" mental model begins by asserting that having adequate income can equip families to overcome poverty and sustain long-term development. If households and communities can generate income, they can provide for their own needs rather than rely on outside organizations or the government. Increases in income can have a spillover

---

[12] Corbett and Fikkert, *When Helping Hurts*, 99–115.

effect in other areas of transformational development, too. For example, a rise from low to higher income generally also delivers gains in nutrition and education.

Approaches to poverty alleviation that focus on enterprise development and market access often emphasize an "Income First" model as an on-ramp to other avenues of development. "Income First" advocates, however, must be careful not to promote or embrace an unquestioning adoption of materialism and unfettered capitalism.

Finally, a mental model that embraces a "Community First" approach to transformation advocates that one must start with local voices, affirm self-determination, and defer to the community to set its own poverty-alleviation priorities, possibly inviting others outside the community into the process. This approach begins with a participatory discussion or initiative from within the community rather than with an outside congregation identifying needs or directing initiatives. Not listening carefully and humbly to the community as true partners risks turning transformational development into oppressive, self-focused charity projects that can do more harm than good. That said, a "Community First" approach taken to an extreme may ignore or diminish the needs and considerations of marginalized people within the community. At times, a community's isolation or practices may prevent them from seeing a larger picture about the needs and concerns impacting their lives.

Regardless of which mental model is at work, poverty-alleviation advocates strongly encourage, on both ethical and efficacy grounds, a high level of local voices and self-determination whenever possible. Not listening carefully and humbly to the community as true partners risks turning transformational development into oppressive, self-focused charity projects that can do more harm than good.

One of these mental models is most likely operating in the minds of congregants. It is helpful to recognize the assumptions at work as a church discerns how best to engage. Often, though, an initial mental model will incorporate other models as a congregation experiences the complexity involved in transformational development efforts. It is also helpful to recognize the mental model(s) of potential partners. Awareness of assumptions can lead to clarity in shared expectations.

Root Causes

A second tool in discerning engagement focuses on brainstorming about the possible root causes of a problem.[13] We see this tool as a way of thinking creatively and broadly rather than as a means of validating a cause. Imagining root causes is useful because we can too easily jump into action to treat symptoms without asking what might be causing a problem. Multiple drivers may need to be addressed too. If multiple tributaries to a problem are surfaced, more effective responses can be discerned.

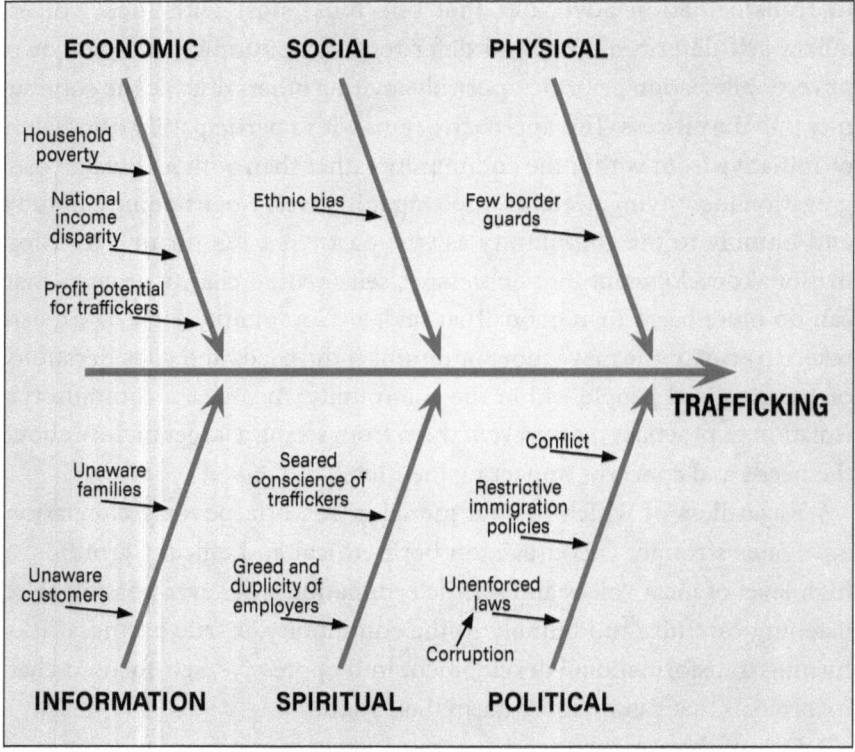

Figure 5.3. Root Causes Fishbone with a Labor-Trafficking Example

---

[13] Churches will learn more about root causes as they dialogue with members of vulnerable communities, as well as through practitioners, partners, and research. Whenever utilized, whether during initial discernment or during implementation, this tool may help in identifying comprehensive drivers of a need.

In disaster relief, ministry leaders might ask how they can help mitigate the risk of disasters before they occur. In trafficking, leaders might consider underlying causes within the community instead of focusing on how best to help survivors of trafficking. Food security might be best addressed by increasing household income. A fishbone diagram can be useful for teasing out possible problem roots.

To use this tool, simply write the problem at the far right of the diagram ("trafficking" is the example used here) and label four to six relevant "spines" as categories of potential causes. Then, possible individual causes to the problem can be detailed for each category by utilizing insights from the community, practitioners, and researchers. Although not all initiatives can or should focus on all causes, sustainable initiatives often try to address (or be aware of) as many of these roots as possible. It can also be helpful, as Duke University professor Anirudh Krishna suggests, to consider the drivers that reverse well-being.[14] A fishbone diagram can be helpful in imagining these.

With a broader awareness of possible root causes, a church can then proceed to focus on gathering more specific insights about causes and responses within a particular context. The goal is not to become an expert—often, seasoned partners have done this work already. But it is helpful to be able to think broadly with others about the issue being considered. As we have mentioned elsewhere, causes and responses vary by locale, so consulting with community members and local partners is essential in understanding potential root causes unique to a community or region.

Theories of Change

The third tool for discerning engagement is to summarize the logical sequence of actions that are believed to lead to a desired outcome. In other words, what is the anticipated impact of Input Y on Outcome Z? Development practitioners call this tool a "theory of change." Here are a few potential examples:

> Agricultural knowledge and skills ➡ access to markets ➡ enhanced productivity ➡ improved income ➡ food security

---

[14] Krishna, *One Illness Away*.

Dance camp ➡ encourages intergroup contact ➡ diminishes intergroup conflict

Improved sanitation ➡ decreases water contamination ➡ decreases incidence of disease ➡ improves health ➡ increases availability to work ➡ increases income

Ideally, insights from research, practitioners, and local friends form the basis of the theory.

Simple theories of change are useful because they distill assumptions about primary drivers and help us stay focused on outcomes instead of activities. They also can help us identify elements that may be missing in planning. Theories of change constitute, in essence, a "best guess" at how an action can lead to an outcome. Assessment then becomes important in confirming the model. Experienced partners should be able to describe their theory of change and supply evidence to support their theory.

Although theories of change can help us think more clearly through a transformational development initiative and its potential impact, it is possible for thinking to become mechanistic and create overly simplistic expectations in poverty alleviation. Brian Fikkert and Kelly Kapic affirm the value of theories of change (or logic models, as they are also called), but they stress the importance of using "participatory rather than blueprint approaches" and remaining humble and prayerful in the process.[15] They recommend broad engagement in constructing a theory of change, and they caution against assuming that change occurs along a linear, predictable, controllable path. Examining and articulating our thinking about change before acting can move congregations past budgets and activities, giving space to plans that bring about sustained positive impact while weighing the potential for harm.

These three tools can serve the church during discernment, but it is critical to continuously listen to vulnerable populations. Once relationships are established, the congregation must subject its assumptions and understanding to the experience and wisdom of the local community. This participatory approach affirms self-determination and locally defined

---

[15] Fikkert and Kapic, *Becoming Whole*.

needs, responses, and assessments.[16] A variety of extremely helpful and practical methods can be used to surface community observations.[17] More importantly, the values that undergird this posture emphasize decentralization, empowerment, cooperation, and emergent change, in contrast to approaches that emphasize linear, generic, top-down, imposed strategies. A participatory approach taps into the local community's insights regarding needs and responses, its awareness of previous initiatives, and its close understanding of the culture. Participation can also engage churches that operate in the context of the vulnerable community. Other perspectives and practices can be used collaboratively, but a participatory approach emphasizes the community's direction and insight from start to finish.

Deciding How to Engage

Once a sector or context has been determined, what should a congregation do next? In a recent conversation, Paul Niehaus, a development economist, asked how local churches discern their role in addressing social needs.[18] Inspired by the conversation, we use the example of medical missions to describe several possible types and levels of engagement. A congregation could

- Opt out, recognizing that health care is an important issue but not one on which a congregation wishes to focus.
- Encourage members to act on their own to support medical missions, such as by individually donating time or money.
- Execute, join, or support short-term medical mission trips.
- Participate in advocacy that supports global health care.

---

[16] Appleby, "The New Name for Peace?," 196, helpfully contrasts "passive participation," which allows for those most directly affected by development programs to provide perspective and carry out initiatives but are not empowered to set the direction with "deliberative participation." He writes, "The optimal mode of collaboration, of course, is deliberative participation, by which non-elites and sometimes elites deliberate together and make decisions." For insights into local and expert views, see Opola et al., "Hybridity of Inclusive Innovation."

[17] For a rationale and methods, see Blackman, *Partnering with the Local Church*, 33–41, 64–76; James, *Inspiring Change*; Njoroge et al , *Umoja*; Gubbels and Koss, *From the Roots Up*.

[18] Paul Niehaus, conversation with Robert Gailey, June 30, 2020.

- Partner with an existing faith-based health delivery organization or initiative.
- Establish, operate, and grow a mission hospital or public health initiative.
- Develop a health-care delivery network in multiple locations.
- Design, test, and propagate innovative models for addressing health-care practices.

Likely, a novice in medical missions might consider the first five options, and large, seasoned congregations or faith-based organizations might consider the last five. But how does one decide among options? Churches might consider three factors as they discern how best to engage: scale, channels, and investment and involvement.

Scale

The scale of the issue in the specific context the church is addressing might stipulate the possible levels of engagement. Addressing malaria in sub-Saharan Africa by building and managing a hospital in Kenya is beyond the capabilities of a single church. On the other hand, providing dental care to a particular community or fundraising locally to purchase fifty treated bed nets (proven to reduce malaria in children) for a nonprofit or church in Kenya to distribute could be viable for a congregation with the relevant skill sets.

Relatedly, the scale of engagement may be governed by the resources available. Although Jesus can do wonders with a few fishes and loaves of bread, we carry a responsibility to consider the impact and sustainability of our efforts. This does not mean big goals should be avoided—that we should not walk by faith—or that mission efforts cannot grow beyond our initial vision. Instead, it means that we consider limits that are healthy and responsible for all involved.

As a cautionary tale from which we can learn, a denomination in Zimbabwe entered a bidding process to be granted an entire school complex from the government as long as it could offer Christian education for the local children. The campus was a significant offering, and educating children was in line with the mission of the denomination. The denomination entered and won the bid, but it quickly found that the operational costs and staffing were a sizable challenge. Further, it had no exit strategy. The denomination was unable to operate the school effectively, irritating the families and government and creating an administrative and financial sinkhole for itself. Lack of foresight about the scale of this endeavor led to an ill-fated attempt at engagement.

Channels

A congregation should also investigate what groups—such as churches, organizations, or government entities—are already addressing the problem. This can help the congregation explore the best channel for engagement (see Figure 5.4). Congregations might consider the following kinds of partnerships:

- *Congregations–denomination partnership:* Some denominations operate their own development agencies or departments. Denominations are often a common link among congregations, North and South, and they are able to build upon shared relationships, theology, and resources. Denominations subsequently may partner with NGOs or congregations at the global level.
- *Congregation–NGO partnership:* Congregations commonly partner with faith-based or secular NGOs that specialize in the sectors highlighted in Chapter Four. Some of these, such as World Relief and Tearfund, among others, commonly work with and through congregations.
- *Congregation–congregation/missionary partnership:* Short-term mission trips and full-time missionary support often provide opportunities for sister churches to collaborate in service projects, medical campaigns, or other needs with the missionary or short-term team coordinator serving as the liaison.[19]
- *Congregation–community partnership:* Some large congregations have bypassed partners and set up their own global operations in direct relation to vulnerable communities. The PEACE plan at Saddleback Church is a well-known example.

---

[19] For insights into sister church relationships, see Bakker, *Sister Churches*.

DEVELOPMENT IN **MISSION**

Figure 5.4. Mission Channels

Investment and Involvement

A third consideration for engagement is to count the cost and assess how much resource investment and member involvement will contribute to the initiative. Do the available financial resources match the scale of the issue and response? How do members envision engaging? For example, they might be involved through praying and giving, participating in short-term trips, or getting training to serve long-term in the field. Projecting the levels of investment and involvement can help clarify the best trajectory for engagement.

Counting the cost is important for every ministry of a church, but it is acutely critical in transformational development. This is because initiatives and relationships require long-term commitment and sustained involvement. Without adequate time and commitment, development becomes a project and truncates transformation. It is natural for the initial excitement to fade and for the congregation to seek a new endeavor or partner after a relatively brief period. Because global development efforts are often criticized for ending too soon or lasting too long, aim for either achieving sustained, lasting benefit or temporary aid that does no harm when it ends.

Being a Good Partner (Friend)
Examining the factors of scale, channels, and investment and involvement can help clarify the role of a church in addressing a particular sector. Although a congregation may consider starting a new project, initiative, or organization, we recommend partnering with churches or organizations that are already at work within the designated sector or context. Partnerships offer potential advantages of sectoral and cultural awareness and experience, and they reduce service duplication. Even if a church decides to launch a new initiative, it can participate in and complement existing efforts and networks among partners.

Establishing Partnerships
Establishing partnerships is an exciting time of discovering where God is leading a church's involvement, but it is also a critical period of setting expectations and roles. We counsel congregations to heed the following recommendations as they seek out and solidify partnerships.

First, identify leaders in the church, whether laity or clergy, who have the relevant passion, giftedness, and, if available, knowledge and experience to be local champions for the effort. Officially commissioning capable leaders for an initiative will help ensure that the church's interests and plans are carried out. Potential partners appreciate clear channels of communication.

Second, as we have suggested throughout this book, it is paramount that a church approaches partners with a posture of listening. While we hope churches, at this point, will be familiar with various facets of transformational development and the specifics of the target sector, people in the vulnerable communities and those working in the field will have greater awareness of the situation on the ground. As Nikki Toyama-Szeto and Femi Adeleye advise:

> Being *with* must precede any *doing*. It is in being together that we begin to understand what God is already doing with people in any given place. Our primary goal must not be to go and provide resources or do things for other people. It should be to strengthen relationships by being with and becoming part

of what God wants to do with us together in any given context. God is already at work in every cultural context, including "unreached people" or "access restricted" contexts. That understanding should free us of any misplaced concept of being messianic interventionists.[20]

The church should inquire about the needs and gaps that it could help fulfill. The church must then trust the partner's recommendations and not insist on its own initiatives. For example, a congregation might have a strong desire to send its members on short-term trips to work with the partner, but the church must be willing to forgo that agenda if it does not align with the needs or desires of the partner.

Third, carefully evaluate the capacity, theory of change, and outcome assessments of potential partners, and weigh how they compare with the congregation's vision, assumptions, and expectations.

Finally, craft a written agreement with the partner. While the relationship should be built on trust and common intentions, a written agreement can clarify expectations and help alleviate possible miscommunication. Delineate the specific roles and tasks of both parties, define the financial arrangement, and outline expectations for the frequency of communication, such as sharing prayer concerns, updates, and reports on outcomes. Finally, consider ways partners can visit and contribute to one another. The hope is that such an agreement lays the foundation for a robust partnership that is sustainable and endures through years to come.

Strengthening Partnerships

Once a partnership is established, maintaining and developing the relationship takes intentionality. It is even more important when partners are separated by borders, oceans, and, at times, language barriers. Congregations must consistently foster relationships and seek opportunities for collaboration. This begins by praying for partners, friends, and vulnerable people engaged in the effort, much like Paul: "I thank God every time I remember you, constantly praying with joy in every one of my prayers for all of you, because of your sharing in the gospel from the

---

[20] Toyama-Szeto and Adeleye, *Partnering with the Global Church*, 9.

first day until now. I am confident of this, that the one who began a good work among you will bring it to completion by the day of Jesus Christ" (Phil. 1:3–6).

A good partner will also find ways to regularly encourage coworkers. The ways to do this are limited only by the creativity of the church, and this is an avenue through which the entire church body can be involved. Letters and art from children and youth are an assured way to lift the spirits of those doing the challenging work of transformational development. The wisdom of seniors in the church can help bolster the determination of the church's partners. Those with the gift of encouragement (Rom. 12:8) can play a significant role in nurturing partnerships.

Encouragement can be one way to fulfill a crucial element of a good partnership: good communication. And communication is a two-way street. A church should utilize various modalities to hear from partners. Emails and reports are obvious examples. However, in our current age, videos and live chats can bring people and the work to life for those in the congregation who may never experience them firsthand. Featuring partners on the church website, through intra-church communications, and in corporate worship gatherings—whether virtually or by inviting them to visit in person—will benefit all involved. Consider asking church members with appropriate language skills to help with translations, or if none is available, perhaps hire a translator or interpreter for special occasions.

A less obvious or intuitive aspect of good communication is informing partners of what God is doing in the life of the church. It is important to give those in the field the opportunity to learn about the congregation and offer prayers on its behalf. Practitioners and those in the community in which they work can be edified by hearing how disciples in their partner church are living out the radical way of Jesus in their own contexts.

Another avenue for strengthening partnerships is sharing human resources. Church members do not have to remain in their home contexts. Certain partnerships might allow for them to engage in global efforts in person. When partners express the need or desire, congregations can send members to live and work alongside those in the communities where transformational development initiatives are happening. This might happen through short-term trips, or there may be occasions for members who have the relevant training and experience to join the work long-term.[21] We also recommend exploring the possibility of inviting partners—members of an organization or church in the foreign context—to visit and serve alongside the congregation. Churches in the Global North should not assume a one-way direction in facilitating learning and service trips. Greater access to financial means should not dictate that congregations in the Global North be the ones who go abroad. Increased benefit and wider impact might come from partners in the Global South coming to share their experience and knowledge with those in the Global North.

Assess the Impact

After a church engages in a specific initiative, most likely through forming and developing a partnership(s), it is important to "close the loop" and return to the initial assumptions to see if an understanding of the context and initiative can be enhanced.

If a church engages in transformational development via a partnership, assessing efficacy should happen on two fronts: (1) the partner should report on progress toward outcomes, and (2) the congregation should evaluate the viability of the partnership and church engagement and transformation. Too often, assessment is one-way, but both parties in a partnership should be measuring their engagement and success and transparently sharing them with each other.

Measures need not be complicated and can be collaboratively designed, but they should incorporate valid and reliable measures. If the partner organization already monitors impact, the church should avoid imposing additional measures that would add to the partner's operational burden. Measurement is important because it informs and influences more faithful and effective practices.

Exiting

Although we have emphasized the desirability of medium- and long-term partnerships, most initiatives and partnerships eventually end. Churches sometimes announce a graduated or sudden cessation of funding, possibly

---

[21] For helpful resources on how to engage in short-term trips well, see Corbett and Fikkert, *When Helping Hurts*; Livermore, *Serving with Eyes Wide Open*.

following an agreed-upon timetable. Even with this, an exit can affect other partners, causing them to scramble for replacement funds. For an effective exit strategy or handover to local partners, consider the following recommendations:[22]

- If possible, plan the handover or exit during initial project planning.
- During the exit, coordinate with the partner to facilitate clarity about roles, minimize disruption, complete any final assessment, and support a smooth transition.
- Affirm a successful exit over a rigid plan; plan for contingencies in scheduling and funding.
- Be transparent on exit timelines, supporting dignity and accountability.

An exit characterized by foresight, attentiveness, and responsiveness will aid all involved, especially direct beneficiaries of the endeavor.

Advocacy

Churches and individuals who are committed to transformational development will want to consider ways in which to advocate for the people and issues related to their work. We suggest thinking of advocacy on two fronts: public advocacy and lifestyle advocacy. Public advocacy is using one's voice, position, and privilege to support justice. A powerful and peaceful way to make positive change in the world is to join forces with other Christians—and with groups that align on a particular issue, even if they are not faith-based—to advocate for public policy changes at local, national, and global levels. The policies and actions of nations in the Global North have clear and direct links to what happens in communities around the world. One way to speak up for those whose voices are often ignored (Prov. 3:8) is to amend and overturn structures that cause or perpetuate abuse.

Many churches in the Global North already have a theological bent toward this type of advocacy, but there are others that resist efforts or actions

---

[22] Recommendations are based on Pal et al., "Ethical Considerations for Closing Humanitarian Projects."

that appear to mix politics and religion. This hesitation is not without warrant, but it can also stem from a dualistic theology—that is, a separation of spiritual and physical realms—as well as from confusing "partisan" with "political." Jesus is "political" in that his life and teachings affect social relationships and the unjust use of religious and governmental power.

There is an alternative way to conceive of this tricky relationship: "The central task of the Church . . . is to live the Lordship of Jesus Christ in all facets of life, seeing the 'spiritual'—that is, God's cosmic plan of redemption—in everything, while acknowledging that in the present ('already but not yet') the two will remain in tension."[23] We live in a world of power structures and political systems that can harm vulnerable populations. Therefore, fidelity to the gospel can propel churches toward creative ways to engage and resist those "powers and principalities." But there is a caution, as Stephen Offutt and his colleagues explain:

> Advocacy should not be about solving problems in our Western sense of the term, but rather building relationships, envisioning new realities, and working together to foster the kind of change that emanates from the Lordship of Jesus Christ. This doesn't mean the Church neglects problem solving, but that it does not approach change with some kind of technological bias that sees the world as some kind of mechanical unit in which, if we can just pull the right lever, the whole world would purr. . . . We undertake advocacy because God advocates for the world. And we undertake advocacy in the way of God, through Jesus Christ, by the power of the Holy Spirit. Advocacy is therefore not a movement away from the gospel but a fundamental response to it.[24]

Some churches might not engage in advocacy because they feel overwhelmed by global issues or are uncertain of what is needed or effective. Fortunately, many faith-based organizations and resources do the hard work of sifting through the complex issues and offering nonpartisan avenues to promote compassion, justice, and flourishing. Churches can glean much from trusted organizations that do the heavy lifting in policy

---

[23] Offutt et al., *Advocating for Justice*, 106.
[24] Offutt et al., *Advocating for Justice*, 116.

research and mobilization. A sampling of faith-based advocacy organizations is listed in Appendix B.

We have one cautionary note for churches that venture into public advocacy work. To speak truth to power, resist inequities, and advocate for real change is not easy. Actors are often praised as saints when offering food to a hungry child but criticized when they ask why there is hunger in the community in the first place[25]—especially if they seek to change the broader, systemic conditions so that all children in a community, not just the one, can be free of hunger. It requires courage and resolve to question injustices or take a stand against policies that benefit one's own nation yet cause immense suffering to people in other nations.

Furthermore, advocacy requires repeated mass efforts with only occasional fruit, yet the harvest can benefit multitudes when it arrives. As Elie Wiesel reminded the world in his 1986 Nobel Peace Prize speech:

> Neutrality helps the oppressor, never the victim. Silence encourages the tormentor, never the tormented. Sometimes we must interfere. When human lives are endangered, when human dignity is in jeopardy, national borders and sensitivities become irrelevant. Wherever men and women are persecuted because of their race, religion, or political views, that place must—at that moment—become the center of the universe.[26]

Opposing oppressive structures happens also through lifestyle advocacy. This type of advocacy is all the more imperative as the interdependency of humans around the world is increasingly evident. What we consume, our standards of living, and how we do business directly impact the experiences of others across the globe. More specifically, our globalized, interconnected, and technologically driven lives clearly intersect with people experiencing poverty and injustice. Those who have eyes to see and ears to hear must be attentive to the ways in which our actions affect people who mine the minerals found in our cell phones and laptops, sew the clothes we wear as we chase the latest fashion trends, and harvest the crops served at our tables each day.

---

[25] McDonagh, *Dom Hélder Câmara*, 11.
[26] Wiesel, "Nobel Peace Prize Speech."

Corporations and governments in the Global North regularly make consequential decisions that impact the lives of the poorest half of the world's population. These decisions are made by leaders who rarely see the impact of their decisions on the lives of people living in poverty. This is where churches in the Global North have an opportunity to listen to and amplify the voices of vulnerable populations in the Global South. For too long, and following in the footsteps of their colonial forbearers, large companies and powerful nations have used their economic and political influence to pressure poorer countries to accept trade and business conditions that hurt or harm their own citizens or environment. The poorer countries often accept these unfair conditions in order to create more jobs, receive aid or debt relief, or gain help with defending their political power from internal or external forces. The harsh realities and severe consequences derived from profit maximization or economic nationalism too frequently are minimized or rationalized by the glorification of success, payouts of quarterly bonuses, and the benefits many of us accrue by the rate of return on our retirement plans.

For consumers, the complexities of the global market, along with the mixing and merging of local, regional, and international political and economic interests, make it challenging to decipher what is good or harmful to others. Many of the purchases we make, particularly those we are surprised to find so cheap, benefit from complex tax shelters and shady supply chains that utilize exploitative labor practices. To lower costs further, unscrupulous global companies sometimes seek out locales where environmental regulations are weak and bribery is conceivable. Vulnerable workers and neighborhoods have little or no choice in submitting to unsafe working and living conditions and will suffer the most from health and environmental consequences.

As we respond to injustices in the world around us, we can avoid the twin ditches of scrupulosity and obliviousness by living modestly and emphasizing meaningful and ethical consumption and lifestyles. Advocating for others through our daily choices, habits, and purchases allows all to flourish more fully.[27]

---

[27] For a rationale and practical guidance, see Fikkert and Kapic, *Becoming Whole*; Scandrette, *Free*.

Being Transformed

A key component of transformational development is the recognition that all involved are being transformed by God as they pursue God's mission to renew all things (2 Cor. 3:18). We are all in need of God's grace to shape us into the likeness of Christ and experience the fullness of God's *shalom*. Church engagement in transformational development creates unique opportunities for this to happen in the life of a congregation. There are many avenues for growth, but here we suggest three pathways for God's people, both corporately and individually: liturgy, simplicity, and hospitality.

Transformed through Liturgy

The church possesses a unique gift for transformation: liturgy. The corporate act of centering the body's attention and devotion on God is a transformative experience. It shapes the congregants' deepest desires and attunes them to the heart of God.[28] Because the heart of God is for the redemption and restoration of the whole world, the church's liturgy should express lament for a broken world and hope for its healing. This can be achieved through sermons on God's mission or Christ's desire for people of all ethnicities to follow him or the blessedness of those in poverty. For those who do not come from a liturgical tradition, we suggest adding a time for prayers for the nations—a moment to cry out to God on behalf of our global neighbors and the issues that keep them from flourishing. Churches can creatively integrate prayers, songs, or Scripture reading in other languages. Specific to the church's global efforts, it is beneficial to appoint occasions for the whole body to hear about and pray for initiatives and partners within the context of worship. Finally, corporate confession—recognition of our own brokenness and need for grace—allows for the Spirit to convict and transform all those who call upon the name of the Lord.

---

[28] See Smith, *Desiring the Kingdom*, for a theological explanation of the formative power of liturgies. See also Fyfe, "Liturgies of Development," for an articulation of how liturgy is essential for those engaged in global development.

Transformed through Simplicity

In Chapter Three, we explored Amartya Sen's view of development as increasing people's choices. Expanding freedom and capacities is a worthwhile objective. Yet, it is possible to be overwhelmed by choice, as the story of our missionary friend in the grocery store illustrates. In the face of a bombardment of choices, followers of Jesus, particularly in the Global North, can subvert our consumeristic and individualist societies through the practice of simplicity. This aspect of discipleship is an opportunity to participate in transformational development. It is easy to assume that giving money is enough to help alleviate global poverty. Yet, it is transformation, and transformation for all, that is needed. Simplicity is a path in the right direction.

Two ways we believe this happens are illustrated in the phrase "spare and share." Choosing to simplify allows increased generosity. As Shane Claiborne writes:

> Generosity is a virtue not just for those with a special spiritual gifting or an admirable philanthropic passion. It is at the very heart of our rebirth. Popular culture has taught us to believe that charity is a virtue. But for Christians, it is only what is expected. True generosity is measured not by how much we give but by how much we have left, especially when we look at the needs of our neighbors.[29]

Somehow, the meaning of *stewardship* has come to connote its opposite: being cautious with resources so as to maximize one's resources rather than using them to bless others. But in the New Testament, a steward is measured by his or her distribution.[30] Stewardship moves beyond managing resources to generativity, to the willingness to involve the larger world.[31] A theologically informed view of stewardship, then, is to work toward future provision, current distribution, and just and generative engagement in God's world.

---

[29] Claiborne, "Simplicity and the Poor," 87.
[30] Hays, "Slaughtering Stewards."
[31] Coleman, "Stewardship."

Beyond generosity, living simply means sacrificing the desire to acquire the next best thing. It means avoiding being a workaholic so one can invest in relationships. It calls for a reduction in wastefulness and the cultivation of habits that do not exploit others or the environment. It invites communities to share belongings and meals. It calls for God's people to rest and be reminded that God's grace is sufficient for them (2 Cor. 12:9). This is what embodied kenosis looks like in everyday life, and in the end, it is discipline that leads to joy.[32]

Transformed through Hospitality

"Do not neglect to show hospitality to strangers, for by doing that some have entertained angels without knowing it" (Heb. 13:2). Showing hospitality to "strangers" in one's local context can benefit the church's global efforts of transformational development and be a conduit for its own transformation. This might mean connecting with a refugee resettlement agency and inquiring how the church can help welcome its new neighbors. It could entail befriending members of a nearby mosque or other religious houses of worship.[33]

Being open to new and diverse relationships creates space for God to form disciples into global Christians and participants in God's mission around the world. Extending hospitality to vulnerable populations can provide insight into the realities facing those affected by poverty and injustice. Sharing meals with people from other cultures and nations can improve intercultural competency. It might turn out that congregants build relationships with people whose country of origin is where the church is engaged in mission efforts. This could open possibilities for increased knowledge of the conditions there and an expanded network of relationships across the globe. However, the greatest benefit of practicing hospitality, both extending and receiving it, to strangers and vulnerable people is the friendships that will emerge.[34]

---

[32] Mark Scandrette offers several helpful steps toward simplifying, including naming what matters most to a person, valuing and aligning one's time, and practicing gratitude and trust. For a practical and thoughtful guide, see Scandrette, *Free*. See also Foster, *Freedom of Simplicity*.

[33] See Two Faiths, One Friendship, http://missunderstanding.co/.

[34] Sweeden, *Church on the Way*.

Strategize with the Spirit

Surrounded by research and reports, the board members of a small faith-based development organization were weary of trying to think through next steps. One board member asked, "Why don't we just trust God, rely on faith, and skip all this strategizing?" It was a reasonable question. But another board member spoke up with an equally thought-provoking response: "The Holy Spirit can work through planning, too."[35]

Considerable harm has been done by well-meaning but poorly planned, triumphalist ventures into holistic mission. While we cannot eradicate uncertainty and will not trust in our knowledge or plans, we owe it to those who are vulnerable, our partners, and our congregations to approach this task humbly, led by the Spirit, as learners with competence. We invest in partnerships with integrity and care, count and sustain our commitments, and join our partners as disciples of Christ. Transformation requires an ongoing rhythm of prayer, listening, learning, discernment, engagement, and assessment, reflecting virtue and vision that are of Christ and submitting our best efforts to mutual discernment, and to God.

> Trust in the LORD with all your heart,
> > and do not rely on your own insight.
> In all your ways acknowledge him,
> > and he will make straight your paths. (Prov. 3:5–6)

William Abraham wrote of the early church that "the gospel spread and the church grew because the sovereign hand of God was in the midst of the community that found itself surrounded by people who were puzzled and intrigued by what they saw happening."[36] May the same be said of our efforts in transformational development.

---

[35] Eternal Threads Board of Directors meeting, personal communication to Monty Lynn, 2010.
[36] Abraham, *The Logic of Evangelism*, 38.

6

LOOKING AHEAD

Holistic mission is never static. Needs emerge, tragedies unfold, and responses intensify and dissipate. As the world continues to change and adapt to new circumstances, it can be challenging to stay abreast of developments and remain connected with God's broader world. Faced with ongoing complexity, we must choose to remain diligent in seeking mutual understanding and deepening relationships with our partners, together bearing "fruit in every good work and as you grow in the knowledge of God" (Col. 1:10). Change offers fresh opportunities to pursue the heart of Christ and reminds us of our complete dependency upon God.

As we look ahead, we cannot predict what will emerge, but we can highlight a few waves of change that are washing up on global shores. Many of these portend considerable changes in how we think about and engage in holistic mission and transformational development. In this chapter, we highlight four of these changes and suggest possible responses by the church to each.

The Southern, Growing Church

Vince Bantu reminds us that "Christianity is not *becoming* a global religion; it has always been a global religion."[1] Frequent associations of the

---
[1] Bantu, *A Multitude of All Peoples*, 1.

faith with Western history and society distort how we view the church and the kingdom of God. Demographics may be slowly changing perspectives, however.

The growth of Christianity in the Global South over the past century has been well documented, but many of us retain antiquated impressions of global Christianity. In the most recent edition of the *World Christian Encyclopedia*, Todd Johnson and Gina Zurlo describe the global communion of Christians in a representative one hundred people. Of these,[2]

- Twenty-six live in Africa, twenty-four in Latin America, twenty-three in Europe, fifteen in Asia, eleven in North America, and one in Oceania; combined, two-thirds of Christians live outside North America and Europe.
- Thirty-five live in low-income countries, forty-six in middle-income countries, and nineteen in high-income countries; in total, eighty-one live outside of high-income countries.
- Sixty-five live in urban areas, while thirty-five live in rural areas.
- Sixteen speak Spanish, ten English, eight Portuguese, five Russian, and sixty-one other languages; more Christians speak Mandarin than French, German, or Polish.

Statistics like these illustrate that, years ago, the numerical growth of Christianity shifted toward urban and lower- and middle-income settings in the Global South. According to the World Christian Database, the ratio of Christians in the Global North and Global South essentially flip-flopped between 1970 and 2018 (see Figure 6.1).[3] During the same period, the statistical center of the worldwide Christian community migrated from Europe to Africa, reflecting the burgeoning numbers of Christians in Africa and Asia.[4] In the opening years of this century, it is likely that more Christians gathered each week for worship in China than in all of Europe.

---

[2] Zurlo, "The World as 100 Christians."

[3] Johnson and Zurlo, *World Christian Database*. Of course, Asia (the Middle East) was the birthplace of Christianity, and most Christians lived there during the first seven hundred years CE.

[4] Johnson and Chung, "Tracking Global Christianity's Statistical Centre of Gravity."

Looking Ahead

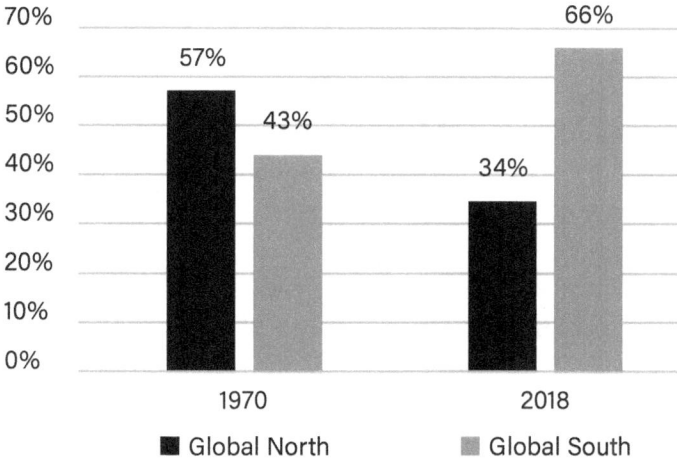

Figure 6.1. Christian Population

Similar population shifts occurred within many denominations. The largest national populations of Methodists, Presbyterians, Catholics, and some other denominations are no longer in the Global North but are scattered across the Global South in countries such as Uganda, Brazil, India, and the Philippines.[5] The United States currently has the most self-identifying Christians in the world, but large populations of Christians are growing elsewhere, expanding the cultural and linguistic diversity of the body of Christ.

Growth in the population of Christians in the Global South has corresponded with an increase in faith-based institutions in these same areas. A 2017 report based on UNESCO data tabulated forty-one higher education institutions in Africa in the 1950s, hosting a combined enrollment of 16,500 students. In 2010, sub-Saharan Africa alone claimed 668 colleges and universities enrolling 5.2 million students. Many of these young institutions are faith-based.[6]

Professional capacity building also is evident in NGOs and multilateral organizations operating in the Global South. For decades, local NGOs (LNGOs) in the Global South have assisted international NGOs

---

[5] Noll, *New Shape of World Christianity*, 20–21. For additional insight into the global growth of Christianity, see Jacobsen, *Global Gospel*.
[6] Carpenter, "Rise of Private Universities in Africa."

(INGOs), serving as partners and subcontractors in development projects. Because LNGOs are generally closer to the front lines in the fight against poverty, they often implement agricultural, education, disaster relief, and other projects for faith-based INGOs, such as World Vision. Faith-based organizations, both INGOs and LNGOs, employ Christians who know the local culture and apply expert knowledge and professional skills in development programming.

Finally, in the Global South, we see growth in the number of indigenous missionaries and holistic mission efforts. Over the past two decades, mission agencies increasingly have relied on indigenous missionaries and staff. Interdenominational organizations, in particular, have employed large numbers of their staff from the Global South.[7] Christian churches also have expanded their own church-planting and poverty-alleviation efforts. The Redeemed Christian Church of God is a prime example. This Pentecostal denomination, which began in Nigeria, has spread to more than eighty countries and engages in health-care delivery, education, and other poverty-alleviation works.[8]

Each of these examples demonstrates that the capacity and availability of Christian leaders and practitioners in the Global South have mushroomed. The distribution is uneven, and despite their education and experience, many are attempting livelihoods in sputtering economies subject to oppressive corruption and limited in material resources. And yet their numbers and capacity continue to increase. It is clear that the global body of Christ is not centered in Europe and North America.

But what are the implications of the growing presence of Christians and Christian leaders in the Global South? We suggest two that are relevant to holistic mission. The first is that the church in the Global North has increasing opportunities to partner with leaders and organizations based in or staffed by Christians in the Global South. Global mission presents abundant needs and abundant possibilities. As the number of Christians and professionals in the Global South grows, so do opportunities to engage in locally envisioned and led efforts.

---

[7] For statistics, see Newell, *North American Mission Handbook*, 53–56.

[8] Redeemed Christian Church of God, "CSR," http://csr.rccg.org/. For a background on the church, see Ukah, "New Paradigm."

A related benefit of this shift is the potential for transformation through Christian relationships and mutuality. Partnerships can be more than merely a transfer of funds; ideally, they form a meeting place of reciprocal learning and engagement. Congregations in the Global North, as they grow in appreciation of and learn from Global South leadership, theologies, and cultural insights, can replicate and adapt the transformational development efforts of their global partners within their own communities, as we explored in Chapter Five.[9]

Despite the growth in population and capacity in the Global South, a disproportionate amount of material resources remains in the hands of Global North churches. The church in the Global North has an opportunity to consider ways to combine assets with the church in the Global South. Crucially, though, it must avoid postures of superiority, imperialism, and dependency. By embracing global relationships built on mutual exchange and respect, we can embody a Christian faith that is both transformational and inspirational.

Local-Led Development

A second wave of change underscores the first but comes from the global development sector. It emphasizes a two-pronged initiative: to advocate for (a) more investment in predisaster planning and (b) greater localization of development and relief efforts to enhance the speed, efficiency, and effectiveness of aid and to contribute more to local capacity building. Daniel J. Clarke of the Centre for Disaster Protection and Stefan Dercon of the University of Oxford lay out this argument.[10] Instead of waiting until disaster strikes and then deciding whether, how to, and how much to respond, they advocate applying an insurance model that determines ahead of time who will respond, how to respond, and to what degree.

Currently, relief aid provided in the moment of crisis is often chaotic and disjointed, which delays responses and mismatches the response to the need—providing too much or too little aid or the wrong kind of assistance. Too often, governments and humanitarian agencies do not have sufficient

---

[9] Hill, *Salt, Light, and a City*, amplifies voices from the diverse and global church to call God's people deeper into faithful and effective mission.

[10] Clarke and Dercon, *Dull Disasters?*

contingency funds from which they can draw during crises. The result is that those in need are left to plead for assistance and hope they receive a response. Clarke and Dercon argue, "The model creates ambiguity about who owns the risk: who will need to act and who will need to pay for it."[11] This results in unnecessary delays, amplification of the crisis, and a fragmented and uncoordinated response. In lieu of a "begging bowl" model, Clarke and Dercon advocate for a financing model that resembles insurance, in which multiple governments and organizations decide on funding protocols and amounts of backing before disaster strikes.

While Clarke and Dercon primarily direct their argument toward governments, the insurance model is relevant to NGOs and churches as well. The Start Network in the United Kingdom is an example. It represents a group of NGOs that commits to plans and funding ahead of disasters and specifically targets historically underfunded emergencies, supplementing the aid often provided by governments. Included in the Start Network's planning is partnering with and investing in local humanitarian organizations in locations where disasters often strike to strengthen the capacity of national and local responders and increase their confidence and response time. Funding is pooled from different NGOs and coordinated to deliver amounts that fit the need. A report from the group states, "The Start Network aims to shift the centre of humanitarian gravity, so that decision-making and leadership take place at the front line and affected people are empowered to improve their lives."[12]

In the Christian community, coordinating mechanisms exist in large faith-based humanitarian organizations such as World Relief, World Vision, and Church World Service. Additionally, congregations and denominations could establish pre-disaster procedures, partnerships, and funding so they are prepared to respond more effectively and efficiently if and when needs arise. Planning ahead and working through local partners enhances capacity building in the long run and response effectiveness in times of need.[13]

---

[11] Clarke and Dercon, *Dull Disasters?*, 17.

[12] Start Network, "Start Fund," 4.

[13] Although focused more on preparedness in the United States, this work may spark thoughts in congregational planning for global missions. See Aten and Boan, *Disaster Ministry Handbook*.

Diversity and Postcolonial Mission

A third wave of change we see affecting holistic mission is the increasing balkanization of cultural diversity in the Global North. Since World War II, flows of emigrants and immigrants across borders have gradually but drastically changed the demography of Europe and North America. Ethnic diversity is evident in some, though not all, congregations, but the makeup of the church in general clearly has changed.

As of 2016, half of all Evangelicals in the United States under thirty were nonwhite, and one-third of all US Evangelicals were people of color. Pentecostals, Catholics, and Baptists are relatively diverse as denominational families.[14] Yet, as Janelle Wong documents, White Evangelicals appear not to have budged on issues that disproportionately affect Christians of other ethnic backgrounds—issues such as immigration, economic inequality, mass incarceration, race relations, and climate change.[15] Surveys consistently indicate that White Evangelicals are the least likely to support offering shelter to undocumented children who arrive in the United States without their parents and are the least likely to support refugees.[16] Similar views are also pervasive among Christians in some European nations.[17]

Embracing diversity and inclusion is also lacking in regard to economic levels. As we mentioned in Chapter Three, churches in the Global North often support holistic mission, but too often these efforts have been *to* "the poor" rather than *with* people living in poverty. People in poverty remain distinguished and objectified, a group to which the church ministers at arm's length instead of embracing them as full participants in the body. Mental segregation and bias can be subtle, invisible, and deniable but, once seen, it is unmistakable.

Lydia Bean observed this in-group and out-group division when she compared Evangelicals in the United States and Canada. Canadian Evangelicals tended to view national social programs as acts of solidarity, uniting all Canadians. US Evangelicals, on the other hand, tended

---

[14] Jones and Cox, "America's Changing Religious Identity."

[15] Wong, *Immigrants, Evangelicals, and Politics.*

[16] Hartig, "Republicans Turn More Negative toward Refugees"; Jones, Cox, and Navarro-Rivera, "Nearly 7-in-10."

[17] Krekó, Hunyadi, and Szicherle, "Anti-Muslim Populism"; Pew Research Center, "Being Christian in Western Europe."

to view people in poverty as a separate group of second-class citizens. Bean noted that churches extended compassion but seldom inclusion. In Canada, people in material poverty were viewed as "Canadians." In the United States, people with low incomes or few resources were "the poor."[18]

From the time of the ancient church, worldly distinctions have divided the body of Christ: Jews and Greeks, slave and free, male and female, rich and poor (Gal. 3:28; James 2:1–7). The church today continues to carve up humanity along such social and cultural boundaries. And with what has been labeled "super-diversity"—an increase in the complexity of diversity itself—society is becoming increasingly fractured.[19] Yet, because the church exists in particular cultures and is called to unity, we need a gospel response of hospitality, fellowship, and reconciliation in and through Christ, where we see, hear, and learn from one another as one body. Some argue for the objectification of "the poor" and "the stranger" and for perpetuating racial bias, but our desire, our longing, is for the church to resist, drawing nearer to the transforming Spirit of God and modeling to the world a better way.[20]

The call to resistance includes those in the Global North who set out with the noble intention to love and serve their global neighbors. Mission that flows from the Global North to the Global South often brings with it the residue of colonialism. Namsoon Kang observes how the ghosts of expansionism and triumphalism haunt our language and thinking as we consider missions to "*foreign* countries to 'help' and 'spread' the Gospel to the *heathen* people in the underdeveloped countries. . . . As long as we try to *patronize, dominate,* and *control* others . . . the colonial mentality permeates and operates in the very act of mission."[21]

The reason we highlight neocolonial thinking in the local and global church is that too often a lack of authentic unity blocks mutual learning, virtue development, and trusting partnerships, even in the midst of abundant humanitarian activity. Elevated status in unequal partnerships

---

[18] Bean, *Politics of Evangelical Identity*.

[19] Vertovec, "Super-Diversity and Its Implications."

[20] For examples, see Charles and Rah, *Unsettling Truths*; Jones, *White Too Long*; Wong, *Immigrants, Evangelicals, and Politics*.

[21] Kang, "Constructing Postcolonial Mission in World Christianity," 106, 111.

prevents transformation. Yet, as Kang writes, "Christian postcolonial mission can be a movement and practice of geopolitical alliances across the globe, transcending boundaries between different identities, nations, cultures, or religions: Participating in God's 'yes' to the entire world and to humans."[22] Paul entreats us to "welcome one another, therefore, just as Christ has welcomed you, for the glory of God" (Rom. 15:7), and that requires seeing the *imago Dei* in others, having the same mind as Christ Jesus by emptying and humbling ourselves (Phil. 2:1–11), looking to the interests of others, and transcending boundaries in our minds and hearts, not merely in our neighborhoods or world. It will take humility and diligence to increase our awareness of our colonial baggage and adopt postcolonial language and practices; yet, through Christ, it is possible.

Faith, Hope, and Love in the Face of Need

Finally, although substantial gains have occurred in poverty reduction, as we explored in Chapter One, inequality and need will continue to be with us. Today, record numbers of martyrs and migrants are mounting, and global food insecurity is ticking up after years of decline. Disasters will not cease, nor will famines, pestilence, violence, or structural and individual brokenness. Climate change portends new challenges, and global pandemics and war can erase decades of development progress.[23] The immensity of needs and suffering in the world is daunting.

In the face of such need, discouragement can come easily—even more so when transformation happens slowly and obstacles stand in our way. I (Monty) know this feeling. A few years ago, I approached a foundation about possibly funding an initiative to provide capital for women entrepreneurs in India and Madagascar. The executive director responded that the donor to the foundation likes to work in sectors "where change is possible," which did not include the Global South. Obviously, the director had not witnessed the great difference global engagements can make, as many initiatives and organizations have demonstrated (see Appendix B for organizations that are making an impact in various sectors). But even for those

---

[22] Kang, "Constructing Postcolonial Mission," 123–24.
[23] The World Bank estimates that the COVID-19 pandemic forced 88–150 million persons back into extreme poverty in 2021. See World Bank, "Reversals of Fortune."

of us who have seen lives and communities forever shaped by transformational development, needs can seem endless and setbacks disheartening.

It is when those feelings of discouragement arise that we put our faith in the One who has proven to be faithful. We recall the lessons of history when the early Christians were small in number, yet by the power of God's Spirit at work in them, they bore faithful witness and were transformed through perseverance and sacrificial service. Or, more directly, we remember and draw strength from God's transforming power in our own lives. Ultimately, we remain steadfast because God, through Jesus Christ, has transformed darkness into light and death into life.

Our perseverance in faith is sustained by our hope in God. Hope for the Christian is not wish fulfillment or even optimism but, rather, confidence in God and in seeing the fruit of God's Spirit at work. As Andrew Root states, "Optimism clothes itself in the present, seeking to make the present good through positive thinking." Instead, "it is through our broken places that we find the resurrected Lord bringing a new reality from within this one. Hope springs from death, because our hope is in the man of the future, in Jesus Christ, who though he is overcome by death on the cross conquers death with life in the Resurrection."[24] We do not deny the needs or the challenges; we look through them to see God's *shalom* breaking in, and we are humbled that God often uses human vessels to help usher in this *shalom* to the world. Therefore, may we not grow weary in doing what is right (Gal. 6:9), but may we encourage one another, through hope, as we journey together toward transformation.[25]

Holding to faith and hope, those who participate in transformational development heed Christ's call: "From everyone to whom much has been given, much will be required" (Luke 12:48). Those of us who have been given abundant material resources are to be generous and sacrificial within God's economy. Those of us with training and expertise related to poverty alleviation should use our talents and knowledge to wisely and effectively work toward justice and well-being. The millions of Christ followers in the

---

[24] Root, *The Promise of Despair*, 141–46.
[25] Considerable research has been devoted to the ways Christianity provides hope and coping. Two development-related studies are Bryan, Choi, and Karlan, "Randomizing Religion," and Lybbert and Wydick, "Poverty, Aspirations, and the Economics of Hope."

Global South who are receiving a fresh current of the Spirit's movement can model the radical way of Jesus in diverse contexts. For the image-bearers who are currently vulnerable, the presence of Christ can be offered to the world. Mutually sharing that which has been given to each of us—time, treasure, talents, insight, experience (even our own brokenness)—is essential to the work of transformation.

But what all of us have been given much of—indeed, an abundant and infinite amount—is love. Therefore, it is love that is required of us. As Pope Benedict affirms in *Deus Caritas Est* (*God Is Love*):

> Love—*caritas*—will always prove necessary, even in the most just society. There is no ordering of the State so just that it can eliminate the need for a service of love. . . . The State which would provide everything, absorbing everything into itself, would ultimately become a mere bureaucracy incapable of guaranteeing the very thing which the suffering person—every person—needs; namely, loving personal concern.[26]

We may at times be limited by resources or ability or knowledge, but we can always love with a love that is defined by the love of the One who "laid down his life for us" (1 John 3:16).

As followers of Christ, we live between the already and the not yet, knowing that God will make all things right. In the interim, we desire to align our hearts and lives with God, knowing that God is the source of wholeness to all of humanity, including us. Those of us rich in material resources need transforming as much, if not more, than anyone in economic poverty, for each one of us is impoverished in one way or another. Yet, because we have faith in God, we rest in God's love and hope in God's renewal of all things.

---

[26] Benedict XVI, *God Is Love*, 69.

AFTERWORD

FROM THE CHURCH
IN THE GLOBAL SOUTH

Ruth Padilla DeBorst

The quilts were beautiful, with colored patches sewn together by loving hands. The women from the US church had happily dedicated long hours preparing these gifts for the rural community. The mission committee had then packed and shipped them, paying a pretty penny given their significant weight. On the other end, a missionary had spent several days and paid heavy import dues to get the packages out of customs. She delivered them to the villagers, who received them with open arms and proceeded to cut them up for use as floor rags. You see, they lived in a tropical climate where the temperature never dropped below 90 degrees!

The book you have just read graciously warns against misguided initiatives such as this one as well as against "voluntourism," the self-justifying service that so often characterizes short-term mission forays by Christians from the Global North in the Global South. Beyond that needed critique, the authors offer sound biblical grounding for a thoroughly Christlike outreach. "Gospeled" poverty alleviation is co-laboring with God in God's mission of salvation of the whole planet, and the means must be shaped by the way of Jesus, which is characterized by emptying of self, power, and privilege; focuses on long-term relationships of proximity, reciprocity, and collaboration; recognizes the dignity of people; and attends to local context and self-determination.

Moving from the *what* and the *why*, this book elaborates on the nuts and bolts of development in mission, honest and helpfully assessing the various sectors in which congregations typically engage, challenging misguided mindsets and practices, and recommending further resources as well as potential partnerships for holistic, contextually appropriate, and mutually transformational development initiatives.

The story at the beginning of this afterword is simply one of the broad repertoire I have acquired throughout my lifetime in Latin America. I am pretty sure that if the churches I encountered along the way had had access to the recommendations offered in these pages, their mission initiatives might have contributed more significantly to God's restorative purposes and their members might have experienced deeper conversions into God's heart for justice. I especially appreciate the call to attend to the root causes of poverty and for people from wealthier contexts to recognize the interdependency of humans around the world and how their personal standards of living, their consumption, and their actions in general impact people across the globe.

This, I believe at the same time, is an area that merits yet further elaboration. For example, the authors highlight the big gap that exists in churches' involvement in creation care in spite of how critical it is to poverty alleviation. They rightly detail how poor families are vulnerable to environmental changes, unable to mitigate or adjust, at risk of losing their lives, and forced to migrate in search of sustenance. However, their call for "sparing and sharing," limiting expenditures and conserving resources, which, in turn, makes awareness of others and sharing of resources more possible, is far too mild, in my estimation, in light of the current disparity in responsibility for the state of our planet. In our world, "the people who are most vulnerable to the threats of climate change are also the least responsible for causing it," given that "the richest 10 percent of people produce half of the planet's individual-consumption-based fossil fuel emissions, while the poorest 50 percent—about 3.5 billion people—contribute only 10 percent."[1] Given the inextricable connection between climate change and economic inequality, the search for transformation will require change, not merely in the conditions of the "have-nots" but especially in those of the "haves." No number of climate mitigation measures or relief response "over there" will bridge the widening and deadening vulnerability gap. Only systemic change and radical lifestyle shifts on the part of the responsible parties hold any promise of correcting our global trajectory. While much of the development imaginary rests on the assumption of limitless growth, creation care requires honest assessment of limits and concrete relinquishment of privilege for the sake of a just Jubilee redistribution of resources.

Christians need to recognize that care of creation is both humankind's original mandate at creation as well as an essential expression of love of God and love of neighbor. In addition, following Jesus in emptying ourselves must be embodied in concrete, corrective action on the "home front" even more importantly than in trying to right wrongs "in the field." May God's Spirit work in us God's goodwill as we discern what that embodiment should look like for each person, family, and congregation! And thanks to the authors for launching this needed revision of mind, heart, and life so that, as the global body of Christ, we might constitute a brightly colored patchwork useful for God's lifegiving purposes in God's world!

—Ruth Padilla DeBorst
    Theologian and educator, Resonate Global Mission, Costa Rica

---

[1] Colarossi, "The World's Richest People Emit the Most Carbon."

APPENDIX A

FURTHER READING

Bauman, Belinda. *Brave Souls: Experiencing the Audacious Power of Empathy*. Downers Grove: InterVarsity Press, 2019.

Cho, Eugene. *Overrated: Are We More in Love with the Idea of Changing the World Than Actually Changing the World?* Colorado Springs: David C. Cook, 2014.

Christian, Jayakumar. *God of the Empty-Handed: Poverty, Power and the Kingdom of God*. Monrovia: MARC, 1999.

Corbett, Steve, and Brian Fikkert. *When Helping Hurts: How to Alleviate Poverty without Hurting the Poor . . . and Yourself*. Chicago: Moody, 2014.

Fikkert, Brian, and Kelly M. Kapic. *A Field Guide to Becoming Whole: Principles for Poverty Alleviation Ministries*. Chicago: Moody, 2019.

Fikkert, Brian, and Russell Mask. *From Dependence to Dignity: How to Alleviate Poverty through Church-Centered Microfinance*. Grand Rapids: Zondervan, 2015.

Harper, Lisa Sharon. *The Very Good Gospel: How Everything Wrong Can Be Made Right*. New York: WaterBrook, 2016.

Hill, Graham. *Relentless Love: Living Out Integral Mission to Combat Poverty, Injustice and Conflict*. Carlisle, UK: Langham, 2020.

Ji-Sun Kim, Grace, and Graham Hill. *Healing Our Broken Humanity: Practices for Revitalizing the Church and Renewing the World*. Downers Grove: InterVarsity Press Books, 2018.

Kuperus, Tracy, and Roland Hoksbergen. *When Helping Heals*. Grand Rapids: Calvin College Press, 2016.

Lynn, Monty L. *Christian Compassion: A Charitable History*. Eugene: Wipf & Stock, 2021.

Martin, Jim. *The Just Church: Becoming a Risk-Taking, Justice-Seeking, Disciple-Making Congregation*. Carol Stream, IL: Tyndale Momentum, 2012.

Mitchell, Bob. *Faith-Based Development: How Christian Organizations Can Make a Difference*. Maryknoll: Orbis, 2017.

Myers, Bryant L. *Walking with the Poor: Principles and Practices of Transformational Development*. Rev. and expanded. Maryknoll: Orbis, 2011.

Offutt, Stephen, F. David Bronkema, Krisanne Vaillancourt Murphy, Robb Davis, and Gregg Okesson. *Advocating for Justice: An Evangelical Vision for Transforming Systems and Structures*. Grand Rapids: Baker Academic, 2016.

Sider, Ronald J. *Rich Christians in an Age of Hunger: Moving from Affluence to Generosity*. Nashville: W Publishing, 2015.

Sweeden, Nell Becker. *Church on the Way: Hospitality and Migration*. Eugene: Pickwick, 2015.

Tizon, Al. *Whole and Reconciled*. Grand Rapids: Baker Academic, 2018.

Warren, Michelle Ferrigno. *The Power of Proximity: Moving Beyond Awareness to Action*. Downers Grove: InterVarsity Press, 2017.

Wydick, Bruce. *Shrewd Samaritan: Faith, Economics, and the Road to Loving Our Global Neighbor*. Nashville: W Publishing, 2019.

APPENDIX B

DEVELOPMENT ORGANIZATIONS

This sampling of faith-based (†) and secular nongovernmental organizations, para-church agencies, and intergovernmental organizations represent potential partners or models and information via examples, networks, and research. Our intent is not to endorse or exclude but to prime your search. We encourage you to assess the fit and effectiveness of these or other organizations.

ADVOCACY

Partners
- Bread for the World† – bread.org
- Church World Service† – cwsglobal.org/our-work/advocacy
- Evangelical Environmental Network† – creationcare.org
- General Board of Church and Society, United Methodist Church† – umcjustice.org
- JustFaith Ministries† – justfaith.org
- NETWORK† – networklobby.org
- World Council of Churches† – oikoumene.org
- World Relief† – worldrelief.org/advocate
- World Vision† – worldvision.org

Information
- Bread for the World Institute† – bread.org/about-bread-world-institute

DEVELOPMENT IN MISSION

Christians for Social Action† – christiansforsocialaction.org
SojoAction† – sojo.net/sojoaction/vision

ASSESSMENT AND EVALUATION

Information
3ie – International Initiative for Impact Evaluation – 3ieimpact.org
Abdul Latif Jameel Poverty Action Lab (J-PAL) – povertyactionlab.org
Candid/GuideStar – guidestar.org
Charity Navigator – charitynavigator.org
Feedback Labs – feedbacklabs.org
GiveWell – givewell.org
Innovations for Poverty Action – poverty-action.org
INTRAC – intrac.org
NGO Advisor – ngoadvisor.net
Poverty Probability Index – povertyindex.org

CHILDREN, YOUTHS, AND OLDER PERSONS

Partners/Organizations
Alongsiders International† – alongsiders.org
Bethany Christian Services† – bethany.org
Buckner International† – buckner.org
The Charis Project – thecharisproject.org
ChildFund – childfund.org
Compassion International† – compassion.org
Fairstart Foundation – fairstartfoundation.com
Girl Effect – girleffect.org
International Care Ministries† – caremin.com
Made in the Streets† – madeinthestreets.org
OneChild† – onechild.org
New Horizons – noi-orizonturi.ro/en
Save the Children – savethechildren.org
Unbound – unbound.org
Zoe Empowers† – zoeempowers.org

Information
Age International – ageinternational.org.uk
Faith to Action Initiative† – faithtoaction.org
Global Ageing Network – globalageing.org

Global Alliance for the Rights of Older People – rightsofolderpeople.org
Help Age International – helpage.org
UNICEF – unicef.org

CREATION CARE

Partners/Organizations
A Rocha International† – arocha.org/en/
Evangelical Environmental Network† – creationcare.org
Plant with Purpose† – plantwithpurpose.org

Information
Forest Action – forestaction.org
International Institute for Environment and Development (IIED) – iied.org
International Institute for Sustainable Development (IISD) – iisd.org
United Nations Environment Programme (UNEP) – unep.org
UN-REDD – un-redd.org
World Resources Institute – wri.org

EDUCATION

Partners/Organizations
Alfalit – alfalit.org
Arab Baptist Theological Seminary† – abtslebanon.org
Bethlehem Bible College† – bethbc.edu
Edify† – edify.org
International Teams Canada† – iteams.ca
Langham Partnership† – us.langham.org
Nations University† – nationsu.edu
Oxford Centre for Mission Studies† – ocms.ac.uk
Room to Read – roomtoread.org
Village Schools International – villageschools.org

FOOD

Partners/Organizations
Bread for the World† – bread.org
Canadian Foodgrains Bank† – foodgrainsbank.ca
CGIAR – cgiar.org
Church World Service† – cwsglobal.org

EcoVentures International – eco-ventures.org
Food for the Hungry† – fh.org
Foundations for Farming† – foundationsforfarming.org
Heifer International† – heifer.org
One Acre Fund – oneacrefund.org
Winrock International – winrock.org

Information

Bread for the World Institute† – bread.org/about-bread-world-institute
CIMMYT – cimmyt.org
ECHO† – echonet.org
Food and Agriculture Organization of the United Nations (FAO) – fao.org
IFAD – ifad.org/en/
Marketlinks (USAID) – marketlinks.org
World Fish Center – worldfishcenter.org
World Food Programme – wfpusa.org

FREEDOM AND LIBERATION

Partners/Organizations

Aid to the Church in Need† – churchinneed.org
Anti-Slavery International – antislavery.org
Arise – arisefdn.org
Association for a More Just Society† – ajs-us.org
Chab Dai – chabdai.org
Christian Aid† – christianaid.org.uk
Christian Solidarity Worldwide† – csw.org.uk/home.htm
Eden Ministry† – thisiseden.jewelry
Faith in Action International† – faithinactioninternational.org
International Justice Mission† – ijm.org
Justice Defenders – justice-defenders.org
Love Does† – lovedoes.org
Love146 – love146.org
Open Doors USA† – opendoorsusa.org
Poetice† – poetice.org
Prison Fellowship International† – pfi.org
Unbound† – unboundnow.org
Urban Light – urban-light.org
Vital Voices – vitalvoices.org
Voice of the Martyrs USA† – persecution.com

Information

Empower Women – empowerwomen.org/en
UN Women – unwomen.org

HEALTH

Partners/Organizations – Health

Blessings International† – blessing.org
Christian Health Service Corps† – healthservicecorps.org
Doctors of the World – doctorsoftheworld.org
Global CHE Network† – chenetwork.org
Global Partners in Care – globalpartnersincare.org
Heart to Heart International – hearttoheart.org
The Leprosy Mission – leprosymission.org.uk
LifeNet International† – lninternational.org
MAP International – map.org
Medecins sans Frontiers/Doctors without Borders (MSF) – msf.org
Medical Ambassadors International† – medicalambassadors.org
MedSend† – medsend.org
Mercy Ships† – mercyships.org
Operation Smile – operationsmile.org
Partners in Health – pih.org
VillageReach – villagereach.org

Information – Health

Christian Connections for International Health† – ccih.org
Christian Medical and Dental Associations (CMDA)† – cmda.org
Consortium of Street Children – streetchildren.org
Institute for Health Metrics and Evaluation – healthdata.org
World Health Organization (WHO) – who.int

Partners/Organizations – Disabilities

CBM – cbm.org
Deaf Child Hope† – deafchildhope.org
EYElliance – eyelliance.org
Free Wheelchair Mission† – freewheelchairmission.org
Handicap International – hi.org
IAPB Vision Atlas – atlas.iapb.org
Joni and Friends Wheels for the World† – joniandfriends.org/ministries/wheels-for-the-world
LIMBS International – limbsinternational.org

DEVELOPMENT IN **MISSION**

Seva – seva.org
Shonaquip – shonaquip.co.za
Sightsavers – sightsavers.org
Walkabout Foundation – walkaboutfoundation.org
Wheels for Humanity – ucpwheels.org
Whirlwind Wheelchair – whirlwindwheelchair.org

Information – Disabilities

Convention on the Rights of Persons with Disabilities – un.org/development/desa/disabilities/convention-on-the-rights-of-persons-with-disabilities.html
International Disability Alliance – internationaldisabilityalliance.org
Messiah University Collaboratory† – messiah.edu/info/21317/collaboratory
RESNA – resna.org
World Health Organization – who.int/health-topics/disability

INCOME GENERATION

Partners/Organizations

BRAC USA – bracusa.org
Crossworld† – crossworld.org
Eternal Threads† – eternalthreads.org
Five Talents† – fivetalents.org.uk
GiveDirectly – givedirectly.org
HOPE International† – hopeinternational.org
Kiva – kiva.org
Nehemiah Center† – nehemiahcenter.net
Oikocredit† – oikocredit.coop/en/
Opportunity International† – opportunity.org
Partners Worldwide† – partnersworldwide.org
SERRV† – serrv.org
Sinapis† – sinapis.org
Ten Thousand Villages† – tenthousandvillages.com
Traidcraft† – traidcraft.co.uk
Upaya Social Ventures – upayasv.org
Village Enterprise – villageenterprise.org

Information

Aid to Artisans – ata.creativelearning.org
BEAM Exchange – beamexchange.org
Business as Mission – businessasmission.com

Development Organizations

Business as Mission, Lausanne Movement – lausanne.org/networks/issues/business-as-mission
Business as Mission Training – bamtraining.org
Chalmers Center† – chalmers.org
Faith Driven Entrepreneur – faithdrivenentrepreneur.org
Family Independence Initiative – fii.org
International Labour Organization – ilo.org
Making Cents International – makingcents.com
Praxis Labs – praxislabs.org
SEEP Network – seepnetwork.org
Transformational SME – transformationalsme.org

MIGRATION AND REFUGE

Partners/Organizations

Catholic Charities USA† – catholiccharitiesusa.org
Church World Service – cwsglobal.org
Episcopal Migration Ministries† – episcopalchurch.org/ministries/episcopal-migration-ministries
Ethiopian Community Development Council – ecdcus.org
Hebrew Immigrant Aid Society – hias.org/
International Rescue Committee – rescue.org
Lutheran Immigration and Refugee Service† – lirs.org
US Committee for Refugees and Immigrants – refugees.org
World Relief† – worldrelief.org

Information

Christian Community Development Association† – ccda.org
Evangelical Immigration Table† – evangelicalimmigrationtable.com
International Association for Refugees – iafr.org
International Organization for Migration – iom.int
National Immigration Forum† – immigrationforum.org
Norwegian Refugee Council (NRC) – nrc.no
UNHCR – United Nations High Commissioner for Refugees – unhcr.org

MULTISECTORAL

Partners/Organizations – General

North America
ACT Alliance† – actalliance.org

DEVELOPMENT IN **MISSION**

 Barefoot College – barefootcollege.org
 Bright Hope International† – brighthope.org
 CARE – care.org
 Christians for Social Action† – christiansforsocialaction.org
 Church Mission Society† – churchmissionsociety.org
 Cross International† – crossinternational.org
 ICCO-Cooperation – icco-cooperation.org/en
 Kairos† (Canada) – kairoscanada.org
 Mercy Corps – mercycorps.org
 Pact – pactworld.org
 Partners Relief and Development (Canada) – partners.ngo/ca
 Samaritan's Purse† – samaritanspurse.org
 Universal Giving – universalgiving.org
 World Concern† – worldconcern.org
 World Hope† – worldhope.org
 World Neighbors – wn.org
 World Relief† – worldrelief.org
 World Vision† – worldvision.org

Global North
Tearfund† (UK) – tearfund.org
Uniting World† (Australia) – unitingworld.org.au

Global South
Department of Service to Middle East Churches, Middle East Council of Churches† (Israel/Palestine) – dsprme.org
Evangelical Fellowship of India Commission on Relief† (India) – eficor.org
Interserve† – interserve.org

Partners/Organizations – Denominational

North America
Adventist Development and Relief Agency (ADRA)† – adra.org
African Methodist Episcopal Church Service and Development Agency (AME-SADA) † – ame-sada.org
American Friends Service Committee (AFSC)† – afsc.org
Brethren Disaster Ministries† – brethren.org/bdm
Brethren Volunteer Service (BVS)† – brethren.org/bvs
CAMA (Christian and Missionary Alliance)† – camaservices.org
Caritas† – caritas.org
Catholic Relief Services† – crs.org
Children's Disaster Services† – brethren.org/cds
CMF International† – cmfi.org

Development Organizations

Episcopal Relief and Development† – episcopalrelief.org
ERDO (Pentecostal Assemblies of Canada) † – erdo.ca
Foursquare Disaster Relief† – foursquare.org/get-involved/relief/
Global Food Initiative (Church of the Brethren)† – brethren.org/gfi/
Global Ministries (Disciples of Christ and United Church of Christ)† – globalministries.org
Global Strategy (Church of God, Anderson, Indiana)† – chogglobal.org
International Ministries (American Baptist Church)† – internationalministries.org
International Orthodox Christian Charities† – iocc.org
Latter-Day Saint Charities† – latterdaysaintcharities.org
Lutheran World Relief† – lwr.org
MCC Canada† – mcccanada.ca
Mennonite Central Committee† – mcc.org
Mission to the World (Presbyterian Church in America) † – mtw.org
Nazarene Compassionate Ministries† – ncm.org
NCM Canada (Church of the Nazarene)† – ncmcanada.ca
Presbyterian Disaster Assistance† – pda.pcusa.org
Presbyterian World Service and Development (Canada)† – presbyterian.ca/pwsd
The Primate's World Relief and Development Fund (Anglican)† – pwrdf.org
RCA Global Mission (Reformed Church in America)† – rca.org/global-mission
Salesian Missions† – salesianmissions.org
Salvation Army World Service† – sawso.org
Send Relief (Southern Baptist)† – sendrelief
Serve Globally (Evangelical Covenant Church)† – covchurch.org/sg
UMCOR/United Methodist Global Ministries† – umcmission.org/umcor
The United Church of Canada, Social Action – united-church.ca/social-action
Vineyard Justice Network† – vineyardjusticenetwork.org
World Partners (Evangelical Missionary Church of Canada)† – emcc.ca
World Partners (Missionary Church)† – wpartners.org
World Renew (Christian Reformed Church)† – worldrenew.net

Global North

Anglican Alliance (UK)† – anglicanalliance.org
Anglican Board of Mission (Australia)† – abmission.org
Anglican Overseas Aid (Australia)† – anglicanoverseasaid.org.au
Baptist World Mission (UK)† – bmsworldmission.org
Christian Aid (UK)† – christianaid.org.uk
Cordaid (The Netherlands)† – cordaid.org/en
FELM/Evangelical Lutheran Church of Finland† – felm.org

DEVELOPMENT IN **MISSION**

Diakonia (Sweden)† – diakonia.se/en
Lutheran World Federation World Service (Switzerland)† – lutheranworld.org/content/about-dws
Norwegian Church Aid† – kirkensnodhjelp.no/en
Salvation Army International† – salvationarmy.org/ihq

Information

Accord Network† – accordnetwork.org
Afrobarometer – afrobarometer.org
Christian Community Development Association† – ccda.org
Devex – devex.com
DevTech – devtechsys.com
Eldis – eldis.org
Interaction – interaction.org
Gapminder – gapminder.org
Jubilee USA Network† – jubileeusa.org
Micah Global† – micahnetwork.org
Overseas Development Institute (ODI) – odi.org
Organisation for Economic Co-operation and Development (OECD) – oecd.org
Our World in Data – ourworldindata.org
Transparency International – transparency.org
United States Agency for International Aid (USAID) – usaid.gov
UN Sustainable Development Goals (SDGs) – sdgs.un.org
The World as 100 Christians – gordonconwell.edu/blog/100christians
World Bank – worldbank.org
World Christian Database – worldchristiandatabase.org

PEACEMAKING AND PEACEBUILDING

Partners/Organizations

Anglican Pacifist Fellowship† – anglicanpeacemaker.org.uk
Christian Peacemaker Teams† – cpt.org
Cord† – cord.org.uk
Cure Violence Global – cvg.org
Development and Peace – Caritas Canada† – devp.org
Global Immersion Project – globalimmerse.org
Institute for Middle East Studies† – abtslebanon.org/institute-of-middle-east-studies/peacebuilding/
Musalaha† – musalaha.org

Development Organizations

One Million Thumbprints† – onemillionthumbprints.org
Pax Christi International† – paxchristi.net
Preemptive Love – preemptivelove.org

Information

Catholic Peacebuilding Network† – cpn.nd.edu
Fellowship of Reconciliation – for.org.uk
Kroc Institute for International Peace Studies, University of Notre Dame† – kroc.nd.edu
Peace Direct – peacedirect.org/us/
Peace Insight – peaceinsight.org
Uppsala Conflict Data Program – ucdp.uu.se

PHILANTHROPY

Partners/Organizations

The Gathering† – thegathering.com

Information

Bill and Melinda Gates Foundation – gatesfoundation.org
Skoll Foundation – skoll.org

RELIEF

Partners/Organizations

Convoy of Hope† – convoyofhope.org
International Committee of the Red Cross (ICRC) – icrc.org
Medair† – medair.org
Missionary Church Disaster Relief† – mcusa.org/disaster-relief
Moravian Disaster Relief† – moravian.org/mission/engagement/mdr
UN Volunteers – unv.org
Also see Multisectoral

Information

ALNAP – alnap.org
Emergency Events Database (EM-DAT) – emdat.be
Harvard Humanitarian Initiative – hhi.harvard.edu
International Network of Crisis Mappers – crisismapping.ning.com
Sphere Standards and Handbook – spherestandards.org
Wheaton College Humanitarian Disaster Institute† – wheaton.edu/academics/academic-centers/humanitarian-disaster-institute/

DEVELOPMENT IN **MISSION**

SCRIPTURE TRANSLATION

Partners/Organizations
Jesus Film Project† – jesusfilm.org
Pioneer Bible Translators† – pioneerbible.org
Wycliffe† – wycliffe.org

SHELTER

Partners/Organizations
Habitat for Humanity† – habitat.org

Information
Cardus† – cardus.ca/research/social-cities
Cities Alliance – citiesalliance.org
Fuller Center for Housing† – fullercenter.org
Landesa – landesa.org
Lazarian World Homes† – lazarianworldhomes.com
MASS Design Group – massdesigngroup.org
Proximity Project – proximityprojectinc.com
Shelter Cluster – sheltercluster.org
Shelter Projects – shelterprojects.org
Slum Dwellers International – knowyourcity.info
UN-Habitat – unhabitat.org
World Habitat – world-habitat.org

SPORT

Partners/Organizations
Athletes in Action† – goaia.org
Cross Cultures – ccpa.eu
Fellowship of Christian Athletes† – fca.org
Laureus Sport for Good – laureus.com/sport-for-good
Missionary Athletes International† – maisoccer.com
SCORE International Ministries† – scoreintl.org
Sports Outreach† – sportsoutreach.net
SRS International† – srs-international.org

Development Organizations

TECHNOLOGY

Partners/Organizations
    Engineering Ministries International† – emiworld.org
    Engineers without Borders – ewb-usa.org
    Lighting Africa – lightingafrica.org
    Liter of Light – literoflight.org
    PATH – path.org

Information
    DreamStart Labs – dreamstartlabs.com
    Energia – energia.org
    Energy Sector Management Assistance Program (ESMAP) – esmap.org
    Global Voices – globalvoices.org
    Hedon – hedon.info
    Samasource – samasource.com
    We Robotics – blog.werobotics.org

WATER, SANITATION, AND HYGIENE

Partners/Organizations
    CharityWater – charitywater.org
    Healing Waters International† – healingwaters.org
    Lifewater International† – lifewater.org
    Living Water International† – water.cc

Information
    IRC – ircwash.org
    Rural Water Supply Network (RWSN) – rural-water-supply.net/en/
    Sustainable Sanitation and Water Management Toolbox – sswm.info

NEWS, TRAINING, AND RESEARCH

News
    The New Humanitarian – thenewhumanitarian.org

Training
    Disaster Ready – disasterready.org

University-Based Research
    Abdul Latif Jameel Poverty Action Lab (J-Pal) – povertyactionlab.org

Center for Justice and Peacebuilding, Eastern Mennonite University† – emu.edu/cjp
Center for the Study of Global Christianity, Gordon-Conwell Theological Seminary† – gordonconwell.edu/center-for-global-christianity
Harvard Center for International Development – hks.harvard.edu/centers/cid
International Humanitarian Studies Association – ihsa.info
IssueLab – issuelab.org
Oxford Centre for Mission Studies† – ocms.ac.uk
Center for International Development, Point Loma Nazarene University† – pointloma.edu/centers-institutes/center-international-development

Research

American Journal of Disaster Medicine
Christian Relief, Development and Advocacy†
Community Development Journal
Comparative Migration Studies
Development and Change
Development in Practice
Disasters
Enterprise Development & Microfinance
Food Policy
Forced Migration Review
Habitat International
International Migration
Journal of Development Effectiveness
Journal of Development Studies
Journal of Refugee Studies
Peace and Conflict
Torture Journal
Transformation: An International Journal of Holistic Mission Studies†
Water Lines
World Development

BIBLIOGRAPHY

Abebe, Tatek. "Orphanhood, Poverty, and the Challenges for Care: Review of Global Policy Trends." In *Orphan Care: A Comparative View*, edited by Jo Daugherty Bailey, 155–81. Sterling, VA: Kumarian Press, 2012.
Abraham, William J. *The Logic of Evangelism*. Grand Rapids: Eerdmans, 1989.
Abu-Nimer, Mohammed. *Nonviolence and Peace Building in Islam: Theory and Practice*. Gainesville: University of Florida Press, 2003.
Accad, Martin. *Sacred Misinterpretation: Reaching across the Muslim-Christian Divide*. Grand Rapids: Eerdmans, 2019.
Accord Network. "Principles of Excellence in Integral Mission." Accessed November 12, 2019. https://www.accordnetwork.org/integral.
Ackerman, Evan, and Eliza Strickland. "Medical Delivery Drones Take Flight in East Africa." *IEEE Spectrum* 55 (2018): 34–35.
ADD International. Accessed October 25, 2019. https://www.add.org.uk.
Ae-Ngibise, Kenneth Ayuurebobi, Victor Christian Korley Doku, Kwaku Poku Asante, and Seth Owusu-Agyei. "The Experience of Caregivers of People Living with Serious Mental Disorders: A Study from Rural Ghana." *Global Health Action* 8 (2015): 26957.
Ae-Ngibise, Kenneth, Sara Cooper, Edward Adiibokah, Bright Akpalu, Crick Lund, Victor Doku, and Mhapp Research Programme Consortium. "'Whether You Like It or Not People with Mental Problems Are Going to Go to Them': A Qualitative Exploration into the Widespread Use of Traditional and Faith Healers in the Provision of Mental Health Care in Ghana." *International Review of Psychiatry* 22 (2010): 558–67.
African Christian Health Associations Platform. https://africachap.org/.
Afrobarometer. http://www.afrobarometer.org/.

Ajulu, Deborah. "Development as Holistic Mission." In *Holistic Mission: God's Plan for God's People*, edited by Wonsuk Ma and Brian Woolnough, 160–74. Eugene: Wipf & Stock, 2010.

Al-Samarrai, Samer, and Paul Bennell. "Where Has All the Education Gone in Sub-Saharan Africa? Employment and Other Outcomes among Secondary School and University Leavers." *Journal of Development Studies* 43 (2007): 1270–1300.

Allen, Tim, Jackline Atingo, Dorothy Atim, James Ocitti, Charlotte Brown, Costanza Torre, Cristin A. Fergus, and Melissa Parker. "What Happened to Children Who Returned from the Lord's Resistance Army in Uganda?" *Journal of Refugee Studies* 33 (2020): 663–83.

Alexander, Michelle. *The New Jim Crow: Mass Incarceration in an Age of Colorblindness*. New York: New Press, 2012.

Alongsiders International. Accessed October 29, 2019. https://www.alongsiders.org.

Anderson, Stephen J., and David J. McKenzie. "Improving Business Practices and the Boundary of the Entrepreneur: A Randomized Experiment Comparing Training, Consulting, Insourcing and Outsourcing." Policy Research Working Paper, no. WPS 9502. Washington, DC: World Bank Group, 2020. http://documents.worldbank.org/curated/en/377351608212969114/Improving-Business-Practices-and-the-Boundary-of-the-Entrepreneur-A-Randomized-Experiment-Comparing-Training-Consulting-Insourcing-and-Outsourcing.

Appleby, R. Scott. "The New Name for Peace? Religion and Development as Partners in Strategic Peacebuilding." In *The Oxford Handbook of Religion, Conflict, and Peacebuilding*, edited by Atalia Omer, R. Scott Appleby, and David Little. Oxford: Oxford University Press, 2015.

Arbuckle, Gerald A. *Culture, Inculturation, and Theologians: A Postmodern Critique*. Collegeville, MN: Liturgical Press, 2010.

Arbuckle, Matthew B., and David M. Konisky. "The Role of Religion in Environmental Attitudes." *Social Science Quarterly* 96 (2015): 1244–63.

Aten, Jamie D., and David M. Boan. *Disaster Ministry Handbook*. Downers Grove: InterVarsity Press, 2016.

Azzarri, Carlo, and Sara Signorelli. "Climate and Poverty in Africa South of the Sahara." *World Development* 125 (2020): 1–19.

Bailey, Jo Daugherty, ed. *Orphan Care: A Comparative View*. Sterling, VA: Kumarian Press, 2012.

Baker, David L. *Tight Fists or Open Hands? Wealth and Poverty in Old Testament Law*. Grand Rapids: Eerdmans, 2009.

Bakker, Janel Kragt. *Sister Churches: American Congregations and Their Partners Abroad*. New York: Oxford University Press, 2014.

Banerjee, Abhijit, Dean Karlan, and Jonathan Zinman. "Six Randomized Evaluations of Microcredit: Introduction and Further Steps." *American Economic Journal: Applied Economics* 7 (2015): 1–21.

Banerjee, Abhijit V., and Esther Duflo. *Poor Economics: A Radical Rethinking of the Way to Fight Global Poverty*. New York: PublicAffairs, 2011.

Bantu, Vince L. *A Multitude of All Peoples: Engaging Ancient Christianity's Global Identity*. Downers Grove: IVP Academic, 2020.

Barbier, Edward B., and Joanne C. Burgess. "Sustainable Development Goal Indicators: Analyzing Trade-Offs and Complementarities." *World Development* 122 (2019): 295–305.

Bardhan, Ronita, Sayantani Sarkar, Arnab Jana, and Nagendra R. Velaga. "Mumbai Slums since Independence: Evaluating the Policy Outcomes." *Habitat International* 50 (2015): 1–11.

Barnard, Tanguy, Stefan Dercon, and Alemayehu Seyoum Taffesse. "The Future in Mind: Aspirations and Forward-Looking Behaviour in Rural Ethiopia." Centre for Economic Policy Research, 2014. https://repec.cepr.org/repec/cpr/ceprdp/DP10224.pdf.

Batchelor, Simon. "Christian and Secular Approaches to Development: Reflections on a Community Development Programme in Cambodia (Kampuchea)." *Transformation: An International Journal of Holistic Mission Studies* 20 (2003): 125–33.

Bauman, Stephan, Matthew Soerens, and Issam Smeir. *Seeking Refuge: On the Shores of the Global Refugee Crisis*. Chicago: Moody, 2016.

Bays, Daniel, and Ellen Widmer, eds. *China's Christian Colleges: Cross-Cultural Connections, 1900-1950*. Stanford: Stanford University Press, 2009.

Bealt, Jennifer, and S. Afshin Mansouri. "From Disaster to Development: A Systematic Review of Community Driven Humanitarian Logistics." *Disasters* 42 (2018): 124–48.

Bean, Lydia. *The Politics of Evangelical Identity: Local Churches and Partisan Divides in the United States and Canada*. Princeton: Princeton University Press, 2016.

Beckmann, David. *Exodus from Hunger: We Are Called to Change the Politics of Hunger*. Louisville: Westminster/John Knox, 2010.

Bediako, Kwame. *Jesus and the Gospel in Africa: History and Experience*. Maryknoll: Orbis Books, 2004.

Beltramo, Theresa, Garrick Blalock, David I. Levine, and Andrew M. Simons. "The Effect of Marketing Messages and Payment over Time on Willingness to Pay for Fuel-Efficient Cookstoves." *Journal of Economic Behavior & Organization* 118 (2015): 333–45.

Benedict XVI. *God Is Love: Deus Caritas Est, Encyclical Letter*. San Francisco: Ignatius, 2006.

Berneking, Steve. "A Sociology of Translation and the Central Role of the Translator." *The Bible Translator* 67 (2016): 265–81.

Bevans, Stephen B., and Roger P. Schroeder. *Constants in Context: A Theology of Mission for Today*. Maryknoll: Orbis, 2004.

Biavaschi, Costanza, Janneke Pieters, Werner Eichhorst, Nuria Rodriguez-Planas, Corrado Giulietti, Ricarda Schmidl, Michael J. Kendzia, Klaus F. Zimmermann,

and Alexander Muravyev. "Youth Unemployment and Vocational Training." *Foundations and Trends in Microeconomics* 9 (2013): 1–157.
Bill and Melinda Gates Foundation. "2014 Gates Annual Letter." https://www.gates-foundation.org/ideas/annual-letters/annual-letter-2014.
Blackman, Rachel. *Partnering with the Local Church*. Teddington, UK: Tearfund, 2007.
———. "Partnering with the Local Church (Roots 11)." Tearfund, 2007. https://learn.tearfund.org/en/resources/publications/roots/partnering_with_the_local_church/.
Blom, Lindsey C., Lawrence Judge, Meredith A. Whitley, Lawrence Gerstein, Ashleigh Huffman, and Sarah Hillyer. "Sport for Development and Peace: Experiences Conducting U.S. and International Programs." *Journal of Sport Psychology in Action* 6 (2015): 1–16.
Blumenfeld, Stephen, and Ashish Malik. "Human Capital Formation under Neo-Liberalism: The Legacy of Vocational Education Training in Australasia and Implications for the Asia-Pacific Region." *Asia Pacific Business Review* 23 (2017): 290–98.
Bonk, Jonathan J. *Missions and Money*. 2nd ed. Maryknoll: Orbis, 1991.
Bosch, David J. *Transforming Mission: Paradigm Shifts in Theology of Mission*. Maryknoll: Orbis, 1991.
Brantly, Kent, and Amber Brantly. *Called for Life: How Loving Our Neighbor Led Us into the Heart of the Ebola Epidemic*. Colorado Springs: WaterBrook, 2015.
Bredenoord, Jan, and Paul van Lindert. "Pro-Poor Housing Policies: Rethinking the Potential of Assisted Self-Help Housing." *Habitat International* 34 (2010): 278–87.
Bronkema, David, and Christopher M. Brown. "Business as Mission through the Lens of Development." *Transformation* 26 (2009): 82–88.
Browne, Stanley George, Frank Davey, and William Archibald Robson Thomson, eds. *Heralds of Health: The Saga of Christian Medical Initiatives*. London: Christian Medical Fellowship, 1985.
Bruce, Nigel, Rogelio Perez-Padilla, and Rachel Albalak. "Indoor Air Pollution in Developing Countries: A Major Environmental and Public Health Challenge." *Bulletin of the World Health Organization* 78 (2000): 1078–1092.
Bryan, Gharad, James J. Choi, and Dean Karlan. "Randomizing Religion: The Impact of Protestant Evangelism on Economic Outcomes." *The Quarterly Journal of Economics* 136 (2021): 293–380.
Bryant, Katharine, and Todd Landman. "Combatting Human Trafficking since Palermo: What Do We Know about What Works?" *Journal of Human Trafficking* 6, no. 2 (March 14, 2020): 119–40.
Busch-Geertsema, Volker, Dennis Culhane, and Suzanne Fitzpatrick. "Developing a Global Framework for Conceptualising and Measuring Homelessness." *Habitat International* 55 (2016): 124–32.

Cahill, Lisa Sowle. "A Theology for Peacebuilding." In *Peacebuilding: Catholic Theology, Ethics, and Praxis*, edited by Robert J Schreiter, R. Scott Appleby, and Gerard F. Powers, 300–331. Maryknoll: Orbis, 2010.
Calhoun, Adele Ahlberg. *Spiritual Disciplines Handbook: Practices That Transform Us*. 2nd ed. Downers Grove: InterVarsity Press, 2015.
Calvi, Rossella, Federico Mantovanelli, and Lauren Hoehn-Velasco. "The Protestant Legacy: Missions and Human Capital in India," 2019. http://dx.doi.org/10.2139/ssrn.3354891.
Calvocoressi, Elfrida. "Leadership in Peacemaking: A Christian View." In *Business, Ethics and Peace*, edited by Luk Bouckaert and Manas Chatterji, 183–97. Bingley, UK: Emerald, 2015.
Campbell, J., G. Dussault, J. Buchan, F. Pozo-Martin, and A. Guerra. *A Universal Truth: No Health without a Workforce. Forum Report, Third Global Forum on Human Resources for Health*. Recife and Geneva: Global Health Workforce Alliance and World Health Organization, 2013.
Candid and the Center for Disaster Philanthropy. "Measuring the State of Disaster Philanthropy 2020: Data to Drive Decisions." https://www.issuelab.org/resources/37649/37649.pdf.
CARE and World Habitat. "Soaring High: Self-Recovery through the Eyes of Local Actors." CARE, World Habitat, Care Philippines, 2019. https://world-habitat.org/publications/soaring-high-self-recovery-through-the-eyes-of-local-actors/.
Carpenter, Joel. "The Rise of Private Universities in Africa Is Being Dominated by Christian Schools." *Quartz Africa*. Accessed August 30, 2020. https://qz.com/africa/1024955/christian-universities-are-growing-across-africa/.
Carpenter, Joel, Perry L. Glanzer, and Nicholas S. Lantinga, eds. *Christian Higher Education: A Global Reconnaissance*. Grand Rapids: Eerdmans, 2014.
Carr, Marilyn, and Maria Hartl. *Lightening the Load: Labour-Saving Technologies and Practices for Rural Women*. Rugby, UK: Practical Action, 2010.
Carter, Richard C. "Can and Should Sanitation and Hygiene Programmes Be Expected to Achieve Health Impacts?" *Waterlines* 36 (2017): 92–103.
Carter, Richard C., and Ian Ross. "Beyond 'Functionality' of Handpump-Supplied Rural Water Services in Developing Countries." *Waterlines* 35 (2016): 94–110.
Castro, Emilio. "Liberation, Evangelism, and Development: Must We Choose in Mission?" *Occasional Bulletin of Missionary Research* 2, no. 3 (1978): 87–90.
Cavanaugh, William T. "The Unfreedom of the Free Market." In *Wealth, Poverty, and Human Destiny*, edited by Doug Bandow and David L. Schindler, 103–28. Wilmington: Intercollegiate Studies Institute, 2003.
Chang, Angela Y., Krycia Cowling, Angela E. Micah, Abigail Chapin, Catherine S. Chen, Gloria Ikilezi, Nafis Sadat, Golsum Tsakalos, Junjie Wu, and Theodore Younker. "Past, Present, and Future of Global Health Financing: A Review of Development Assistance, Government, Out-of-Pocket, and Other Private Spending on Health for 195 Countries, 1995–2050." *The Lancet* 393, no. 10187 (2019): 2233–260.

Charles, Mark, and Soong-Chan Rah. *Unsettling Truths: The Ongoing, Dehumanizing Legacy of the Doctrine of Discovery*. Downers Grove: InterVarsity Press, 2019.

Charlson, Fiona, Mark van Ommeren, Abraham Flaxman, Joseph Cornett, Harvey Whiteford, and Shekhar Saxena. "New WHO Prevalence Estimates of Mental Disorders in Conflict Settings: A Systematic Review and Meta-Analysis." *The Lancet* 394, no. 10,194 (2019): 240–48.

Chea, Lyda, and Roy Huijsmans. "Rural Youth and Urban-Based Vocational Training: Gender, Space and Aspiring to 'Become Someone.'" *Children's Geographies* 16 (2018): 39–52.

Chesterman, Clement C. *In the Service of Suffering: Phases of Medical Missionary Enterprise*. London: Cargate, 1940.

Chilcote, Paul W. "The Integral Nature of Worship and Evangelism." In *The Study of Evangelism: Exploring a Missional Practice of the Church*, edited by Paul W. Chilcote and Laceye C. Warner, 246–63. Grand Rapids: Eerdmans, 2008.

Cho, Bernardo. "Subverting Slavery: Philemon, Onesimus, and Paul's Gospel of Reconciliation." *Evangelical Quarterly* 86 (2014): 99–115.

Cho, Eugene. *Overrated: Are We More in Love with the Idea of Changing the World Than Actually Changing the World?* Colorado Springs: David C. Cook, 2014.

Chowdhury, Rafi M. M. I. "Religiosity and Voluntary Simplicity: The Mediating Role of Spiritual Well-Being." *Journal of Business Ethics* 152 (2018): 149–74.

Christian, Jayakumar. *God of the Empty-Handed: Poverty, Power and the Kingdom of God*. Monrovia, CA: MARC, 1999.

"Christian Alliance for Orphans." Accessed August 1, 2019. https://cafo.org/global/.

Christian International Peace Service. https://chipspeace.org/.

Christian Medical and Dental Associations. "About Us." https://cmda.org/about-us/.

Claiborne, Shane. "Simplicity and the Poor." In *Following Jesus: Journeys in Radical Discipleship*, by Paul Alexander and Al Tizon, 83–93. Oxford: Regnum, 2013.

Clapp, Jennifer. *Hunger in the Balance: The New Politics of International Food Aid*. Ithaca: Cornell University Press, 2015.

Clarke, Daniel J., and Stefan Dercon. *Dull Disasters? How Planning Ahead Will Make a Difference*. Oxford: Oxford University Press, 2016.

Clarke, Matthew, and Brett W. Parris. "Understanding Disasters: Managing and Accommodating Different Worldviews in Humanitarian Response." *Journal of International Humanitarian Action* 4, no. 19 (2019).

Coakley, Sarah. *Powers and Submissions: Spirituality, Philosophy and Gender*. Oxford: Blackwell, 2002.

Coalter, Fred. "Sport-for-Development: Going beyond the Boundary?" *Sport in Society* 13 (2010): 1374–91.

Cochrane, James R. "Trustworthy Intermediaries: Role of Religious Agents on the Boundaries of Public Health." In *When Religion and Health Align: Mobilizing Religious Health Assets for Transformation*, edited by James R. Cochrane, Barbara Schmid, and Teresa Cutts, 150–63. Pietermaritzburg: Cluster, 2011.

Colarossi, Jess. "The World's Richest People Emit the Most Carbon." *Our World*. December 5, 2015. https://ourworld.unu.edu/en/the-worlds-richest-people-also-emit-the-most-carbon.

Coleman, Gerald. "Stewardship." In *The New Dictionary of Catholic Social Thought*, edited by Judith A. Dwyer, 920–24. Collegeville, MN: Liturgical Press, 1994.

Collins, Daryl, Jonathan Morduch, Stuart Rutherford, and Orlanda Ruthven. *Portfolios of the Poor: How the World's Poor Live on $2 a Day*. Princeton: Princeton University Press, 2009.

Compassion International. Accessed October 29, 2019. https://www.compassion.com/.

Consortium for Street Children. "Advocacy and Action Guide: Making Rights a Reality for Street-Connected Children," 2019. https://www.streetchildren.org/resources/advocacy-action-guide/.

Copestake, James. "Well-Being in Development: Comparing Global Designs with Local Views in Peru." *European Journal of Development Research* 23 (2011): 94–110.

———. "Wellbeing in International Development: What's New?" *Journal of International Development* 20 (2008): 577–97.

Corbett, Steve, and Brian Fikkert. *When Helping Hurts: How to Alleviate Poverty without Hurting the Poor . . . and Yourself*. Chicago: Moody, 2014.

Cornelius, Kirk J. Franklin, and J. P. Niemandt. "Vision 2025 and the Bible Translation Movement." *HTS Theological Studies* 69 (2013): 1–8.

Crawford, Christa Foster, Glenn Miles, and Gundelina Velazco, eds. *Finding Our Way through the Traffick: Navigating the Complexities of a Christian Response to Sexual Exploitation and Trafficking*. Eugene: Wipf & Stock, 2017.

Crawford, Lynn, and Julien Pollack. "Hard and Soft Projects: A Framework for Analysis." *International Journal of Project Management* 22 (2004): 645–53.

Crisp, Oliver D. *Approaching the Atonement: The Reconciling Work of Christ*. Downers Grove: IVP Academic, 2020.

Cross Cultures. Accessed November 26, 2019. https://ccpa.eu/.

Dabir, Neela, and Naina Athale. *From Street to Hope: Faith Based and Secular Programs in Los Angeles, Mumbai and Nairobi for Street Living Children*. New Delhi: Sage, 2011.

Dale, Reidar. *Development Planning: Concepts and Tools for Planners, Managers and Facilitators*. London: Zed, 2004.

Das, Ashok. "Slum Upgrading with Community-Managed Microfinance: Towards Progressive Planning in Indonesia." *Habitat International* 47 (2015): 256–66.

Das, Rupen, and Brent Hamoud. *Strangers in the Kingdom: Ministering to Refugees, Migrants and the Stateless*. Carlisle, UK: Langham, 2017.

Davey, T. F. "Introduction." In *Heralds of Health: The Saga of Christian Medical Initiatives*, edited by Stanley G. Browne, Frank R. C. Davey, and William A. R. Thompson, 1–16. London: Christian Medical Fellowship, 1985.

De Haan, Robert. "Production Principles for 'Good' Agriculture." In *Biblical Holism and Agriculture: Cultivating Our Roots*, edited by David J. Evans, Ronald J. Vos, and Keith P. Wright, 56–67. Pasadena: William Carey Library, 2003.

de Waal, Alex. *Mass Starvation: The History and Future of Famine*. Cambridge, UK: Polity, 2018.

DeCamp, Matthew, Lisa Soleymani Lehmann, Pooja Jaeel, and Carrie Horwitch. "Ethical Obligations Regarding Short-Term Global Health Clinical Experiences: An American College of Physicians Position Paper." *Annals of Internal Medicine* 168, no. 9 (2018): 651–57.

Dickson-Gómez, Julia. "Substance Abuse Disorders Treatment in El Salvador: Analysis of Policy-Making-Related Failure." *Substance Use & Misuse* 47 (2012): 1546–51.

Dickson-Gómez, Julia, Gloria Bodnar, Carmen Eugenia Guevara, Karla Rodriguez, Lorena Rivas De Mendoza, and A. Michelle Corbett. "With God's Help I Can Do It: Crack Users' Formal and Informal Recovery Experiences in El Salvador." *Substance Use & Misuse* 46 (2011): 426–39.

Dieleman, Joseph L., Matthew T. Schneider, Annie Haakenstad, Lavanya Singh, Nafis Sadat, Maxwell Birger, Alex Reynolds et al. "Development Assistance for Health: Past Trends, Associations, and the Future of International Financial Flows for Health." *The Lancet* 387, no. 10037 (2016): 2536–44.

Dimmock, Franck, Jill Olivier, and Quentin Wodon. "Half a Century Young: The Christian Health Associations of Africa." November 2012. https://mpra.ub.uni-muenchen.de/45369.

DuBois, Heather M., and Janna Hunter-Bowman. "The Intersection of Christian Theology and Peacebuilding." In *The Oxford Handbook of Religion, Conflict, and Peacebuilding*, edited by Atalia Omer, R. Scott Appleby, and David Little, 569–96. Oxford: Oxford University Press, 2015.

Duflo, Esther. "The Economist as Plumber." Presented at the American Economics Association, Boston, January 2017. https://economics.mit.edu/files/12569.

Dwyer, Judith A., ed. "Preferential Option for the Poor." In *The New Dictionary of Catholic Social Thought*, 755–59. Collegeville, MN: Liturgical Press, 1994.

Easterly, William. *The Tyranny of Experts: Economists, Dictators, and the Forgotten Rights of the Poor*. New York: Basic, 2013.

Ebrahim, Alnoor, and V. Kasturi Rangan. "What Impact? A Framework for Measuring the Scale and Scope of Social Performance." *California Management Review* 56 (2014): 118–41.

Eikenberry, Angela M. "The Hidden Costs of Cause Marketing." *Stanford Social Innovation Review* 7 (2009): 50–55.

Engen, Charles Van. *Transforming Mission Theology*. Pasadena: William Carey Library, 2017.

Epstein, Keith. "Crisis Mentality." *Stanford Social Innovation Review* 4 (2006): 48–57.

Escobar, Samuel. "Refugees: A New Testament Perspective." *Transformation* 35 (2018): 102–8.

Evans, David J., Ronald J. Vos, and Keith P. Wright, eds. *Biblical Holism and Agriculture: Cultivating Our Roots*. Pasadena: William Carey Library, 2003. https://www.disciplenations.org/media/BHA-Conference-Papers-Full-text.pdf.

Eyben, Rosalind, and Rebecca Napier-Moore. "Choosing Words with Care? Shifting Meanings of Women's Empowerment in International Development." *Third World Quarterly* 30 (2009): 285–300.

Faith to Action. "Guiding Principles." Accessed August 1, 2019. https://www.faithtoaction.org/guiding-principles/.

Faith to Action Initiative. *The Continuum of Care for Orphans and Vulnerable Children*. Faith to Action Initiative, 2015. http://faithtoaction.org/wp-content/uploads/2015/08/Faith2Action_ContinuumOfCare.pdf.

Famine Early Warning Systems Network. Accessed November 12, 2019. https://fews.net/.

Faramelli, Norman. "*Missio Dei* and Eco-Justice and Earth Care." In *Creation Care in Christian Mission*, edited by Kapya J. Kaoma. Eugene: Wipf & Stock, 2015.

Farmer, Paul. "Health, Healing, and Social Justice: Insights from Liberation Theology." In *In the Company of the Poor: Conversations with Dr. Paul Farmer and Fr. Gustavo Gutiérrez*, edited by Michael Griffin and Jeannie Weiss Block. Maryknoll: Orbis Books, 2013.

Farquhar, Carey, Ruth W. Nduati, and Judith N. Wasserheit. "Ethical Obligations in Short-Term Global Health Clinical Experiences: The Devil Is in the Details." *Annals of Internal Medicine* 168, no. 9 (2018): 672–73.

Fiddian-Qasmiyeh, Elena. "The Pragmatics of Performance: Putting 'Faith' in Aid in the Sahrawi Refugee Camps." *Journal of Refugee Studies* 24 (2011): 533–47.

Fikkert, Brian, and Kelly M. Kapic. *Becoming Whole: Why the Opposite of Poverty Isn't the American Dream*. Chicago: Moody, 2019.

Fikkert, Brian, and Russell Mask. *From Dependence to Dignity: How to Alleviate Poverty through Church-Centered Microfinance*. Grand Rapids: Zondervan, 2015.

Finke, Roger. "Origins and Consequences of Religious Freedoms: A Global Overview." *Sociology of Religion* 74 (2013): 297–313.

Flachs, Andrew. *Cultivating Knowledge: Biotechnology, Sustainability, and the Human Cost of Cotton Capitalism in India*. Tucson: University of Arizona Press, 2019.

Fletcher, Richard. *The Barbarian Conversion: From Paganism to Christianity*. New York: Henry Holt, 1997.

Food and Agriculture Organization. "Rome Declaration on World Food Security." Food and Agriculture Organization, 1996. http://www.fao.org/docrep/003/w3613e/w3613e00.HTM.

Food and Agriculture Organization of the United Nations. *The State of Food Insecurity and Nutrition in the World 2019: Safeguarding against Economic Slowdowns and Downturns*. Rome: Food and Agriculture Organization of the United Nations, 2019. http://www.fao.org/3/ca5162en/ca5162en.pdf.

Food for the Hungry. "Redemptive Agriculture: Working the Land God Entrusted to Us," 2006. https://www.disciplenations.org/media/Redemptive-Agriculture-Curriculum.pdf.

Foot, Kirsten A., Amoshaun Toft, and Nina Cesare. "Developments in Anti-Trafficking Efforts: 2008–2011." *Journal of Human Trafficking* 1 (2015): 136–55.

Foster, Richard. *Freedom of Simplicity*. San Francisco: Harper & Row, 1981.

Fountain, Daniel E. *Health for All: The Vanga Story*. Pasadena: William Carey Library, 2014.

Franceys, Richard, Sue Cavill, and Andrew Trevett. "Who Really Pays? A Critical Overview of the Practicalities of Funding Universal Access." *Waterlines* 35, no. 1 (2016): 78–93.

Francis. "Fratelli Tutti: On Fraternity and Social Friendship." 2020. http://www.vatican.va/content/francesco/en/encyclicals/documents/papa-francesco_20201003_enciclica-fratelli-tutti.html.

———. *Praise Be to You (Laudato Si'): On Care for Our Common Home*. San Francisco: Ignatius, 2015.

Freeman, Dena. *The Role of Faith in Tearfund's Work during Its First Fifty Years*. Teddington, UK: Tearfund, 2019.

Freeman, Scott, and Mark Schuller. "Aid Projects: The Effects of Commodification and Exchange." *World Development* 126 (2020): 104,731.

Freidus, Andrea Lee. "Unanticipated Outcomes of Voluntourism among Malawi's Orphans." *Journal of Sustainable Tourism* 25, no. 9 (2017): 1306–21.

Fyfe, Rosie. "Liturgies of Development: Formation for Working among the Poor." *Christian Relief, Development, and Advocacy* 2, no. 1 (2020): 13–19.

Galea, Sandro, and Margaret E. Kruk. "Forty Years after Alma-Ata: At the Intersection of Primary Care and Population Health." *The Milbank Quarterly* 97, no. 2 (2019): 383–86.

Garchitorena, Andres, Ann C. Miller, Laura F. Cordier, Victor R. Rabeza, Marius Randriamanambintsoa, Hery-Tiana R. Razanadrakato, Lara Hall, Djordje Gikic, Justin Haruna, and Meg McCarty. "Early Changes in Intervention Coverage and Mortality Rates Following the Implementation of an Integrated Health System Intervention in Madagascar." *BMJ Global Health* 3, no. 3 (2018): e000762.

Garcia, Jonathan, Miguel Muñoz-Laboy, and Richard Parker. "Vulnerable Salvation: Evangelical Protestant Leaders and Institutions, Drug Use and HIV and AIDS in the Urban Periphery of Rio de Janeiro." *Global Public Health* 6 (2011): 243–S256.

Gates, Jamie, Larry Bollinger, and Rob Gailey. "Nurturing a Prophetic Imagination: Missiology as Ecclesiology." In *Nurturing the Prophetic Imagination*, edited by Jamie Gates and Mark H. Mann, 229–43. San Diego: Point Loma Press, 2012.

Germond, Paul, and James R. Cochrane. "Healthworlds: Conceptualizing Landscapes of Health and Healing." *Sociology* 44 (2010): 307–24.

Gibson, Stephen W., and Bette M. Gibson. *Where There Are No Jobs*. Vol. 2–26. Complete MicroEnterprise Lessons. Provo: Academy for Creating Enterprise, n.d.

Gibson, Stephen W., and Tina J. Huntsman. *Where There Are No Jobs*. Vol. 1. Twenty-Five Rules of Thumb for MicroEnterprise Success. Provo: Academy for Creating Enterprise, n.d.
Glanzer, Perry L. "Growing on the Margins: Global Christian Higher Education." *International Higher Education*, no. 88 (2017): 23–25.
Global CHE Network. https://www.chenetwork.org/.
"Goal Area 1: Every Child Survives and Thrives." In *Global Annual Results Report 2018*. New York: UNICEF, 2018. https://www.unicef.org/media/54971/file/Global_Annual_Results_Report_2018_Goal_Area_1.pdf.
Goheen, Michael W. *Introducing Christian Mission Today: Scripture, History and Issues*. Downers Grove: InterVarsity Press, 2014.
"The Good News about Global Poverty: What Americans Believe about the World's Poor—and What Churches Can Do to Help." Barna Group, 2018.
Gorman, Michael J. *Becoming the Gospel: Paul, Participation, and Mission*. Grand Rapids: Eerdmans, 2015.
———. *Inhabiting the Cruciform God: Kenosis, Justification, and Theosis in Paul's Narrative Soteriology*. Grand Rapids: Eerdmans, 2009.
Gort, Gea, and Mats Tunehag. *BAM Global Movement: Business as Mission, Concepts and Stories*. Peabody, MA: Hendrickson, 2018.
Goudeau, Jessica. *After the Last Border: Two Families and the Story of Refuge in America*. New York: Viking, 2020.
Graddy-Lovelace, Garrett, and Adam Diamond. "From Supply Management to Agricultural Subsidies—and Back Again? The U.S. Farm Bill & Agrarian (in) Viability." *Journal of Rural Studies* 50 (2017): 70–83.
Green, Joel. *Salvation*. St. Louis: Chalice, 2003.
Green, Joel B., and Mark D. Baker. *Recovering the Scandal of the Cross: Atonement in New Testament and Contemporary Contexts*. Downers Grove: IVP Academic, 2000.
Greenberg, Jeffrey, Christine Gamble, Bayard Pickens, Kaitlyn Wallett, David Edgren, Chris Keil, Raymond Lewis, and James Clark. "Small-Scale Waste-Stabilization Ponds for Rural Communities: An Undergraduate Experimental Venture." *Waterlines* 34 (2015): 435–44.
Greenfield, Craig. "Can We Talk about the Anti-Trafficking Industry? Things Are Getting Out of Control." Blog. August 15, 2018. https://www.craiggreenfield.com/blog/anti-trafficking-industrial-complex.
———. *The Urban Halo*. Milton Keynes, UK: Authentic, 2007.
Grigg, Viv. *Companion to the Poor: Christ in the Urban Slums*. Waynesboro, GA: Authentic, 2004.
Gubbels, Peter, and Catheryn Koss. *From the Roots Up: Strengthening Organizational Capacity through Guided Self-Assessment*. Oklahoma City: World Neighbors, 2000.
Gutiérrez, Gustavo. *A Theology of Liberation: History, Politics, and Salvation*. Maryknoll: Orbis, 1973.

Guttentag, Daniel A. "The Possible Negative Impacts of Volunteer Tourism." *International Journal of Tourism Research* 11 (2009): 537–51.

Gyimah-Brempong, Kwabena. "Education and Economic Development in Africa." *African Development Review* 23 (2011): 219–36.

Haakenstad, Annie, Elizabeth Johnson, Casey Graves, Jill Olivier, Jean Duff, and Joseph L. Dieleman. "Estimating the Development Assistance for Health Provided to Faith-Based Organizations, 1990–2013." *PLOS One* 10, no. 6 (2015): e0128389.

Halvorson, Britt. *Conversionary Sites: Transforming Medical Aid and Global Christianity from Madagascar to Minnesota*. Chicago: University of Chicago Press, 2018.

Hamilton, Mark W. *Jesus, King of Strangers: What the Bible Really Says about Immigration*. Grand Rapids: Eerdmans, 2019.

Hanna, Rema, Esther Duflo, and Michael Greenstone. "Up in Smoke: The Influence of Household Behavior on the Long-Run Impact of Improved Cooking Stoves." *American Economic Journal: Economic Policy* 8 (2016): 80–114.

Hanushek, Eric A., and Ludger Woessmann. "Do Better Schools Lead to More Growth? Cognitive Skills, Economic Outcomes, and Causation." *Journal of Economic Growth* 17 (2012): 267–321.

Harries, Jim. *Vulnerable Mission: Insights into Christian Mission to Africa from a Position of Vulnerability*. Pasadena: William Carey, 2011.

Hartig, Hannah. "Republicans Turn More Negative toward Refugees as Number Admitted to U.S. Plummets." Pew Research Center, May 24, 2018. https://www.pewresearch.org/fact-tank/2018/05/24/republicans-turn-more-negative-toward-refugees-as-number-admitted-to-u-s-plummets/.

Hartmann, Douglas, and Christina Kwauk. "Sport and Development: An Overview, Critique, and Reconstruction." *Journal of Sport and Social Issues* 35 (2011): 284–305.

Hauerwas, Stanley. "Worship, Evangelism, Ethics: On Eliminating the 'And.'" In *The Study of Evangelism: Exploring a Missional Practice of the Church*, edited by Paul W. Chilcote and Laceye C. Warner, 205–14. Grand Rapids: Eerdmans, 2008.

Haugen, Gary A., and Victor Boutros. *The Locust Effect: Why the End of Poverty Requires the End of Violence*. New York: Oxford University Press, 2014.

Hays, Christopher M. "Slaughtering Stewards and Incarcerating Debtors: Coercing Charity in Luke 12:35–13:9." *Neotestamentica* 46 (2012): 41–60.

Headey, Derek, and Kalle Hirvonen. "Is Exposure to Poultry Harmful to Child Nutrition? An Observational Analysis for Rural Ethiopia." *PLOS One* 11, no. 8 (August 16, 2016): e0160590.

Heidebrecht, Doug. "Toward a Mennonite Brethren Peace Theology: Reading the Bible through an Anabaptist Lens." *Direction* 43 (2014): 228–42.

Heim, S. Mark. *The Depth of the Riches: A Trinitarian Theology of Religious Ends*. Grand Rapids: Eerdmans, 2001.

Hill, Graham Joseph. *Salt, Light, and a City: Conformation—Ecclesiology for a Global Missional Community*. 2nd ed. Eugene: Wipf & Stock, 2020.
Holman, Susan R. *Beholden: Religion, Global Health and Human Rights*. New York: Oxford University Press, 2015.
Horner, Rory. "Towards a New Paradigm of Global Development? Beyond the Limits of International Development." *Progress in Human Geography* 44, no. 3 (June 1, 2020): 415–36.
Hotez, Peter J. *Blue Marble Health: An Innovative Plan to Fight Diseases of the Poor Amid Wealth*. Baltimore: Johns Hopkins University Press, 2016.
Hunt, Cherryl, David G. Horrell, and Christopher Southgate. "An Environmental Mantra? Ecological Interest in Romans 8:19–23 and a Modest Proposal for Its Narrative Interpretation." *Journal of Theological Studies* 59 (2008): 546–79.
Innovations for Poverty Action. "Graduating the Ultra Poor in Ghana," February 4, 2011. https://www.poverty-action.org/study/graduating-ultra-poor-ghana.
Innovations for Poverty Action. "The Impact of Maternal Cash Transfers on Child Malnutrition in Myanmar," 2017. https://www.poverty-action.org/study/impact-maternal-cash-transfers-child-malnutrition-myanmar.
Institute for Health Metrics and Evaluation, University of Washington. "Financing Global Health." Accessed August 1, 2019. http://vizhub.healthdata.org/fgh.
Inter-Agency Standing Committee. *Guidelines for Integrating Gender-Based Violence Interventions in Humanitarian Action: Reducing Risk, Promoting Resilience and Aiding Recovery*. Geneva: Inter-Agency Standing Committee, 2015.
———. "Inclusion of Persons with Disabilities in Humanitarian Action." Inter-Agency Standing Committee, 2019. https://interagencystandingcommittee.org/iasc-task-team-inclusion-persons-disabilities-humanitarian-action/case-studies-inclusion-persons.
International Disaster Database. https://www.emdat.be/.
International Federation of Red Cross and Red Crescent Societies. "World Disasters Report 2018." International Federation of Red Cross and Red Crescent Societies, 2018. https://media.ifrc.org/ifrc/world-disaster-report-2018/.
International Federation of Red Cross and Red Crescent Societies and the ICRC. "The Code of Conduct: Principles of Conduct for the International Red Cross and Red Crescent Movement and Non-Governmental Organizations (NGOs) in Disaster Relief." International Federation of Red Cross and Red Crescent Societies and the ICRC, 1994. https://www.icrc.org/en/doc/resources/documents/publication/p1067.htm.
International Labour Office. "Upgrading Informal Apprenticeships: A Resource Guide for Africa." International Labour Office, 2012. https://www.ilo.org/skills/pubs/WCMS_171393/lang--en/index.htm.
International Labour Organization. "Global Estimates of Modern Slavery: Forced Labour and Forced Marriage." International Labour Organization, September 19, 2017. http://www.ilo.org/global/publications/books/WCMS_575479/lang--en/index.htm.

Isaak, Paul John. "Mission as Praxis for Peace-Building, Healing, and Reconciliation: Critical Appraisal of the Praxis of CWM." In *Postcolonial Mission: Power and Partnership in World Christianity*, edited by Desmond van der Water, Isabel Apawo Phiri, Namsoon Kang, Roderick Hewitt, and Sarojini Nadar, 237–64. Upland, CA: Sopher, 2011.

Jack, Kristen, ed. *The Sound of Worlds Colliding: Stories of Radical Discipleship from Servants to Asia's Urban Poor*. Phnom Penh: Servants to Asia's Urban Poor, 2009.

Jacobsen, Douglas. *Global Gospel: An Introduction to Christianity on Five Continents*. Grand Rapids: Baker Academic, 2015.

James, Rick. *Inspiring Change: Creating More Space for Grace in Organisations*. Oslo: Digni, n.d. https://spaceforgrace.network/resources/.

Johnson, C. Neal. *Business as Mission: A Comprehensive Guide to Theory and Practice*. Downers Grove: InterVarsity Press, 2011.

Johnson, Todd M., and Sun Young Chung. "Tracking Global Christianity's Statistical Centre of Gravity, AD 33–AD 2100." *International Review of Mission* 93, no. 369 (2004): 166–81.

Johnson, Todd M., and Gina A. Zurlo, eds. *World Christian Database*. Leiden: Brill, 2020.

Johnson, Todd M., Gina A. Zurlo, Albert W. Hickman, and Peter F. Crossing. "Christianity 2018: More African Christians and Counting Martyrs." *International Bulletin of Mission Research* 42, no. 1 (2018): 20–28.

"Joint Declaration of Religious Leaders against Modern Slavery," 2014. http://www.endslavery.va.

Jones, Robert P. *White Too Long: The Legacy of White Supremacy in American Christianity*. New York: Simon & Schuster, 2020.

Jones, Robert P., and Daniel Cox. "America's Changing Religious Identity: Findings from the 2016 American Values Atlas." Public Religion Research Institute, 2017.

Jones, Robert P., Daniel Cox, and Juhem Navarro-Rivera. "Nearly 7-in-10 See Unaccompanied Children Coming to U.S. as Refugees, Not Illegal Immigrants." Public Religion Research Institute, July 29, 2014. https://www.prri.org/research/july-2014-unaccompanied-minors/.

Juran, Sabrina, P. Niclas Broer, Stefanie J. Klug, Rachel C. Snow, Emelda A. Okiro, Paul O. Ouma, Robert W. Snow, Andrew J. Tatem, John G. Meara, and Victor A. Alegana. "Geospatial Mapping of Access to Timely Essential Surgery in Sub-Saharan Africa." *BMJ Global Health* 3, no. 4 (2018): e000875.

Kaemingk, Matthew. *Christian Hospitality and Muslim Immigration in an Age of Fear*. Grand Rapids: Eerdmans, 2018.

Kang, Namsoon. "Constructing Postcolonial Mission in World Christianity: Mission as Radical Affirmation to the World." In *Postcolonial Mission: Power and Partnership in World Christianity*, edited by Desmond van der Water, Isabel Apawo Phiri, Namsoon Kang, Roderick Hewitt, and Sarojini Nadar, 105–30. Upland, CA: Sopher, 2011.

Kara, Siddharth. *Sex Trafficking: Inside the Business of Modern Slavery*. New York: Columbia University Press, 2009.

Kennedy, Jim, Joseph Ashmore, Elizabeth Babister, and Ilan Kelman. "The Meaning of 'Build Back Better': Evidence from Post-Tsunami Aceh and Sri Lanka." *Journal of Contingencies and Crisis Management* 16 (2008): 24–36.

Kern, Kathleen. *In Harm's Way: A History of Christian Peacemaker Teams*. Eugene: Cascade, 2009.

Khandelwal, Meena, Matthew E. Hill Jr., Paul Greenough, Jerry Anthony, Misha Quill, Marc Linderman, and H. S. Udaykumar. "Why Have Improved Cook-Stove Initiatives in India Failed?" *World Development* 92 (2017): 13–27.

Kidd, Bruce. "A New Social Movement: Sport for Development and Peace." *Sport in Society* 11 (2008): 370–80.

Kim, Young-Suk G., Hansol Lee, and Stephanie S. Zuilkowski. "Impact of Literacy Interventions on Reading Skills in Low- and Middle-Income Countries: A Meta-Analysis." *Child Development* 91 (2020): 638–60.

Kivisto, Peter. *Religion and Immigration: Migrant Faiths in North America and Western Europe*. Cambridge, UK: Polity, 2014.

Klassen, Pamela. *Spirits of Protestantism: Medicine, Healing, and Liberal Christianity*. Berkeley: University of California Press, 2011.

Krakauer, Eric L., and M. R. Rajagopal. "End-of-Life Care across the World: A Global Moral Failing." *The Lancet* 388, no. 10043 (2016): 444–46.

Krekó, Péter, Bulcsú Hunyadi, and Patrik Szicherle. "Anti-Muslim Populism in Hungary: From the Margins to the Mainstream." Brookings Institution, July 24, 2019. https://www.brookings.edu/research/anti-muslim-populism-in-hungary-from-the-margins-to-the-mainstream/.

Krishna, Anirudh. *One Illness Away: How People Escape Poverty and Why They Become Poor*. New York: Oxford University Press, 2010.

Kuma, Tadesse, Mekdim Dereje, Kalle Hirvonen, and Bart Minten. "Cash Crops and Food Security: Evidence from Ethiopian Smallholder Coffee Producers." *Journal of Development Studies* 55 (2019): 1267–84.

Landesa. https://www.landesa.org.

Lasker, Judith N. *Hoping to Help: The Promises and Pitfalls of Global Health Volunteering*. Ithaca: Cornell University Press, 2016.

Laureus Sport. "Using the Power of Sport to End Violence, Discrimination and Disadvantage," n.d. https://www.laureus.com/sport-for-good.

Lederach, John Paul. *Building Peace: Sustainable Reconciliation in Divided Societies*. Washington, DC: Institute of Peace Press, 1997.

———. *Preparing for Peace: Conflict Transformation across Cultures*. Syracuse: Syracuse University Press, 1995.

Lederleitner, Mary T. *Cross-Cultural Partnerships: Navigating the Complexities of Money and Mission*. Downers Grove: IVP Books, 2010.

Legros, Gwenaelle, Ines Havet, Nigel Bruce, Sophie Bonjour, Kamal Rijal, Minoru Takada, and C. Dora. "The Energy Access Situation in Developing Countries: A

Review Focusing on the Least Developed Countries and Sub-Saharan Africa." World Health Organization, 2009.

Leo, Ben. "Is Anyone Listening? Does US Foreign Assistance Target People's Top Priorities? – Working Paper 348." Center for Global Development, 2013. https://www.cgdev.org/publication/anyone-listening-does-us-foreign-assistance-target-peoples-top-priorities-working-paper.

"Let Innovation Thrive: Solutions from the World Habitat Awards to End the Global Housing Crisis." World Habitat, 2020. https://www.world-habitat.org/publications/let-innovation-thrive/.

Levine, Simon, and Lewis Sida. "Multi-Year Humanitarian Funding: A Thematic Evaluation." Humanitarian Policy Group. July 2019. https://www.odi.org/sites/odi.org.uk/files/resource-documents/12809.pdf.

Li, Zhihui, Mingqiang Li, George C. Patton, and Chunling Lu. "Global Development Assistance for Adolescent Health from 2003 to 2015." *JAMA Network Open* 1, no. 4 (2018): e181072–e181072.

Litsios, Socrates. "The Christian Medical Commission and the Development of the World Health Organization's Primary Health Care Approach." *American Journal of Public Health* 94 (2004): 1884–93.

Livermore, David A. *Serving with Eyes Wide Open: Doing Short-Term Missions with Cultural Intelligence.* Grand Rapids: Baker, 2016.

Lizarralde, Gonzalo. "Stakeholder Participation and Incremental Housing in Subsidized Housing Projects in Colombia and South Africa." *Habitat International* 35 (2011): 175–87.

Loeser, John, Berk Özler, and Patrick Premand. "What Have We Learned about Cash Transfers?" World Bank Blog: *Development Impact.* May 10, 2021.

Lozano, Rafael, Nancy Fullman, Degu Abate, Solomon M. Abay, Cristiana Abbafati, Nooshin Abbasi, Hedayat Abbastabar, Foad Abd-Allah, Jemal Abdela, and Ahmed Abdelalim. "Measuring Progress from 1990 to 2017 and Projecting Attainment to 2030 of the Health-Related Sustainable Development Goals for 195 Countries and Territories: A Systematic Analysis for the Global Burden of Disease Study 2017." *The Lancet* 392, no. 10159 (2018): 2091–138.

Lybbert, Travis J., and Bruce Wydick. "Poverty, Aspirations, and the Economics of Hope." *Economic Development and Cultural Change* 66 (2018): 709–53.

Lynn, Monty L. *Christian Compassion: A Charitable History.* Eugene: Wipf & Stock, 2021.

———. "Congregational Aid: North American Protestant Engagement in International Relief and Development." *Journal of Development Studies* 52 (2016): 965–85.

Magezi, Vhumani. "Church-Driven Primary Health Care: Models for an Integrated Church and Community Primary Health Care in Africa (a Case Study of the Salvation Army in East Africa)." *HTS Teologiese Studies/Theological Studies* 74, no. 2 (2018): 1–11.

Maki, Jesse, Munirih Qualls, Benjamin White, Sharon Kleefield, and Robert Crone. "Health Impact Assessment and Short-Term Medical Missions: A Methods Study to Evaluate Quality of Care." *BMC Health Services Research* 8, no. 1 (2008): 121.

Martin, Jim. *The Just Church: Becoming a Risk-Taking, Justice-Seeking, Disciple-Making Congregation*. Carol Stream, IL: Tyndale Momentum, 2012.

Maundeni, Tapologo. "Care for Children and Botswana: Current Limitations, Future Possibilities." In *Orphan Care: A Comparative View*, edited by Jo Daugherty Bailey, 19–37. Sterling, VA: Kumarian Press, 2012.

Maxey, James A. *From Orality to Orality: A New Paradigm for Contextual Translation of the Bible*. Eugene: Cascade, 2009

McDonagh, Francis, ed. *Dom Hélder Câmara: Essential Writings*. Maryknoll: Orbis Books, 2009.

McKay, Johnston. *The Kirk and the Kingdom: A Century of Tension in Scottish Social Theology, 1830–1929*. Edinburgh: Edinburgh University Press, 2012.

McKenzie, David J. "Small Business Training to Improve Management Practices in Developing Countries: Reassessing the Evidence for 'Training Doesn't Work,'" Policy Research Paper 9408. World Bank, 2020. http://documents1.worldbank.org/curated/en/593081600709463800/pdf/Small-Business-Training-to-Improve-Management-Practices-in-Developing-Countries-Reassessing-the-Evidence-for-Training-Doesn-t-Work.pdf.

McKnight, Scot. *The King Jesus Gospel: The Original Good News Revisited*. Grand Rapids: Zondervan, 2001.

McLaughlin, Levi. "What Have Religious Groups Done after 3.11? Part 1: A Brief Survey of Religious Mobilization after the Great East Japan Earthquake Disasters." *Religion Compass* 7, no. 8 (2013): 294–308.

MDG Monitor. "MDG 2: Achieve Universal Primary Education." Millennium Development Goals, 2017. https://www.mdgmonitor.org/mdg-2-achieve-universal-primary-education/.

Meara, John G., Andrew JM Leather, Lars Hagander, Blake C. Alkire, Nivaldo Alonso, Emmanuel A. Ameh, Stephen W. Bickler, Lesong Conteh, Anna J. Dare, and Justine Davies. "Global Surgery 2030: Evidence and Solutions for Achieving Health, Welfare, and Economic Development." *The Lancet* 386, no. 9993 (2015): 569–624.

"Measuring the Information Society Report 2018, Vol. 1." International Telecommunication Union, 2018. https://www.itu.int/en/ITU-D/Statistics/Pages/publications/misr2018.aspx.

Merton, Thomas. *Confessions of a Guilty Bystander*. New York: Image, 1966.

Miles, Glenn, and Christa Foster Crawford, eds. *Stopping the Traffick: A Christian Response to Sexual Exploitation and Trafficking*. Oxford: Regnum, 2014.

Millennium Ecosystem Assessment. *Ecosystems and Human Well-Being: Synthesis*. Washington, DC: Island Press, 2005.

Mim, Nusrat Jahan. "Religion at the Margins: Resistance to Secular Humanitarianism at the Rohingya Refugee Camps in Bangladesh." *Religions* 11, no. 8 (2020): 1–17.

Mitchell, Bob. *Faith-Based Development: How Christian Organizations Can Make a Difference*. Maryknoll: Orbis, 2017.

Msabah, Barnabé Anzuruni. "'And the Greatest of These Is Hope': Reframing the Global Refugee Crisis." *Transformation* 35 (2018): 117–23.

Mukhija, Vinit. "The Value of Incremental Development and Design in Affordable Housing." *Cityscape: A Journal of Policy Development and Research* 16, no. 2 (2014): 11–20.

Mullainathan, Sendhil, and Edlar Shafir. *Scarcity: Why Having Too Little Means So Much*. New York: Times Books, 2013.

Musalaha. Accessed November 26, 2019. https://musalaha.org/.

Myers, Bryant L. *Engaging Globalization: The Poor, Christian Mission, and Our Hyperconnected World*. Grand Rapids: Baker Academic, 2017.

———. *Walking with the Poor: Principles and Practices of Transformational Development*. Revised and Expanded. Maryknoll: Orbis, 2011.

Neill, Stephen. *Creative Tension*. London: Edinburgh House, 1959.

Newbigin, Lesslie. *The Gospel in a Pluralist Society*. Grand Rapids: Eerdmans, 1989.

———. *The Household of God: Lectures on the Nature of Church*. Eugene: Wipf & Stock, 2008.

Newell, Peggy. *North American Mission Handbook: US and Canadian Protestant Ministries Overseas, 2017–2019*. 22nd ed. Pasadena: William Carey Library, 2017.

Niehaus, Paul. Conversation with Rob Gailey. June 30, 2020.

Njoroge, Francis, Tulo Raistrick, Bill Crooks, and Jackie Mouradian. *Umoja: Transforming Communities*. Teddington, UK: Tearfund, 2009.

Noll, Mark A. *The New Shape of World Christianity: How American Experience Reflects Global Faith*. Downers Grove: IVP Academic, 2009.

Norell, Dan, and Margie Brand. "Integrating Extremely Poor Producers into Markets Field Guide, 4th ed.," 2017. https://www.marketlinks.org/sites/marketlinks.org/files/resources/markets_field_guide_iv.pdf.

Norell, Dan, Emily Janoch, Elly Kaganzi, Malini Tolat, Monty L. Lynn, and Emily C. Riley. "Value Chain Development with the Extremely Poor: Evidence and Lessons from CARE, Save the Children, and World Vision." *Enterprise Development and Microfinance* 28 (2017): 44–62.

Norman, Ray, and Odoi Odotei. "Faith Integration and Christian Witness in Relief and Development: Reflections and Practical Guidance for Field Teams." *Christian Relief, Development, and Advocacy* 1 (2019): 31–43.

Ó Gráda, Cormac. *Famine. A Short History*. Princeton: Princeton University Press, 2009.

OECD. "Development Co-operation Profiles." Paris: OECD Publishing, 2020. https://doi.org/10.1787/2dcf1367-en.

Office of the Special Representative of the Secretary-General for Children and Armed Conflict. "Children and Justice during and in the Aftermath of Armed Conflict." United Nations, September 2011. https://childrenandarmedconflict.un.org/publications/WorkingPaper-3_Children-and-Justice.pdf.

Offutt, Stephen, F. David Bronkema, Krisanne Vaillancourt Murphy, Robb Davis, and Gregg Okesson. *Advocating for Justice: An Evangelical Vision for Transforming Systems and Structures*. Grand Rapids: Baker Academic, 2016.

Oliver, Caroline, Rianne Dekker, Karin Geuijen, and Jacqueline Broadhead. "Innovative Strategies for the Reception of Asylum Seekers and Refugees in European Cities: Multi-level Governance, Multi-sector Urban Networks and Local Engagement." *Cooperative Migration Studies* 8, no. 30 (2020): 1–14.

Olson, Kerry, Zanele Sibanda Knight, and Geoff Foster. *From Faith to Action: Strengthening Family and Community Care for Orphans and Vulnerable Children in Sub-Saharan Africa: A Resource for Faith-Based Groups and Donors Seeking to Help Children and Families Affected by HIV/AIDS*. Santa Cruz: Firelight Foundation, 2005.

Opola, Felix Ouko, Laurens Klerkx, Cees Leeuwis, and Catherine W. Kilelu. "The Hybridity of Inclusive Innovation Narratives between Theory and Practice: A Framing Analysis." *European Journal of Development Research* 33 (2021): 626–48.

Orlinsky, Harry M., and Robert G. Bratcher. *A History of Bible Translation and the North American Contribution*. Atlanta: Scholars Press, 1991.

Ott, Craig. *The Mission of the Church: Five Views in Conversation*. Grand Rapids: Baker Academic, 2016.

Ottonelli, Valeria, and Tiziana Torresi. "When Is Migration Voluntary?" *International Migration Review* 47 (2013): 783–813.

"PACK – Practical Approach to Care Kit." Accessed August 1, 2019. https://pack.bmj.com/.

Padilla, C. René. "The Biblical Basis for Social Ethics." In *Transforming the World? The Gospel and Social Responsibility*, edited by Jamie A. Grant and Dewi A. Hughes. Nottingham: Apollos, 2009.

———. "Holistic Mission." In *Lausanne Occasional Paper 33*, 2004. https://www.lausanne.org/content/lop/holistic-mission-lop-33#hm.

———. "Integral Mission and Its Historical Development." In *Justice, Mercy and Humility: Integral Mission and the Poor*, edited by Tim Chester, 42–58. Waynesboro, GA: Paternoster, 2002.

Pal, Nicole E., Lisa Eckenwiler, Shelley-Rose Hyppolite, John Pringle, Ryoa Chung, and Matthew Hunt. "Ethical Considerations for Closing Humanitarian Projects: A Scoping Review." *Journal of International Humanitarian Action*, 1-9, 4, no. 17 (2019).

Palazuelos, Daniel, Paul E. Farmer, and Joia Mukherjee. "Community Health and Equity of Outcomes: The Partners in Health Experience." *The Lancet Global Health* 6 (2018): e491–e493.

Pallant, Dean. *Keeping Faith in Faith-Based Organizations: A Practical Theology of Salvation Army Health Ministry*. Eugene: Wipf & Stock, 2012.

Patton, William M. "Philanthropic Grantmaking for Disasters: Lessons Learned at the Conrad N. Hilton Foundation." Conrad N. Hilton Foundation, March 2012. https://www.issuelab.org/resources/13210/13210.pdf.

Pega, Frank, Sze Yan Liu, Stefan Walter, Roman Pabayo, Ruhi Saith, and Stefan K. Lhachimi. "Unconditional Cash Transfers for Reducing Poverty and Vulnerabilities: Effect on Use of Health Services and Health Outcomes in Low- and Middle-Income Countries." *Cochrane Database of Systematic Reviews* 11 (2017): CD011135.

Petersen, Elizabeth. "Working with Religious Leaders and Faith Communities to Advance Culturally Informed Strategies to Address Violence against Women." *Agenda* 30, no. 3 (2016): 50–59.

Pew Research Center. "Being Christian in Western Europe," May 29, 2018. https://www.pewforum.org/2018/05/29/being-christian-in-western-europe/.

———. "The Religious Affiliation of International Migrants," March 8, 2012. https://www.pewforum.org/2012/03/08/religious-migration-exec/.

Pinckaers, Servais. *Morality: The Catholic View*. South Bend: St. Augustine's, 2001.

Pope, Stephen J. "Love in Contemporary Christian Ethics." *Journal of Religious Ethics* 23 (1995): 167–97.

Pritchett, Lant. *The Rebirth of Education: Schooling Ain't Learning*. Washington, DC: Center for Global Development, 2013.

Pryce, Joseph, Marty Richardson, and Christian Lengeler. "Insecticide-Treated Nets for Preventing Malaria." *Cochrane Database of Systematic Reviews* 11, no. CD000363 (2018).

Pui-lan, Kwok. "Sustainability, Earth Care and Christian Mission." In *Creation Care in Christian Mission*, edited by Kapya J. Kaoma. Eugene: Wipf & Stock, 2015.

Rawlence, Ben. *City of Thorns: Nine Lives in the World's Largest Refugee Camp*. New York: Picador, 2016.

Rawlins, Rosemary, Svetlana Pimkina, Christopher B. Barrett, Sarah Pedersen, and Bruce Wydick. "Got Milk? The Impact of Heifer International's Livestock Donation Programs in Rwanda on Nutritional Outcomes." *Food Policy* 44 (2014): 202–13.

Reese, Robert. *Roots & Remedies of the Dependency Syndrome in World Missions*. Pasadena: William Carey, 2010.

ReliefWeb. "Disasters." Accessed November 26, 2019. https://reliefweb.int/disasters.

Richter, Linda M., and Amy Norman. "AIDS Orphan Tourism: A Threat to Young Children in Residential Care." *Vulnerable Children and Youth Studies* 5, no. 3 (2010): 217–29.

Ridley, Matthew, Gautam Rao, Frank Schilbach, and Vikram Patel, "Poverty, Depression, and Anxiety: Causal Evidence and Mechanisms." *Science* 370 (Dec. 11, 2020).

Root, Andrew. *The Promise of Despair: The Way of the Cross as the Way of the Church*. Nashville: Abingdon, 2010.

Ross, Cathy, and Andrew Walls, eds. *Mission in the 21st Century: Exploring the Five Marks of Global Mission*. Maryknoll: Orbis, 2008.

Rowe, Nicholas, and Ray Aldred. "Healthy Leadership and Power Differences in the Postcolonial Community: Two Reflections." In *Evangelical Postcolonial*

Conversations: Global Awakenings in Theology and Praxis, edited by Kay Higuera Smith, Jayachitra Lalitha, and Daniel Hawk, 211–23. Downers Grove: IVP Academic, 2014.

Russell, Mark L. *The Missional Entrepreneur: Principles and Practices for Business as Mission*. Birmingham: New Hope, 2011.

Salsich, Peter W., Jr. "Toward a Property Ethic of Stewardship: A Religious Perspective." In *The Community Land Trust Reader*, edited by John Emmeus Davis, 48–65. Cambridge, MA: Lincoln Institute of Land Policy, 2010.

Samuel, Vinay. "Mission as Transformation." *Transformation: An International Journal of Holistic Mission Studies* 19 (2002): 243–47.

Sanneh, Lamin. *Translating the Message: The Missionary Impact on Culture*. Maryknoll: Orbis, 2015.

———. *Whose Religion Is Christianity? The Gospel beyond the West*. Grand Rapids: Eerdmans, 2003.

Santos, Narry F. "'Diaspora Missions': Contemporary Missiological Significance of People on the Move." In *Rejection: God's Refugees in Biblical and Contemporary Perspective*, edited by Stanley E. Porter, 191–208. Eugene: Pickwick, 2015.

Scandrette, Mark. *Free: Spending Your Time and Money on What Matters Most*. Downers Grove: InterVarsity Press, 2013.

Scherer, James A., and Stephen B. Bevans. "Introduction: Faith and Culture in Perspective." In *New Directions in Mission and Evangelization*, edited by James A. Scherer and Stephen B. Bevans, 3:1–16. Maryknoll: Orbis, 1999.

Schirch, Lisa. *The Little Book of Strategic Peacebuilding*. Intercourse, PA: Good Books, 2005.

Schwartz, Glenn. *When Charity Destroys Dignity: Overcoming Unhealthy Dependency in the Christian Movement: A Compendium*. Lancaster, PA: World Mission Associates, 2007.

Scott, Kerry, S. W. Beckham, Margaret Gross, George Pariyo, Krishna D. Rao, Giorgio Cometto, and Henry B. Perry. "What Do We Know about Community-Based Health Worker Programs? A Systematic Review of Existing Reviews on Community Health Workers." *Human Resources for Health* 16, no. 1 (2018): 39.

Seager, Greg. *When Healthcare Hurts: An Evidence Based Guide for Best Practices in Global Health Initiatives*. Bloomington, IN: AuthorHouse, 2012.

Sen, Amartya. "Equality of What?" In *Tanner Lectures on Human Values*, edited by Stirling M. McMurrin, Vol. 1. Salt Lake City: University of Utah Press, 1980.

———. *Inequality Reexamined*. Cambridge, MA: Harvard University Press, 1995.

Shelley, Louise. *Human Trafficking: A Global Perspective*. New York: Cambridge University Press, 2010.

Shepherd, Andrew, Tom Mitchell, Kirsty Lewis, Amanda Lenhardt, Lindsey Jones, Lucy Scott, and Robert Muir-Wood. "The Geography of Poverty, Disasters and Climate Extremes in 2030." London: ODI, October 2013. https://www.odi.org/sites/odi.org.uk/files/odi-assets/publications-opinion-files/8633.pdf.

Shore, Chris. "How Climate Affects the Poor: A Development Worker's Perspective." In *Loving the Least of These: Addressing a Changing Environment*, by Dorothy Boorse, 29–36. Washington, DC: National Association of Evangelicals, 2011.

Singal, Jesse. "For 80 Years, Young Americans Have Been Getting More Anxious and Depressed, and No One Is Quite Sure Why." *New York Magazine*. March 13, 2016.

Singla, Daisy R., Brandon A. Kohrt, Laura K. Murray, Arpita Anand, Bruce F. Chorpita, and Vikram Patel. "Psychological Treatments for the World: Lessons from Low-and Middle-Income Countries." *Annual Review of Clinical Psychology* 13 (2017): 149–81.

Small Arms Survey. "Global Violent Deaths: Interactive Map and Charts on the Global Burden of Armed Violence." Small Arms Survey. Accessed November 12, 2019. http://www.smallarmssurvey.org/tools/interactive-map-charts-on-armed-violence.html.

Smalley, William Allen. *Translation as Mission: Bible Translation in the Modern Missionary Movement*. Macon, GA: Mercer University Press, 1991.

Smith, Aaron. *Slums Reimagined: How Informal Settlements Help the Poor Overcome Poverty and Model Sustainable Neighborhoods for All*. Skyforest, CA: Urban Loft, 2019.

Smith, James K. A. *Awaiting the King: Reforming Public Theology*. Grand Rapids: Baker Academic, 2017.

———. *Desiring the Kingdom: Worship, Worldview, and Cultural Formation*. Grand Rapids: Baker Academic, 2009.

Sobrino, Jon. *No Salvation Outside the Poor: Prophetic-Utopian Essays*. Maryknoll: Orbis, 2008.

———. *Where Is God?: Earthquake, Terrorism, Barbarity, and Hope*. Maryknoll: Orbis, 2004.

Social Value UK. "A Guide to Social Return on Investment," 2012. http://www.socialvalueuk.org/resources/sroi-guide/.

———. "Tools by Principle." Accessed September 1, 2020. http://www.socialvalueuk.org/resources/tools-by-principle/.

Soerens, Matthew, and Jenny Yang. *Welcoming the Stranger: Justice, Compassion and Truth in the Immigration Debate*. Rev. ed. Downers Grove: InterVarsity Press, 2018.

Soini, Eija, and Richard Coe. "Principles for Design of Projects Introducing Improved Wood-Burning Cooking Stoves." *Development in Practice* 24 (2014): 908–20.

Spaling, Harry. "Enabling Creation's Praise: Lessons in Agricultural Stewardship from Africa." In *Biblical Holism and Agriculture: Cultivating Our Roots*, edited by David J. Evans, Ronald J. Vos, and Keith P. Wright, 68–83. Pasadena: William Carey Library, 2003.

Speak, Suzanne. "'Values' as a Tool for Conceptualising Homelessness in the Global South." *Habitat International* 38 (2013): 143–49.

Stambach, Amy. *Faith in Schools: Religion, Education, and American Evangelicals in East Africa*. Stanford, CA: Stanford University Press, 2009.

Stanaway, Jeffrey D., Ashkan Afshin, Emmanuela Gakidou, Stephen S. Lim, Degu Abate, Kalkidan Hassen Abate, Cristiana Abbafati, Nooshin Abbasi, Hedayat Abbastabar, and Foad Abd-Allah. "Global, Regional, and National Comparative Risk Assessment of 84 Behavioural, Environmental and Occupational, and Metabolic Risks or Clusters of Risks for 195 Countries and Territories, 1990–2017: A Systematic Analysis for the Global Burden of Disease Study 2017." *The Lancet* 392, no. 10159 (2018): 1923–94.

Start Network. "Start Fund," September 22, 2016. https://startnetwork.org/start-fund.

———. "Start Fund: Learning from Partnerships." Start Network, 2018. https://startnetwork.org/resource/start-fund-learning-partnerships.

Stassen, Glen H. *Just Peacemaking: Transforming Initiatives for Justice and Peace*. Louisville: Westminster/John Knox, 1992.

Steinert, Janina I., Juliane Zenker, Ute Filipiak, Ani Movsisyan, Lucie D. Cluver, and Yulia Shenderovich. "Do Saving Promotion Interventions Increase Household Savings, Consumption, and Investments in Sub-Saharan Africa? A Systematic Review and Meta-Analysis." *World Development* 104 (2018): 238–56.

Stine, Philip C. *Let the Words Be Written: The Lasting Influence of Eugene A. Nida*. Atlanta: Society of Biblical Literature, 2004.

Stone, Bryan. *Evangelism after Christendom: The Theology and Practice of Christian Witness*. Grand Rapids: Brazos, 2007.

Strom, Bruce D. *Gospel Justice: Joining Together to Provide Help and Hope for Those Oppressed by Legal Injustice*. Chicago: Moody, 2013.

Stuart-Shor, Eileen M., Elizabeth Cunningham, Laura Foradori, Elizabeth Hutchinson, Martha Makwero, Jill Smith, Jane Kasozi, Esther M. Johnston, Aliasgar Khaki, and Elisa Vandervort. "The Global Health Service Partnership: An Academic–Clinical Partnership to Build Nursing and Medical Capacity in Africa." *Frontiers in Public Health* 5 (2017): 174.

Sullivan, Winnifred Fallers, Elizabeth Shakman Hurd, Saba Mahmood, and Peter G. Danchin, eds. *Politics of Religious Freedom*. Chicago: University of Chicago Press, 2015.

Sweeden, Nell Becker. *Church on the Way: Hospitality and Migration*. Eugene: Wipf & Stock, 2015.

Sykes, Kevin J. "Short-Term Medical Service Trips: A Systematic Review of the Evidence." *American Journal of Public Health* 104, no. 7 (2014): e38–e48.

Tankari, Mahamadou Roufahi. "Cash Crops Reduce the Welfare of Farm Households in Senegal." *Food Security* 9 (2017): 1105–15.

Tanner, Kathryn. *Jesus, Humanity and the Trinity: A Brief Systematic Theology*. Minneapolis: Fortress, 2001.

———. *Theories of Culture: A New Agenda for Theology*. Minneapolis, MN: Fortress, 1997.

Tazelaar, Grace, and Carolyn "Care" Newhof. "Empowering toward Shalom, the Lay Health Movement." In *Health, Healing, and Shalom: Frontiers and Challenges for Christian Health Missions*, edited by Bryant L. Myers, Erin Dufault-Hunter, and Isaac B. Voss, 233–47. Pasadena: William Carey Library, 1985.

Telleria, Juan. "Development and Participation: Whose Participation? A Critical Analysis of UNDP's Participatory Research Methods." *European Journal of Development Research* 33 (2021): 459–81.

"The Good News about Global Poverty: What Americans Believe about the World's Poor—and What Churches Can Do to Help." Barna Group, 2018.

Thiagarajan, R. I., M. A. Scheurer, and J. W. Salvin. "Great Need, Scarce Resources, and Choice: Reflections on Ethical Issues Following a Medical Mission." *Journal of Clinical Ethics* 25 (2014): 311–13.

Thistlethwaite, Susan Brooks, ed. *Interfaith Just Peacemaking: Jewish, Christian, and Muslim Perspectives on the New Paradigm of Peace and War*. New York: Palgrave MacMillan, 2011.

Thomas, Terry. "The Limitations of Roofwater Harvesting in Developing Countries." *Waterlines* 33 (2014): 139–45.

Thurow, Roger. *The First 1,000 Days: A Crucial Time for Mothers and Children—And the World*. New York: PublicAffairs, 2017.

Tinker, Melvin. "The Servant Solution: The Coordination of Evangelism and Social Action." In *Transforming the World? The Gospel and Social Responsibility*, edited by Jamie A. Grant and Dewi A. Hughes. Nottingham: Apollos, 2009.

Tizon, Al. "Precursors and Tensions in Holistic Mission: An Historical Overview." In *Holistic Mission: God's Plan for God's People*, edited by Wonsuk Ma and Brian Woolnough, 61–75. Oxford: Regnum, 2010.

———. *Whole and Reconciled: Gospel, Church, and Mission in a Fractured World*. Grand Rapids: Baker Academic, 2018.

Toyama-Szeto, Nikki A., and Femi Adeleye. *Partnering with the Global Church*. Downers Grove: InterVarsity Press, 2012.

Tsimpo, Clarence, and Quentin Wodon. "Faith Affiliation, Religiosity, and Attitudes towards the Environment and Climate Change." *Review of Faith and International Affairs* 14, no. 3 (2016): 51–64.

Tumwesigye, Nazarius M., Lynn Atuyambe, Simon P. S. Kibira, Fred Wabwire-Mangen, Florence Tushemerirwe, and Glenn J. Wagner. "Do Religion and Religiosity Have Anything to Do with Alcohol Consumption Patterns? Evidence from Two Fish Landing Sites on Lake Victoria Uganda." *Substance Use & Misuse* 48 (2013): 1130–37.

UK Foreign and Commonwealth Office. "Chair's Summary—Global Summit to End Sexual Violence in Conflict." June 13, 2014. https://www.gov.uk/government/publications/chairs-summary-global-summit-to-end-sexual-violence-in-conflict/chairs-summary-global-summit-to-end-sexual-violence-in-conflict.

Ukah, Asonzeh. *A New Paradigm of Pentecostal Power: A Study of the Redeemed Christian Church of God in Nigeria*. Trenton, NJ: Africa World Press, 2008.

UN-Habitat. "Participatory Slum Upgrading." Accessed September 24, 2020. https://www.mypsup.org/.
———. "Slums of the World: The Face of Urban Poverty in the New Millennium?" 2003. https://unhabitat.org/slums-of-the-world-the-face-of-urban-poverty-in-the-new-millennium.
———. "Strategies to Combat Homelessness." 2006, 2002. https://unhabitat.org/sites/default/files/download-manager-files/Strategies%20To%20Combat%20Homelessness.pdf.
———. "The Strategic Plan 2020–2023." United Nations Human Settlements Programme. n.d. https://mirror.unhabitat.org/downloads/docs/13555_1_596472.pdf.
UNHCR. "Global Trends: Forced Displacement in 2019." United Nations. 2020. https://www.unhcr.org/globaltrends2019/.
———. "Resettlement." n.d. https://www.unhcr.org/en-us/resettlement.html.
———. "UNHCR Viewpoint: 'Refugee' or 'Migrant'—Which Is Right?" 2016. https://www.unhcr.org/news/latest/2016/7/55df0e556/unhcr-viewpoint-refugee-migrant-right.html.
———. "What Is a Refugee?" Accessed May 19, 2021. https://www.unrefugees.org/refugee-facts/what-is-a-refugee/.
UNICEF. "Gender Equality." n.d. https://www.unicef.org/gender-equality.
———. *Reimagine the Future: Innovation for Every Child*. The State of the World's Children 2015. New York: UNICEF, 2014.
UN. "The Millennium Development Goals Report 2015." 2015. https://www.un.org/millenniumgoals/2015_MDG_Report/pdf/MDG%202015%20rev%20(July%201).pdf.
UN Department of Economic and Social Affairs. "Goal 17: Strengthen the Means of Implementation and Revitalize the Global Partnership for Sustainable Development." Accessed September 1, 2020. https://sdgs.un.org/goals/goal17.
———. "Sustainable Development Goal 8." n.d. https://sdgs.un.org/goals/goal8.
UN General Assembly. "Trafficking in Persons, Especially Women and Children." July 18, 2019. https://undocs.org/A/74/189.
———. "Transforming Our World: The 2030 Agenda for Sustainable Development." September 25, 2015. https://sdgs.un.org/2030agenda.
UN Office on Drugs and Crime. *Global Report on Trafficking in Persons 2018*. 2018.
UN Population Fund. *State of World Population 2007: Unleashing the Potential of Urban Growth*. State of World Population. 2007. New York: UNFPA, 2007.
USAID Learning Lab. "Worksheet: Six Simple Questions to Identify Your Complexity-Aware Monitoring Need." Text. 2017. https://usaidlearninglab.org/library/worksheet-six-simple-questions-identify-your-complexity-aware-monitoring-need.
Van Duzer, Jeff. *Why Business Matters to God (And What Still Needs to Be Fixed)*. Downers Grove: InterVarsity Press Academic, 2010.
Van Reken, David E. *Mission and Ministry: Christian Medical Practices in Today's Changing World Cultures*. Wheaton, IL: EMIS, 1987.

Ver Beek, Kurt Alan. "The Impact of Short-Term Missions: A Case Study of House Construction in Honduras after Hurricane Mitch." *Missiology* 34 (2006): 477–95.

Vertovec, Steven. "Super-Diversity and Its Implications." *Ethnic and Racial Studies* 30 (2007): 1,024–54.

Walls, Andrew. *The Missionary Movement in Christian History: Studies in the Transmission of Faith*. Maryknoll: Orbis, 1996.

Warren, Michelle Ferrigno. *The Power of Proximity: Moving Beyond Awareness to Action*. Downers Grove: InterVarsity Press, 2017.

Water.org. "Microfinancing Toolkits." Accessed August 2, 2019. https://water.org/about-us/our-work/watercredit/watercredit-toolkits/.

Weber, Jeremy. "World Vision Flips the Script on Child Sponsorship." *Christianity Today*. September 20, 2019.

Welty Peachey, Jon, Allison Musser, Na Ri Shin, and Adam Cohen. "Interrogating the Motivations of Sport for Development and Peace Practitioners." *International Review for the Sociology of Sport* 53 (2018): 767–87.

Wheaton College. "WASTE: A Project with Global Implications." Wheaton College. Accessed August 2, 2019. https://www.wheaton.edu/academics/programs/geology/student-opportunities-in-geology/waste-a-project-with-global-implications/.

White, Robert. "Sustainability: Interaction between Science, Ethics and Theology." In *Our Common Cosmos: Exploring the Future of Theology, Human Culture and Space Sciences*, edited by Zoë Lehmann Imfeld and Andreas Losch, 83–94. London: T&T Clark, 2019.

White, Robert S. *Who Is to Blame? Disasters, Nature and Acts of God*. Oxford: Monarch, 2014.

WHO and UNICEF. "Progress on Sanitation and Drinking Water: 2015 Update and MDG Assessment." Geneva, Switzerland: WHO and UNICEF, 2015. https://www.unicef.org/publications/index_82419.html.

Wiesel, Elie. "Nobel Peace Prize Speech." Stockholm, Sweden: December 10, 1986. https://eliewieselfoundation.org/elie-wiesel/nobelprizespeech/.

Wong, Janelle S. *Immigrants, Evangelicals, and Politics in an Era of Demographic Change*. New York: Russell Sage, 2018.

Woolnough, Brian E. "But How Do We Know We Are Making a Difference? Issues Related to the Evaluation of Christian Development Work." *Transformation* 25, no. 2–3 (2008): 134–43.

World Bank. "Reversals of Fortune." 2020. https://www.worldbank.org/en/publication/poverty-and-shared-prosperity.

———. "World Bank Country and Lending Groups." n.d. https://datahelpdesk.worldbank.org/knowledgebase/articles/906519-world-bank-country-and-lending-groups.

World Gospel Mission. "Farming God's Way." n.d. https://www.wgm.org/issue/farming.

World Health Organization. "Climate Change and Health." 2019. https://www.who.int/news-room/fact-sheets/detail/climate-change-and-health.
———. "Disability and Health." Accessed October 25, 2019. https://www.who.int/news-room/fact-sheets/detail/disability-and-health.
———. *The Economics of Social Determinants of Health and Health Inequalities: A Resource Book.* Geneva: World Health Organization, 2013.
———. "Global Health Expenditure Database." n.d. http://apps.who.int/nha/database.
———. "Mental Health in Emergencies." June 11, 2019. https://www.who.int/news-room/fact-sheets/detail/mental-health-in-emergencies.
World Vision. "Farming as Business (FAAB) Manual for Smallholder Farmers." World Vision. 2019. https://www.fsnnetwork.org/farming-business-faab-manual-smallholder-farmers.
Wright, Christopher J. H. *The Mission of God: Unlocking the Bible's Grand Narrative.* Downers Grove: InterVarsity Press, 2013.
Wright, Christopher J. H., and Marcel V. Măcelaru. "The Refugee Crisis—A Shared Human Condition: An Old Testament Perspective." *Transformation* 35 (2018): 91–101.
Wright, N. T. *Simply Good News: Why the Gospel Is News and What Makes It Good.* New York: HarperCollins, 2015.
———. *Surprised by Hope: Rethinking Heaven, the Resurrection, and the Mission of the Church.* New York: HarperOne, 2008.
Wrogemann, Henning. *Intercultural Hermeneutics.* Translated by Karl E. Böhmer. Downers Grove: InterVarsity Press Academic, 2016.
———. *Theologies of Mission.* Translated by Karl E. Böhmer. Downers Grove: InterVarsity Press Academic, 2018.
Wycliffe Global Alliance. "Scripture & Language Statistics 2018." Accessed July 15, 2019. http://www.wycliffe.net/en/statistics.
Wydick, Bruce. *Shrewd Samaritan: Faith, Economics, and the Road to Loving Our Global Neighbor.* Nashville: W Publishing, 2019.
Wydick, Bruce, Paul Glewwe, and Laine Rutledge. "Does International Child Sponsorship Work? A Six-Country Study of Impacts on Adult Life Outcomes." *Journal of Political Economy* 121 (2013): 393–436.
Zhang, Xing Quan. "The Trends, Promises and Challenges of Urbanisation in the World." *Habitat International* 54 (2016): 241–52.
Zurlo, Gina A. "The World as 100 Christians." January 29, 2020. https://www.gordonconwell.edu/blog/100christians/.

www.ingramcontent.com/pod-product-compliance
Lightning Source LLC
Chambersburg PA
CBHW020521080526
44583CB00013B/686